WRITING WITH EASE, REVISED EDITION

Level Two

part of *The Complete Writer*

INSTRUCTOR SECTION

By

Susan Wise Bauer

and Susanna Jarrett

WELL-TRAINED MIND PRESS

18021 The Glebe Lane
Charles City, VA 23030
www.welltrainedmind.com

Names:
Bauer, Susan Wise, author. | Jarrett, Susanna, author.
Title:
Writing with ease. Level two, Instructor section / by Susan Wise Bauer and Susanna Jarrett.
Other titles: Writing with ease. Level two, complete.
Description:
Revised edition. | Charles City, VA : Well-Trained Mind Press, [2024] | Series: The complete writer | Also known as: Writing with ease. Level two, complete. | For instructors of students ages 7 to 8.
Identifiers: ISBN: 978-1-944481-50-6 (paperback)
Subjects:
LCSH: English language--Rhetoric--Study and teaching (Elementary) | English language-- Composition and exercises--Study and teaching (Elementary) | LCGFT: Teachers' guides. | BISAC: EDUCATION / Teaching / Subjects / Language Arts. | JUVENILE NONFICTION / Language Arts / Composition & Creative Writing.
Classification:
LCC: LB1576 .B382 2024 | DDC: 372.62/3--dc23

1 2 3 4 5 6 7 8 9 10 B&B 32 31 30 29 28 27 26 25 24

© 2024 Well-Trained Mind Press
All rights reserved.
Cover Design by Shane Klink

CONTENTS

READING SELECTIONS

Week 1: "The Owl and the Grasshopper" by Aesop and "The Fox and the Stork" by Aesop

Week 2: *The Patchwork Girl of Oz* by L. Frank Baum

Week 3: *Mrs. Piggle-Wiggle* by Betty MacDonald

Week 4: *Doctor Dolittle* by Hugh Lofting

Week 5: *Misty of Chincoteague* by Marguerite Henry

Week 6: "My Shadow" by Robert Louis Stevenson and "The Owl and the Pussycat" by Edward Lear

Week 7: *Ginger Pye* by Eleanor Estes

Week 8: *The Jungle Book* by Rudyard Kipling

Week 9: *Pippi Longstocking* by Astrid Lindgren

Week 10: *Nurse Matilda* by Christianna Brand

Week 11: *The Hundred and One Dalmatians* by Dodie Smith

Week 12: *Pilgrim's Progress* by John Bunyan

Week 13: *The Borrowers* by Mary Norton

Week 14: *The Boxcar Children* by Gertrude Chandler Warner

Week 15: *Mrs. Frisby and the Rats of NIMH* by Robert C. O'Brien

Week 16: "The Young Man and the Cat" from *The Crimson Fairy Book* by Andrew Lang

Week 17: "The Pied Piper of Hamelin" by Robert Browning

Week 18: "The Midnight Ride" from *Fifty Famous People* by James Baldwin

Week 19: *Five Children and It* by Edith Nesbit

Week 20: "Alexander the Great and His Horse" from *Tales from Far and Near* by Arthur Guy Terry and *The Story of the World, Volume One* by Susan Wise Bauer

Week 21: *Nurse Matilda* by Christianna Brand and "The Horse That Aroused the Town" from *Junior Classics: Animal and Nature Stories* by Lillian M. Gask, abridged by Susan Wise Bauer

Week 22: "The Hare That Ran Away" from *Eastern Stories and Legends* by Marie L. Shedlock

Week 23: *Little Women* by Louisa May Alcott and *Invincible Louisa* by Cornelia Meigs

Week 24: *The Plant That Ate Dirty Socks* by Nancy McArthur

Week 25: "The Elephant's Child" by Rudyard Kipling

Week 26: *Moominland Midwinter* by Tove Jansson

Week 27: "The Real Princess" by Hans Christian Andersen and "The Brave Tin Soldier" by Hans Christian Andersen

Week 28: *The Magic of Oz* by L. Frank Baum

Week 29: *The Story of Mankind* by Hendrik Van Loon

Week 30: *The Story of the Greeks* by H. A. Guerber

Week 31: "The Duel" by Eugene Field and "Rebecca, Who Slammed Doors for Fun and Perished Miserably" by Hilaire Belloc

Week 32: *A Child's Geography of the World* by V. M. Hillyer

Week 33: *The Hobbit* by J. R. R. Tolkien

Week 34: *Bunnicula: A Rabbit-Tale of Mystery* by Deborah and James Howe

Week 35: *Doctor Dolittle* by Hugh Lofting

Week 36: *Peter Pan* by J. M. Barrie

NOTE TO THE REVISED EDITION: HOW TO USE THE NEW CREATIVE WRITING LESSONS

At the end of each week, there is a bonus lesson. These lessons provide fun prompts to spark a young writer's imagination. They will satisfy the needs of students who could benefit from a creative writing outlet, while reinforcing concepts and skills students have practiced throughout the week.

These lessons are completely optional! If you skipped each one, your child would not be at all behind. The first four lessons each week cover everything students need to develop their writing skills.

In this second edition, we want to account for the fact that children think and learn in different ways. At this age, some students are not ready for creative writing, and there is nothing to be gained in forcing them to do it. Meanwhile, other students crave opportunities to practice their new skills in a creative way. You know your child best, and can decide whether or not your student will benefit from this extra practice.

If you decide to use the bonus lessons, be sure to read these parameters first:

The creative writing lessons typically consist of a single writing prompt (exceptions are noted within the lessons). There are three steps to use the prompts:

1. **Verbal Narration:** Read the prompt and have your student narrate their answer to you.
2. **Model Sentence:** Write down the first sentence of their narration (modifying when necessary to simplify or shorten).
3. **Copywork/Dictation:** For weeks 1–28, have your student carefully copy the model sentence onto their Student Page. For weeks 28 on, follow these steps: (1) read the student's sentence back to her and (2) have her repeat it back to you. Then (3) have her write the sentence down on her own, without access to the written model. Repeat steps 1–2 if necessary until the student has written the full sentence.

The prompts in these lessons are designed to awaken a student's creativity. After completing the model sentence, some students may want to draw a picture or write additional sentences on their own. Encourage this, but do not require it. While the model sentence should be checked and edited for grammar and spelling, do not require students to correct or edit any additional writing. Just encourage them!

WEEK 1

DAY ONE: Narration Exercise

Focus: *Identifying central ideas and actions*

Pull out Student Page 1. Ask the student to write his name and the date.

Read the following passage out loud to the student. After reading this passage, you will help the student identify the three central actions that form the "skeleton" of the plot. This will begin to train the student in the skill of summarizing narrative passages.

> The Owl always takes her sleep during the day. Then after sundown, when the rosy light fades from the sky and the shadows rise slowly through the wood, out she comes ruffling and blinking from the old hollow tree. Now her weird "hoo-hoo-hoo-oo-oo" echoes through the quiet wood, and she begins her hunt for the bugs and beetles, frogs and mice she likes so well to eat.
>
> Now there was a certain old Owl who had become very cross and hard to please as she grew older, especially if anything disturbed her daily slumbers. One warm summer afternoon as she dozed away in her den in the old oak tree, a Grasshopper nearby began a joyous but very raspy song. Out popped the old Owl's head from the opening in the tree that served her both for door and for window.
>
> "Get away from here, sir," she said to the Grasshopper. "Have you no manners? You should at least respect my age and leave me to sleep in quiet!"
>
> But the Grasshopper answered saucily that he had as much right to his place in the sun as the Owl had to her place in the old oak. Then he struck up a louder and still more rasping tune.
>
> The wise old Owl knew quite well that it would do no good to argue with the Grasshopper, nor with anybody else for that matter. Besides, her eyes were not sharp enough by day to permit her to punish the Grasshopper as he deserved. So she laid aside all hard words and spoke very kindly to him.
>
> "Well sir," she said, "if I must stay awake, I am going to settle right down to enjoy your singing. Now that I think of it, I have a wonderful wine here, sent me from Olympus, of which I am told Apollo drinks before he sings to the high gods. Please come up and taste this delicious drink with me. I know it will make you sing like Apollo himself."
>
> The foolish Grasshopper was taken in by the Owl's flattering words. Up he jumped to the Owl's den, but as soon as he was near enough so the old Owl could see him clearly, she pounced upon him and ate him up.
>
> Moral: Just because someone flatters you, it doesn't mean that they truly admire you.

—From "The Owl and the Grasshopper"
by Aesop

Ask the following questions to test the student's listening ability. Remind the student to answer in complete sentences; if he answers in a fragment, put the answer in the form of a sentence and then require the student to repeat it back to you.

Instructor: When does the Owl sleep?
Student: *She sleeps during the day.*

Instructor: What did the Grasshopper do to annoy the owl?
Student: *He began a very noisy, raspy song.*

Instructor: When the Owl told the Grasshopper to be quiet, what did the Grasshopper do?
Student: *He began to sing more loudly.*

Instructor: Why did the Owl decide not to punish the Grasshopper at once?
Student: *She couldn't see well enough during the day to catch him.*

Instructor: What did the Owl offer to the Grasshopper?
Student: *She offered him the wine of Apollo.*

Instructor: What happened to the Grasshopper when he jumped up to drink the wine?
Student: *The Owl ate him.*

Your goal now is to teach the student to summarize the basic narrative thread in the passage—the "bones" of the selection—in not more than two sentences. In order to do this, say to the student:

Instructor: What problem did the Owl have?
Student: *The Grasshopper was keeping the Owl awake.*

Instructor: How did the Owl get rid of the Grasshopper?
Student: *She invited the Grasshopper to come drink wine with her, and then she ate him.*

Note: If the student just gives you one part of this answer, encourage him to give a two-part answer by saying:

Instructor: What did the Owl invite the Grasshopper to do?
Student: *She invited him to drink wine.*

Instructor: Then what did she do?
Student: *She ate him.*

Now ask the student, "Can you tell me in one or two sentences what happened in this story?" The student's answer should resemble one of the following (three BRIEF sentences are also acceptable):

"The Grasshopper was making so much noise that the Owl couldn't sleep. He wouldn't be quiet, so she invited him in to have wine, and then she ate him."

"The Grasshopper wouldn't stop singing when the Owl asked him to. So she flattered him, and then she ate him up."

"The Owl couldn't sleep because the Grasshopper was singing. So she told him that he was a wonderful singer and offered him wine. When he flew up to drink it, she ate him."

Write down the student's narration on Student Page 1 as he watches.

Note To Instructor: As you can see, students cannot learn to summarize effectively until they are guided into recognizing the important elements of stories through careful questioning. Your questioning and conversation will help the student learn to discard unimportant details and keep only the central parts of the narrative.

DAY TWO: Copywork Exercise *Student Page 2*

Focus: *Review beginning capitals and ending punctuation; proper use of "a" and "an"*

Pull out Student Page 2. Ask the student to write his name and the date. The following model sentence is already printed on it:

Do not let flattery throw you off your guard against an enemy.

Ask the student to look carefully at the sentence. While he is examining it, tell him that this is another way to phrase the moral of "The Owl and the Grasshopper." Point out that the article before "enemy" is "an" rather than "a" because "enemy" begins with a vowel rather than a consonant. Remind him that a sentence begins with a capital letter and ends with a punctuation mark.

Remember to watch him write, and correct him at once if he begins to make errors in spelling or format.

DAY THREE: The First Dictation Exercise *Student Page 3*

Pull out Student Page 3. Ask the student to write his name and the date.

Tips for Teaching

Now that the student has experience in writing properly while looking at a sentence, he'll learn how to *visualize* a properly written sentence in his head before he puts it down on paper.

For this reason, the first dictation exercise is the sentence which the student copied the day before. Although you won't show the sentence to the student before dictating it, he should have some memory of it.

Just as with beginning copywork, allow the student to write in pencil. Watch him as he writes; if he begins to make a mistake in form or spelling, stop him and tell him the correct answer. Never let him write incorrectly; the point of the exercise is to reinforce *correct* mental pictures of written language.

If the student asks you how to spell a word, tell him; this is not a spelling exercise.

Dictate the following sentence to the student:

Do not let flattery throw you off your guard against an enemy.

This dictation sentence does not contain any punctuation challenges. If necessary, remind the student that this is a command, and that commands are sentences which begin with capital letters and end with periods or exclamation points. Since this is not an urgent command, it ends with a period.

Tell the student that you will read the sentence slowly, twice. He should pay close attention so that he can remember the sentence and write it down.

After you have repeated the sentence the second time, encourage the student to repeat it back to you. After he repeats it, tell him to write it down.

If the student forgets the last part of the sentence, you can read it to him again. However, first tell him to read out loud what he's already written, and see whether he can then say the rest of the sentence himself. (You should continue to follow this procedure for the rest of the dictation exercises in this workbook.)

If you do have to repeat the last part of the sentence out loud, ask the student to repeat the forgotten words back to you before he writes. You are helping the student develop the skill of active listening as he writes, which will be necessary when he does his own original work later.

DAY FOUR: Narration Exercise and Dictation   *Student Pages 4–5*

Focus: *Identifying the central narrative thread in a story*

Pull out Student Pages 4–5. Ask the student to write his name and the date on Student Page 5.

Today's exercise will combine narration and dictation. Tell the student that you will read the following passage to him, ask him a few questions about it, and then help him to summarize in two or three sentences. After you write these sentences down (while the student watches), you will dictate one or two of them back to him.

Read the following passage out loud to the student:

> The Fox one day thought of a plan to amuse himself at the expense of the Stork, at whose odd appearance he was always laughing.
>
> "You must come and dine with me today," he said to the Stork, smiling to himself at the trick he was going to play. The Stork gladly accepted the invitation and arrived in good time and with a very good appetite.
>
> For dinner the Fox served soup. But it was set out in a very shallow dish, and all the Stork could do was to wet the very tip of his bill. Not a drop of soup could he get. But the Fox lapped it up easily, and, to increase the disappointment of the Stork, made a great show of enjoyment.

The hungry Stork was much displeased at the trick, but he was a calm, even-tempered fellow and saw no good in flying into a rage. Instead, not long afterward, he invited the Fox to dine with him in turn.

The Fox arrived promptly at the time that had been set, and the Stork served a fish dinner that had a very appetizing smell. But it was served in a tall jar with a very narrow neck. The Stork could easily get at the food with his long bill, but all the Fox could do was to lick the outside of the jar, and sniff at the delicious odor. And when the Fox lost his temper, the Stork said calmly, "Do not play tricks on your neighbors unless you can stand the same treatment yourself."

—From "The Fox and the Stork"
by Aesop

Ask the following questions to test the student's listening ability. Remind the student to answer in complete sentences; if he answers in a fragment, put the answer in the form of a sentence and then require the student to repeat it back to you.

Instructor: Why did the Fox laugh at the Stork?
Student: *He laughed at the Stork's odd appearance.*

Instructor: What did the Fox serve the Stork for dinner?
Student: *He served soup.*

Instructor: Why did the Stork have trouble eating the soup?
Student: *He could not get his bill down into the shallow dish.*

Instructor: What did the Stork serve the Fox in return?
Student: *He served the Fox fish.*

Instructor: Why couldn't the Fox eat the fish?
Student: *It was in a tall jar with a narrow opening.*

Instructor: What is the moral of this fable?
Student: *If you play tricks on people, you shouldn't be upset when they play tricks on you* OR *Don't play tricks on people unless you don't mind having tricks played on you* OR an equivalent answer.

You will now continue to teach the student to summarize the basic narrative thread in the passage. In order to do this, say to the student:

Instructor: What did the Fox do to the Stork?
Student: *He served the Stork dinner in a dish too shallow for the Stork to eat out of.*

Instructor: What did the Stork do to the Fox in return?
Student: *He served the Fox dinner in a jar with a very narrow top.*

Instructor: What did the Stork say to the Fox at the end of the story?
Student: *Don't play tricks on people if you don't want tricks played on you.*

Now ask the student, "Can you tell me in two sentences what happened in this story?" The student's answer should resemble one of the following (three BRIEF sentences are also acceptable):

> "The Fox played a trick on the Stork, so the Stork played the same trick on the Fox. The moral of the story is that you shouldn't play tricks unless you can put up with tricks played on you."

> "The Fox thought the Stork was funny looking, so he invited the Stork to dinner. But the soup was served in a shallow dish, and the Stork couldn't eat it. So the Stork played the same trick on the Fox."

> "The Fox invited the Stork to dinner and fed him soup in a dish that was too shallow for the Stork to eat from. So the Stork invited the Fox to dinner and gave him fish in a jar with a narrow top."

Write down the student's narration on Student Page 4 as he watches. Then, choose one of the sentences from the narration to use as a dictation exercise (Student Page 5). Follow the same dictation techniques as above.

If the student writes well and easily, you may choose to dictate two sentences instead.

DAY FIVE (optional): Creative Writing   *Student Pages 6–7*

As discussed in the introduction, the fifth lesson of each week is an optional creative writing lesson/prompt. Please refer to page vii for detailed instructions on how to use these prompts.

For creative writing activities in weeks 1–10, student responses to the prompt should be one sentence of roughly 10–12 words. If your student's verbal response is longer than 12 words, shorten it before writing it down.

> Pull out Student Pages 6–7. Write the student's name and the date for him as he watches, or ask him to write the name and date independently.

> **Instructor:** Imagine that the owl, the grasshopper, the fox, and the stork all have dinner together. What does each animal choose to eat? If you like, draw an illustration to accompany your sentence on Student Page 7.

Remind the student to answer you in a complete sentence. If he answers in a fragment, turn the fragment into a complete sentence, say it to him, and then ask him to repeat this sentence back to you. Write the student's answer down on the "Instructor" lines of Student Page 6 as he watches. Then have him copy the sentence onto the "Student" lines.

WEEK 2

DAY ONE: Narration Exercise

Focus: *Identifying central ideas and actions*

Pull out Student Page 8. Ask the student to write her name and the date.

Read the following passage out loud to the student. After reading this passage, you will help the student identify the most important part of the description.

Tell the student that this passage comes from one of the stories about the Land of Oz that L. Frank Baum wrote after he finished *The Wizard of Oz*. Ojo is a little boy from the Munchkin country. On his adventures, he has arrived at the house of a magician and his wife, Margolotte. Margolotte has decided to make herself a household maid out of patchwork.

> Ojo examined this curious contrivance with wonder. The Patchwork Girl was taller than he, when she stood upright, and her body was plump and rounded because it had been so neatly stuffed with cotton. Margolotte had first made the girl's form from the patchwork quilt and then she had dressed it with a patchwork skirt and an apron with pockets in it—using the same gay material throughout. Upon the feet she had sewn a pair of red leather shoes with pointed toes. All the fingers and thumbs of the girl's hands had been carefully formed and stuffed and stitched at the edges, with gold plates at the ends to serve as finger-nails . . . .
>
> The head of the Patchwork Girl was the most curious part of her. While she waited for her husband to finish making his Powder of Life the woman had found ample time to complete the head as her fancy dictated, and she realized that a good servant's head must be properly constructed. The hair was of brown yarn and hung down on her neck in several neat braids. Her eyes were two silver suspender-buttons cut from a pair of the Magician's old trousers, and they were sewed on with black threads, which formed the pupils of the eyes. Margolotte had puzzled over the ears for some time, for these were important if the servant was to hear distinctly, but finally she had made them out of thin plates of gold and attached them in place by means of stitches through tiny holes bored in the metal. Gold is the most common metal in the Land of Oz and is used for many purposes because it is soft and pliable.
>
> The woman had cut a slit for the Patchwork Girl's mouth and sewn two rows of white pearls in it for teeth, using a strip of scarlet plush for a tongue. This mouth Ojo considered very artistic and lifelike, and Margolotte was pleased when the boy praised it. There were almost too many patches on the face of the girl for her to be considered strictly beautiful, for one cheek was yellow and the other red, her chin blue, her forehead purple and the center, where her nose had been formed and padded, a bright yellow.

—From *The Patchwork Girl of Oz*
by L. Frank Baum

Ask the following questions to test the student's listening ability. Remind the student to answer in complete sentences; if she answers in a fragment, put the answer in the form of a sentence and then require the student to repeat it back to you.

Instructor: Who is taller—Ojo or the Patchwork Girl?
Student: *The Patchwork Girl is taller.*

Instructor: What kind of shoes is the Patchwork Girl wearing?
Student: *She is wearing red leather shoes with pointed toes.*

Instructor: What are the Patchwork Girl's fingernails made out of?
Student: *They are made out of gold plates.*

Instructor: What else on the Patchwork Girl is made out of gold?
Student: *Her ears are made out of gold.*

Instructor: What is her hair made from?
Student: *Her hair is made from brown yarn.*

Instructor: What color is her nose?
Student: *Her nose is bright yellow.*

Instructor: What are her teeth made from?
Student: *Her teeth are made from pearls.*

Your goal now is to teach the student to summarize the central idea in the passage. In order to do this, say to the student:

Instructor: What was unusual about the Patchwork Girl?
Student: *She was made out of a patchwork quilt.*

Instructor: List three other things that were used to make her.
Student: *She had gold ears and fingernails, red leather shoes, yarn hair, pearl teeth, button eyes, and a plush tongue.*

Now tell the student, "Describe the Patchwork Girl to me in one sentence." The student's answer should resemble one of the following:

"The Patchwork Girl was made out of a patchwork quilt, with gold ears, button eyes, and pearl teeth."

"The girl was made out of patchwork, and she wore a patchwork skirt, a patchwork apron, and red leather shoes."

"The Patchwork Girl was made out of a quilt, and she had yarn hair, button eyes, and a plush tongue."

Write down the student's narration on Student Page 8 as she watches.

DAY TWO: Copywork Exercise

Focus: *Action verbs, capitalization of the pronoun "I"*

Pull out Student Page 9. Ask the student to write her name and the date. The following model sentence is already printed on it:

> So I cut up the quilt and made from it a girl, which I stuffed
> with cotton.

Ask the student to look carefully at the sentence. While she is examining it, explain that these are Margolotte's words, telling Ojo how she made the Patchwork Girl. Point out that the pronoun *I* is capitalized. Then ask the student to point out the three action verbs in the sentence (cut, made, stuffed). If she has difficulty finding the action verbs, say, "What did Margolotte do with the quilt?" (She *cut* it up.) What did she do with it then? (She *made* a girl.) What did she do with the cotton? (She *stuffed* it into the Patchwork Girl.)

Now ask the student to copy the sentence. Remember to watch her write, and correct her at once if she begins to make errors in spelling or format.

DAY THREE: Dictation Exercise

Pull out Student Page 10. Ask the student to write her name and the date.
Dictate the following sentence to the student:

> So I cut up the quilt and made from it a girl, which I stuffed
> with cotton.

Before she begins to write, remind her that *I* is capitalized. Also, remind her that there is a comma in the sentence, and that she should listen for it. Read the sentence twice. When you reach the comma while dictating, pause while you count silently to three.

Ask the student to repeat the sentence back to you before she writes. If she cannot remember it, repeat it to her until she can.

DAY FOUR: Narration Exercise and Dictation

Focus: *Identifying the central narrative thread in a passage*

Pull out Student Pages 11–12. Ask the student to write her name and the date on Student Page 12.

Today's exercise will combine narration and dictation. Tell the student that you will read the following passage to her, ask her a few questions about it, and then help her to summarize.

After you write these summary sentences down (while the student watches), you will dictate one or two of them back to her.

Read the following passage out loud to the student. Tell her that a "conundrum" is a riddle that can't be answered.

In this scene, Ojo and the Patchwork Girl, whose name is Scraps, have been travelling all morning, along with a Glass Cat. When they stop for a rest, Ojo begins to eat the bread and cheese he has packed for lunch.

"Why do you put those things into your mouth?" asked Scraps, gazing at him in astonishment. "Do you need more stuffing? Then why don't you use cotton, such as I am stuffed with?"

"I don't need that kind," said Ojo.

"But a mouth is to talk with, isn't it?"

"It is also to eat with," replied the boy. "If I didn't put food into my mouth, and eat it, I would get hungry and starve."

"Ah, I didn't know that," she said. "Give me some."

Ojo handed her a bit of the bread and she put it in her mouth.

"What next?" she asked, scarcely able to speak.

"Chew it and swallow it," said the boy.

Scraps tried that. Her pearl teeth were unable to chew the bread and beyond her mouth there was no opening. Being unable to swallow she threw away the bread and laughed.

"I must get hungry and starve, for I can't eat," she said.

"Neither can I," announced the cat; "but I'm not fool enough to try. Can't you understand that you and I are superior people and not made like these poor humans?"

"Why should I understand that, or anything else?" asked the girl. "Don't bother my head by asking conundrums, I beg of you. Just let me discover myself in my own way."

With this she began amusing herself by leaping across the brook and back again.

"Be careful, or you'll fall in the water," warned Ojo.

"Never mind."

"You'd better. If you get wet you'll be soggy and can't walk. Your colors might run, too," he said.

"Don't my colors run whenever I run?" she asked.

"Not in the way I mean. If they get wet, the reds and greens and yellows and purples of your patches might run into each other and become just a blur—no color at all, you know."

"Then," said the Patchwork Girl, "I'll be careful, for if I spoiled my splendid colors I would cease to be beautiful."

—From *The Patchwork Girl of Oz*
by L. Frank Baum

Ask the following questions to test the student's listening ability. Remind the student to answer in complete sentences; if she answers in a fragment, put the answer in the form of a sentence and then require the student to repeat it back to you.

Instructor: What is Ojo doing that confuses Scraps, the Patchwork Girl?
Student: Ojo is eating.

Instructor: Can Scraps eat?
Student: No, she can't chew or swallow.

Instructor: When Ojo says that the Patchwork Girl's colors will "run," what does he mean?
Student: He means that the color will come out of the cloth when it gets wet.

Instructor: When the Patchwork Girl says "run," what does she mean?
Student: She means running with her legs.

Instructor: Both the colors and the Patchwork Girl can run! The same word is used in two different ways in the story. If the Patchwork Girl's colors "run," what will they turn into?
Student: They will turn into a blur.

You will now continue to teach the student to summarize the basic narrative thread in the passage. In order to do this, say to the student:

Instructor: What was Ojo doing that Scraps could not do?
Student: Ojo was eating.

Instructor: What did Scraps do to entertain herself while Ojo was eating?
Student: Scraps jumped across the water.

Instructor: What would have happened if Scraps had gotten wet?
Student: Her colors would run.

Now ask the student, "Can you tell me in two sentences what happened in this story?" The student's answer should resemble one of the following (three BRIEF sentences are also acceptable):

"Ojo was eating, but Scraps could not eat. So she jumped over the water, but she was afraid to get wet."

"Scraps tried to eat because Ojo was eating, but she couldn't. Instead she jumped over the water, but Ojo told her not to fall in."

"Scraps discovered that she could not chew or swallow. While Ojo was eating, she played near the water."

Write down the student's narration on Student Page 11 as she watches. Then, choose one of the sentences from the narration to use as a dictation exercise (Student Page 12). Follow the same dictation techniques as above.

If the student writes well and easily, you may choose to dictate two sentences instead.

DAY **F**IVE **(optional):** Creative Writing   *Student Pages 13–14*

Pull out Student Pages 13–14. Write the student's name and the date for her as she watches, or ask her to write the name and date independently.

> **Instructor:** If you could make something in your house come alive – a toy, a piece of furniture, a blanket, anything – what would you choose? What is one thing it might say? If you like, draw a picture of it on Student Page 14.

Remind the student to answer you in a complete sentence. If she answers in a fragment, turn the fragment into a complete sentence, say it to her, and then ask her to repeat this sentence back to you. Write the student's answer down on the "Instructor" lines of Student Page 13 as she watches. Then have her copy the sentence onto the "Student" lines.

WEEK 3

DAY ONE: Narration Exercise   *Student Page 15*

Focus: Identifying central ideas and actions

Pull out Student Page 15. Ask the student to write his name and the date.

Read the following passage out loud to the student. After reading this passage, you will help the student identify the actions that form the "skeleton" of the plot.

> Up to the time of this story Patsy was just an everyday little girl. Sometimes she was good and sometimes she was naughty but usually she did what her mother told her without too much fuss. BUT ONE MORNING Patsy's mother filled the bathtub with nice warm water and called to Patsy to come and take her bath. Patsy came into the bathroom but when she saw the nice warm tub of water she began to scream and yell and kick and howl like a wild animal.
>
> Naturally her mother was quite surprised to see her little girl acting so peculiarly but she didn't say anything, just took off Patsy's bathrobe and said, "Now, Patsy, stop all this nonsense and hop into the tub."
>
> Patsy gave a piercing shriek and ran from the bathroom stark naked and yelling, "I won't take a bath! I won't ever take a bath! I hate baths! I HATE BATHS! I haaaaaaaaaaaaaaaaaaaaate baaaaaaaaaaaaaaths!" . . . .
>
> The next morning she didn't say one single word to Patsy about a bath and so Patsy was sweet and didn't act like a wild animal. The next day was the same and so was the next and the next.
>
> When Sunday came Patsy was a rather dark blackish gray color so her mother suggested that she stay home from Sunday School . . . .
>
> By the end of the third week they had to keep Patsy indoors all of the time because one morning she skipped out to get the mail and the postman, on seeing her straggly, uncombed, dust-caked hair and the rapidly forming layer of topsoil on her face, neck, and arms, gave a terrified yell and fell down the front steps.

—From *Mrs. Piggle-Wiggle*
by Betty MacDonald

Ask the following questions to test the student's listening ability. Remind the student to answer in complete sentences; if he answers in a fragment, put the answer in the form of a sentence and then require the student to repeat it back to you.

Instructor: What did Patsy do when she saw her nice warm tub of water? Can you remember all four actions?
Student: *Patsy screamed, yelled, kicked, and howled.*

Instructor: What did she do when her mother told her to hop into the tub?
Student: *She ran out of the bathroom yelling, "I hate baths!"*

Instructor: Why was Patsy sweet the next morning?
Student: *Her mother didn't say anything to her about a bath.*

Instructor: Why did Patsy's mother suggest that she stay home from Sunday School?
Student: *Patsy was dark blackish gray.*

Instructor: What was covering her face, neck, and arms?
Student: *She had topsoil on her face, neck, and arms!*

Instructor: What happened when the postman saw her?
Student: *He yelled and fell down the front steps.*

Instructor: What did Patsy's mother and father decide to do then?
Student: *They decided to keep Patsy indoors.*

Your goal now is to teach the student to summarize the basic narrative thread in the passage—the "bones" of the selection—in not more than two sentences. In order to do this, say to the student:

Instructor: What problem did Patsy have?
Student: *She hated her bath.*

Instructor: How did her parents react to this?
Student: *They didn't make her take a bath, and kept her inside.*

Note: If the student just gives you one part of this answer, encourage him to give a two-part answer by saying:

Instructor: Did they make her take a bath?
Student: *No, they did not.*

Instructor: What did they do when she scared the postman?
Student: *They kept her inside.*

Instructor: What happened to Patsy when she stopped taking baths?
Student: *She got a layer of dirt all over her face, hands, and neck.*

Note: If the student says, "She turned blackish gray," ask, "Why did she turn blackish gray?"

Now ask the student, "Can you tell me in two sentences what happened in this story?" The student's answer should resemble one of the following:

"Patsy hated taking baths and refused to have another one. She got so dirty that she had to stay indoors all the time."

"Pasty wouldn't have a bath, and so her parents kept her inside. Dirt started to cover her face, neck, and hands."

"When Patsy saw her bath, she screamed and ran away, so her parents didn't make her take another one. She got so dirty that she frightened the postman and couldn't go to Sunday School."

Write down the student's narration on Student Page 15 as he watches.

DAY TWO: Copywork Exercise

Student Page 16

Focus: *Linking verbs*

Pull out Student Page 16. Ask the student to write his name and the date. The following model sentences are already printed on it:

> Patsy refused to take a bath. She was so dirty that she could not go outside.

Ask the student to look carefully at the sentence. While he is examining it, ask him to point to *refused* in the first sentence. This is an action verb. Then, ask him to point to *was* in the second sentence. This is a linking verb. It connects the subject, Patsy, to the adjective that describes the subject: dirty.

Ask him to copy both sentences. Remember to watch him write, and correct him at once if he begins to make errors in spelling or format.

DAY THREE: Dictation Exercise

Student Page 17

Pull out Student Page 17. Ask the student to write his name and the date.

Dictate the following sentences to the student:

> Patsy refused to take a bath. She was so dirty that she could not go outside.

Before he begins to write, remind him that the dictation exercise has two separate sentences. Tell him to listen for the period, and to capitalize the next word that comes after it. Then read the sentences twice. When you reach the period, pause while you count silently to five.

Ask the student to repeat the sentences back to you before he writes. If he cannot remember them, repeat them to him until he can. If necessary, you may dictate the sentences one at a time (by the end of the year, you will aim for the student to be able to remember two sentences at once).

DAY FOUR: Narration Exercise and Dictation   *Student Pages 18–19*

Focus: *Identifying the central narrative thread in a passage*

Pull out Student Pages 18–19. Ask the student to write his name and the date on Student Page 19.

Today's exercise will combine narration and dictation. Tell the student that you will read the following passage to him, ask him a few questions about it, and then help him to summarize. After you write these summary sentences down (while the student watches), you will dictate one or two of them back to him.

Read the following passage out loud to the student. Tell him that Patsy can't talk clearly because she has so much dried mud on her cheeks and lips.

> That night when she was asleep her mother and father tiptoed into her room and very gently pressed radish seeds into her forehead, her arms, and the backs of her hands. When they had finished and were standing by her bed gazing fondly at their handiwork, Patsy's father said, "Repulsive little thing, isn't she?"
>
> Patsy's mother said, "Why, George, that's a terrible thing to say of your own child!"
>
> "My little girl is buried so deep in that dirt that I can't even remember what she looks like," said Patsy's father and he stamped down the stairs.
>
> The Radish Cure is certainly hard on the parents.
>
> Quite a few days after that Patsy awoke one morning and there on the back of her hand, in fact on the backs of both hands and on her arms and on her FOREHEAD were GREEN LEAVES! Patsy tried to brush them off but they just bent over and sprang right up again.
>
> She jumped out of bed and ran down the stairs to the dining room where her mother and father were eating breakfast. "Ook, ook at y ands!" she squeaked.
>
> Her father said, "Behold the bloom of youth," and her mother said, "George!" then jumped up briskly, went over to Patsy, took a firm hold of one of the plants on her forehead and gave it a quick jerk. Patsy squealed and her mother showed her the little red radish she had pulled. Patsy tried to pull one out of her arm, but her hands were so caked with dirt that they couldn't grasp the little leaves so her mother had to pull them.
>
> When they had finished one hand and part of the left arm, Patsy suddenly said, "Other, I ant a ath!"
>
> "What did you say?" asked her mother, busily pulling the radishes and putting them in neat little piles on the dining room table.
>
> "I oowant a b . . . b . . . ath!" said Patsy so plainly that it cracked the mud on her left cheek.

—From *Mrs. Piggle-Wiggle*
by Betty MacDonald

Ask the following questions to test the student's listening ability. Remind the student to answer in complete sentences; if he answers in a fragment, put the answer in the form of a sentence and then require the student to repeat it back to you.

Instructor: What do Patsy's mother and father put into the dirt on her skin?
Student: *They put radish seeds into the dirt.*

Instructor: What do the seeds do?
Student: *The seeds sprout!*

Instructor: What does Patsy's mother do when she sees the green leaves?
Student: *She pulls the radishes out.*

Instructor: Does Patsy help?
Student: *No, her hands are too dirty.*

Instructor: What does Patsy say to her mother?
Student: *She says, "I want a bath!"*

You will now continue to teach the student to summarize the basic narrative thread in the passage. In order to do this, say to the student:

Instructor: What did Patsy's parents do to convince her to take a bath?
Student: *They planted radish seeds on her dirty skin.*

Instructor: Did this work? What did Patsy do?
Student: *It did work; Patsy took a bath!*

Now ask the student, "Can you tell me in one or two sentences what happened in this story?" The student's answer should resemble one of the following:

"Patsy's mother and father planted radish seeds on her. When they sprouted, she took a bath."

"Patsy's parents convinced her to take a bath by planting radishes on her."

"Patsy's parents put radish seeds into the dirt on her skin. The radishes grew, so Patsy decided to take a bath."

Write down the student's narration on Student Page 18 as he watches. Then, choose one of the sentences from the narration to use as a dictation exercise (Student Page 19). Follow the same dictation techniques as above.

If the student writes well and easily, you may choose to dictate two sentences instead.

DAY FIVE (optional): Creative Writing   *Student Pages 20–21*

Pull out Student Pages 20–21. Write the student's name and the date for him as he watches, or ask him to write the name and date independently.

Instructor: In the story *Mrs. Piggle-Wiggle*, Patsy hates taking a bath and refuses to do it until she gets so dirty that vegetables grow on her body. Listen to the description of Patsy one more time. Try to draw a picture of what she looks like, using the details I read to you.

If you like, write a sentence about what would happen to a kid who refused to brush his teeth for a whole year.

Read the student the following description of Patsy:

Patsy awoke one morning and there on the back of her hand, in fact on the backs of both hands and on her arms and on her forehead, were green leaves! Her hands were so caked with dirt that they couldn't grasp the little leaves, so her mother had to pull them off.

If the student chooses to answer the written prompt, write his answer down on the "Instructor" lines of Student Page 20 as he watches. Then have him copy the sentence onto the "Student" lines.

WEEK 4

DAY ONE: Narration Exercise   *Student Page 22*

Focus: *Identifying central ideas and actions*

Pull out Student Page 22. Ask the student to write her name and the date.

Read the following passage out loud to the student. After reading this passage, you will help the student identify the actions that form the "skeleton" of the plot.

> Once upon a time, many years ago when our grandfathers were little children—there was a doctor; and his name was Dolittle—John Dolittle, M.D. "M.D." means that he was a proper doctor and knew a whole lot.
>
> He lived in a little town called Puddleby-on-the-Marsh. All the folks, young and old, knew him well by sight. And whenever he walked down the street in his high hat everyone would say, "There goes the Doctor!—He's a clever man." And the dogs and the children would all run up and follow behind him; and even the crows that lived in the church-tower would caw and nod their heads.
>
> The house he lived in, on the edge of the town, was quite small; but his garden was very large and had a wide lawn and stone seats and weeping-willows hanging over. His sister, Sarah Dolittle, was housekeeper for him; but the Doctor looked after the garden himself.
>
> He was very fond of animals and kept many kinds of pets. Besides the goldfish in the pond at the bottom of his garden, he had rabbits in the pantry, white mice in his piano, a squirrel in the linen closet and a hedgehog in the cellar. He had a cow with a calf too, and an old lame horse—twenty-five years of age—and chickens, and pigeons, and two lambs, and many other animals. But his favorite pets were Dab-Dab the duck, Jip the dog, Gub-Gub the baby pig, Polynesia the parrot, and the owl Too-Too.
>
> —From *Doctor Dolittle*
> by Hugh Lofting

Ask the following questions to test the student's listening ability. Remind the student to answer in complete sentences; if she answers in a fragment, put the answer in the form of a sentence and then require the student to repeat it back to you.

Instructor: What two initials tell us that John Dolittle is a doctor?
Student: *The initials M.D. tell us that he is a doctor.*

Instructor: Do you remember the name of his town?
Student: *It was called Puddleby-on-the-Marsh.*

Instructor: What was the difference between the size of the house and the size of the garden?
Student: *The house was small and the garden was large.*

Instructor: Who was Doctor Dolittle's housekeeper?
Student: *His sister Sarah was his housekeeper.*

Instructor: Can you remember four different kinds of animals that Doctor Dolittle kept as pets?
Student: *He kept goldfish, mice, a squirrel, rabbits, a hedgehog, a cow and calf, a horse, chickens, pigeons, and lambs.*

Instructor: Can you remember the names of two of his pets?
Student: *They were named Dab-Dab the duck, Jip the dog, Gub-Gub the pig, Polynesia the parrot, and Too-Too the owl.*

Your goal now is to teach the student to summarize the central idea in the passage. In order to do this, say to the student:

Instructor: What was John Dolittle?
Student: *He was a doctor.*

Instructor: What was unusual about him?
Student: *He had many different pets.*

Instructor: Can you name one or two of them?
Student: *He had cats, goldfish, and mice* OR *He had a dog named Jip and a parrot named Polynesia.*

Now tell the student, "Describe Doctor Dolittle to me in one sentence." The student's answer should resemble one of the following:

"John Dolittle was a doctor who had many pets, including cats and mice."

"Doctor Doolittle had cats, mice, goldfish, a squirrel, and many other pets."

"Doctor Doolittle had an owl named Too-Too, a pig named Gub-Gub, and many other animals."

Write down the student's narration on Student Page 22 as she watches.

DAY TWO: Copywork Exercise   *Student Page 23*

Focus: *Commands and questions*

Pull out Student Page 23. Ask the student to write her name and the date. The following model sentences are already printed on it:

> How can you expect sick people to come and see you when you keep all these animals in the house? Do not keep the parlor full of hedgehogs and mice!

Ask the student to look carefully at the sentences. While she is examining them, tell her that these are the words of Doctor Dolittle's sister Sarah. He has so many pets in the house that his human patients stop coming to see him!

Point out that the first sentence is a question and ends with a question mark. The second is a command. Sarah wants Doctor Dolittle to get the animals out of the house. She feels strongly about this—so the command ends with an exclamation point instead of a period!

Ask the student to copy one or both of the sentences, depending on handwriting ability. Remember to watch her write, and correct her at once if she begins to make errors in spelling or format.

DAY THREE: Dictation Exercise   *Student Page 24*

Pull out Student Page 24. Ask the student to write her name and the date.

Read the following sentences to the student:

> How can you expect sick people to come and see you when you keep all these animals in the house?
>
> Do not keep the parlor full of hedgehogs and mice!

Ask her which sentence she would like to write. Before she begins to write, ask her whether the sentence ends with a question mark or an exclamation point. Then read the sentence twice. Ask the student to repeat the sentence back to you before she writes.

DAY FOUR: Narration Exercise and Dictation   *Student Pages 25–26*

Focus: Identifying the central idea in a passage

Pull out Student Pages 25–26. Ask the student to write her name and the date on Student Page 26.

Today's exercise will combine narration and dictation. Tell the student that you will read the following passage to her, ask her a few questions about it, and then help her to summarize in one or two sentences. After you write these sentences down (while the student watches), you will dictate one or two of them back to her.

Read the following passage out loud to the student:

At tea-time, when the dog, Jip, came in, the parrot said to the Doctor, "See, he's talking to you."

"Looks to me as though he were scratching his ear," said the Doctor.

"But animals don't always speak with their mouths," said the parrot in a high voice, raising her eyebrows. "They talk with their ears, with their feet, with their tails—with everything. Sometimes they don't WANT to make a noise. Do you see now the way he's twitching up one side of his nose?"

"What's that mean?" asked the Doctor.

"That means, 'Can't you see that it has stopped raining?'" Polynesia answered. "He is asking you a question. Dogs nearly always use their noses for asking questions."

After a while, with the parrot's help, the Doctor got to learn the language of the animals so well that he could talk to them himself and understand everything they said. Then he gave up being a people's doctor altogether . . . . old ladies began to bring him their pet pugs and poodles who had eaten too much cake; and farmers came many miles to show him sick cows and sheep.

—From *Doctor Dolittle*
by Hugh Lofting

Ask the following questions to test the student's listening ability. Remind the student to answer in complete sentences; if she answers in a fragment, put the answer in the form of a sentence and then require the student to repeat it back to you.

Instructor: What is the dog's name?
Student: *His name is Jip.*

Instructor: What is the parrot's name?
Student: *Her name is Polynesia.*

Instructor: What do animals talk with?
Student: *They talk with their ears, feet, and tails.*

Instructor: What does Jip do to say, "Can't you see that it has stopped raining?"
Student: *He twitches his nose.*

Instructor: Once the Doctor learns animal language, what changes?
Student: *He starts to be an animal doctor instead of a people doctor.*

Your goal now is to teach the student to summarize the central idea in the passage. In order to do this, say to the student:

Instructor: How do animals talk?
Student: *They talk with their ears, feet, tails, and other parts of their bodies.*

Instructor: When Doctor Dolittle learns to talk with animals, what does he become?
Student: *He becomes an animal doctor.*

Now tell the student, "Tell me about animal language and Doctor Dolittle in one or two sentences."

The student's answer should resemble one of the following:

"Doctor Dolittle learned animal language and became an animal doctor."

"Polynesia told Doctor Dolittle how to understand animal language. He stopped being a people doctor and became an animal doctor."

"Doctor Dolittle's parrot told him that animals talked with their ears, feet, and tails. He learned to talk to animals, and started to doctor animals instead of people."

Write down the student's narration on Student Page 25 as she watches. Then, choose one of the sentences from the narration to use as a dictation exercise (Student Page 26). Follow the same dictation techniques as above.

If the student writes well and easily, you may choose to dictate two sentences instead.

Day Five (optional): Creative Writing   *Student Pages 27–28*

Pull out Student Pages 27–28. Write the student's name and the date for her as she watches, or ask her to write the name and date independently.

Instructor: In the story, Dr. Dolittle can talk to animals. If you could ask your pet any question, what would you ask them? What would your pet answer? (And if you don't have a pet, what would you ask a dog in the park? What would the dog tell you in return?) Make sure to use a question mark in your answer. If you like, draw a picture of your talking animal on Student Page 28.

Remind the student to answer you in 1–2 complete sentences. If she answers in fragments, turn the fragment into a complete sentence, say it to her, and then ask her to repeat this sentence back to you. Write the student's answer down on the "Instructor" lines of Student Page 27 as she watches. Then have her copy the sentence onto the "Student" lines.

WEEK 5

DAY ONE: Narration Exercise   *Student Page 29*

Focus: *Identifying central ideas and actions*

Pull out Student Page 29. Ask the student to write his name and the date.

Read the following passage out loud to the student. After reading this passage, you will help the student identify the actions that form the "skeleton" of the plot.

Tell the student that this passage comes from the book *Misty of Chincoteague* by Marguerite Henry. At the beginning of the book, a ship carrying ponies from Spain to the New World, three hundred years ago, sinks. The ponies swim to shore and find themselves on an island off the coast of Virginia.

> The moon was high overhead when the little band came out on grassy marshland. They stopped a moment to listen to the wide blades of grass whisper and squeak in the wind; to sniff the tickling smell of salt grass.
>
> This was it! This was the exciting smell that had urged them on. With wild snorts of happiness they buried their noses in the long grass. They bit and tore great mouthfuls—frantically, as if they were afraid it might not last. Oh, the salty goodness of it! Not bitter at all, but juicy-sweet with rain. It was different from any grass they knew. It billowed and shimmered like the sea. They could not get enough of it. That delicious salty taste! Never had they known anything like it . . . .
>
> When they could eat no more, they pawed shallow wells with their hooves for drinking water. Then they rolled in the wiry grass, letting out great whinnies of happiness. They seemed unable to believe that the island was all their own. Not a human being anywhere. Only grass. And sea. And sky. And the wind.
>
> At last they slept.
>
> —From *Misty of Chincoteague*
> by Marguerite Henry

Ask the following questions to test the student's listening ability. Remind the student to answer in complete sentences; if he answers in a fragment, put the answer in the form of a sentence and then require the student to repeat it back to you.

Instructor: Does this story take place during the day or at night?
Student: *The story takes place at night.*

Note: If the student cannot answer this, read the first sentence of the passage again, and then ask, "Is the moon up during the day or at night?"

Instructor: What did the ponies find?
Student: *They found long grass.*

Instructor: What flavor did the grass have?
Student: The grass was salty.

Instructor: How did the ponies get drinking water?
Student: They pawed holes for water with their hooves.

Instructor: After they drank, what did they do?
Student: They rolled in the grass.

Instructor: What was the last thing the ponies did?
Student: They slept.

You will now continue to teach the student to summarize the basic narrative thread in the passage. In order to do this, say to the student:

Instructor: Where were the ponies?
Student: They were on an island.

Instructor: What two important things did they find on the island?
Student: They found grass and water.

Instructor: After they ate and drank, what did they do?
Student: They slept.

Now say to the student, "Tell me in two sentences where the ponies were and what they did." The student's answer should resemble one of the following:

"The ponies were on an island. They found grass and water there."

"The ponies were all alone on an island. They found grass to eat, and they pawed holes to find water."

"The Spanish ponies were shipwrecked. They found an island where there was salty grass for them to eat and water for them to drink."

Write the student's narration down on Student Page 29 while he watches.

DAY TWO: Copywork Exercise   *Student Page 30*

Focus: *Names of seasons*

Pull out Student Page 30. Ask the student to write his name and the date. The following model sentences are already printed on it:

> The ponies arrived on the island in the summer. Soon winter came, and snow covered the grass.

Ask the student to look carefully at the sentences. Point out that the names of seasons (spring, summer, winter, and fall) are not capitalized. Also point out that the comma in the second sentence separates two complete sentences: "soon winter came" and "snow covered the grass." Two complete sentences must be joined by a comma *and* a coordinating conjunction (and). (They can also be joined by a semicolon without a coordinating conjunction.) If there were no comma and conjunction between "came" and "snow," this would be a run-on sentence.

Now ask the student to copy the sentences. Remember to watch him write, and correct him at once if he begins to make errors in spelling or format.

DAY THREE: Dictation Exercise   *Student Page 31*

Pull out Student Page 31. Ask the student to write his name and the date.

Dictate the following sentences to the student:

> **The ponies arrived on the island in the summer. Soon winter came, and snow covered the grass.**

Before he begins to write, remind him that you will be dictating two separate sentences. There will be a period at the end of the first sentence, and a capital letter at the beginning of the second sentence. There will also be a comma. Tell the student to listen carefully for the difference between commas and periods.

Read the sentences twice to the student. When you reach "summer," be sure to let your voice fall. Pause and count silently to five at the period. When you read the phrase "Soon winter came," keep your voice level (to differentiate between the end of a sentence and the middle), and pause silently for a count of three when you reach the comma.

Ask the student to repeat the sentences back to you before he writes. If he cannot remember the sentences, repeat them together.

DAY FOUR: Narration Exercise and Dictation   *Student Pages 32–33*

Focus: *Identifying the central narrative thread in a passage*

Pull out Student Pages 32–33. Ask the student to write his name and the date on Student Page 33.

Today's exercise will combine narration and dictation. Tell the student that you will read the following passage to him, ask him a few questions about it, and then help him to summarize. After you write these summary sentences down (while the student watches), you will dictate one or two of them back to him.

Read the following passage out loud to the student. Tell him that this is also from Marguerite Henry's book *Misty of Chincoteague*. In this passage, Henry describes what happens as the ponies remain on the island for months, and then for years—and then for centuries.

Snow was a new experience, too. They blew at it, making little snow flurries of their own. They tasted it. It melted on their tongues. Snow was good to drink!

If the Spaniards could have seen their ponies now, they would have been startled at their changed appearance. No longer were their coats sleek. They were as thick and shaggy as the coat of any sheep dog. This was a good thing. On bitter days, when they stood close-huddled for comfort, each pony could enjoy the added warmth of his neighbor's coat as well as his own.

There were no wolves or wildcats on the island, but there was deep, miry mud to trap creatures and suck them down. After a few desperate struggles, the ponies learned how to fall to their knees, then sidle and wriggle along like crabs until they were well out of it.

With each season the ponies grew wiser. And with each season they became tougher and more hardy. Horse colts and fillies were born to them. As the horse colts grew big, they rounded up mares of their own and started new herds that ranged wild—wild as the wind and the sea that had brought them there long ago.

—From *Misty of Chincoteague*
by Marguerite Henry

Ask the following questions to test the student's listening ability. Remind the student to answer in complete sentences; if he answers in a fragment, put the answer in the form of a sentence and then require the student to repeat it back to you.

Instructor: What was a new experience for the ponies?
Student: *Snow was a new experience.*

Instructor: What happened to the ponies' coats?
Student: *They grew thick and shaggy.*

Instructor: What was the biggest danger to the ponies?
Student: *Deep mud could suck them down.*

Instructor: How did the ponies get out of the mud?
Student: *They fell to their knees and wriggled out.*

Instructor: What did the colts start, as they grew older?
Student: *They started new herds.*

Instructor: Were these new herds of ponies tame or wild?
Student: *They were wild.*

You will now continue to teach the student to summarize the basic narrative thread in the passage. In order to do this, say to the student:

Instructor: List two new things that happened to the ponies.
Student: *They saw snow; they grew thick coats; they learned to escape from mud; they formed new herds.*

Instructor: What happened to the ponies as time went on?
Student: *They started new herds of wild ponies.*

Now ask the student, "Can you tell me in two sentences what happened in this story?" The student's answer should resemble one of the following:

"The ponies learned how to eat snow and grew thick coats. More and more ponies were born and new wild herds started."

"The ponies learned how to escape from the mud, and they grew wiser. They had colts and fillies, and new herds formed."

"The ponies learned how to live on the island, and their coats grew thick and shaggy. More ponies were born, and the colts started new herds."

DAY FIVE (optional): Creative Writing   *Student Pages 34–35*

Pull out Student Pages 34–35. Write the student's name and the date for him as he watches, or ask him to write the name and date independently.

Instructor: In *Misty of Chincoteague,* the ponies experience snow for the first time. What is your favorite thing to do in the snow? If you haven't played in the snow before, what is the first thing you would do if you found yourself in a place covered in snow?

Remind the student to answer you in a complete sentence. If he answers in a fragment, turn the fragment into a complete sentence, say it to him, and then ask him to repeat this sentence back to you. Write the student's answer down on the "Instructor" lines of Student Page 34 as he watches. Then have him copy the sentence onto the "Student" lines.

WEEK 6

DAY ONE: Narration Exercise   *Student Page 36*

Focus: *Identify the central theme of a poem*

Pull out Student Page 36. Ask the student to write her name and the date.

Read the following poem out loud to the student. After reading, you will help the student to express the central theme of the poem in her own words.

You may need to tell the student that "arrant" means "wandering" or "going away"—the shadow is "arrant" because he stays in bed instead of going with the little boy. ("Arrant" can also mean "thorough" or "complete"; Stevenson may be saying that the shadow is *very* sleepy.)

> I have a little shadow that goes in and out with me,
> And what can be the use of him is more than I can see.
> He is very, very like me from the heels up to the head;
> And I see him jump before me, when I jump into my bed.
>
> The funniest thing about him is the way he likes to grow—
> Not at all like proper children, which is always very slow;
> For he sometimes shoots up taller like an india-rubber ball,
> And he sometimes gets so little that there's none of him at all.
>
> He hasn't got a notion of how children ought to play,
> And can only make a fool of me in every sort of way.
> He stays so close beside me, he's a coward, you can see;
> I'd think shame to stick to nursie as that shadow sticks to me!
>
> One morning, very early, before the sun was up,
> I rose and found the shining dew on every buttercup;
> But my lazy little shadow, like an arrant sleepy-head,
> Had stayed at home behind me and was fast asleep in bed.

>   —"My Shadow"
>   by Robert Louis Stevenson

Ask the following questions to test the student's listening ability. Remind the student to answer in complete sentences; if she answers in a fragment, put the answer in the form of a sentence and then require the student to repeat it back to you.

Instructor: When the child jumps into bed, what does the shadow do?
Student: *The shadow jumps into bed first.*

Instructor: Does the shadow grow slowly, like a normal person?
Student: *No, it doesn't.*

Instructor: What does the shadow do instead?
Student: *Sometimes it gets suddenly taller, and sometimes it gets shorter.*

Instructor: Does the shadow go off and play?
Student: *No, it stays close to the child.*

Instructor: When the child got up early, did the shadow get up too?
Student: *No, it stayed in bed.*

Instructor: Why does the shadow disappear when the child goes out early?
Student: *The shadow can't be seen because the sun isn't up yet.*

Note: Don't expect the student to know this without assistance! You may wish to show the student how the sun casts a shadow, using a lamp or other bright light; then turn the light off and ask whether the student can still see a shadow.

Your goal now is to teach the student to summarize the central idea in the poem. In order to do this, say to the student:

Instructor: Who is the child's companion?
Student: *The shadow is the child's companion.*

Instructor: Can you tell me two ways in which the shadow is *not* like a regular child?
Student: *The shadow follows him everywhere; the shadow gets very tall and very short; the shadow sticks close to him instead of playing; early in the morning, the shadow disappears.*

Now tell the student, "In two sentences, tell me who the child's companion is, and what it is like." The student's answer should resemble one of the following:

"The child has a shadow that follows him everywhere. The shadow sticks close to him, but it disappears when the sun isn't up."

"The shadow goes everywhere with the child, as long as there is light. It gets bigger and smaller quickly and jumps into bed before him."

"The shadow keeps him company. It stays with him all the time, and jumps into bed with him."

Write the student's narration down on Student Page 36 while she watches.

Day Two: Copywork Exercise   *Student Page 37*

Focus: Proper form for lines of poetry

Pull out Student Page 37. Ask the student to write her name and the date. The following model sentences are already printed on it:

I have a little shadow that goes in and out with me,

And what can be the use of him is more than I can see.

Ask the student to look at the sentences. Can she tell you why the "and" in the second line begins with a capital A, even though a comma and not a period comes before it? In traditional poetry, the first letter of every line is capitalized even if it does not begin a new sentence. Each line is also indented from the margin.

You may also point out the pronoun I, which is capitalized.

Ask the student to copy the sentence. Remember to watch her write, and correct her at once if she begins to make errors in spelling or format. If she needs help in deciding how far to indent, suggest that she indent about three pencil widths.

Day Three: Dictation Exercise   *Student Page 38*

Pull out Student Page 38. Ask the student to write her name and the date.

Dictate the following two lines of poetry to the student:

> I have a little shadow that goes in and out with me,
>
> And what can be the use of him is more than I can see.

Read the lines twice. Before she begins to write, ask her to tell you where the end of the first line is. Ask whether she can remember which punctuation mark comes at the end of this line, and remind her that the next line begins with a capital letter.

Day Four: Narration Exercise and Dictation   *Student Pages 39–40*

Focus: *Identifying the central narrative thread in a story poem*

Pull out Student Pages 39–40. Ask the student to write her name and the date on Student Page 40.

Today's exercise will combine narration and dictation. After reading the poem, you will help the student to express the central story of the poem in her own words.

Read the following poem out loud to the student. Tell her that "pound" is the name of the English money which is (more or less, depending on the exchange rate) like a North American dollar. A "runcible spoon" is a spoon with tines on the end like a fork (in the United States, we sometimes call this a "spork"). Mince is a kind of meat pie, while quince is a fruit (a little bit like a pear).

> The Owl and the Pussy-Cat went to sea
>   In a beautiful pea-green boat;
> They took some honey, and plenty of money
>   Wrapped up in a five-pound note.
> The Owl looked up to the moon above,
>   And sang to a small guitar,

"O lovely Pussy! O Pussy, my love!
  What a beautiful Pussy you are,—
    You are,
  What a beautiful Pussy you are!"

Pussy said to the Owl, "You elegant fowl!
  How charmingly sweet you sing!
Oh, let us be married,—too long we have tarried,—
  But what shall we do for a ring?"

They sailed away for a year and a day
  To the land where the Bong-tree grows,
And there in a wood a piggy-wig stood
  With a ring in the end of his nose,—
    His nose,
  With a ring in the end of his nose.

"Dear Pig, are you willing to sell for one shilling
  Your ring?" Said the piggy, "I will,"
So they took it away, and were married next day
  By the turkey who lives on the hill.
They dined upon mince and slices of quince,
  Which they ate with a runcible spoon,
And hand in hand on the edge of the sand
  They danced by the light of the moon,—
    The moon,
  They danced by the light of the moon.

—"The Owl and the Pussycat"
by Edward Lear

Ask the following questions to test the student's listening ability. Remind the student to answer in complete sentences; if she answers in a fragment, put the answer in the form of a sentence and then require the student to repeat it back to you.

Instructor: What color was the boat the Owl and Cat sailed in?
Student: The boat was pea-green.

Instructor: Can you remember one of the things they took with them?
Student: They took honey and money.

Instructor: What did the Pussy-Cat tell the Owl that they should do?
Student: She said that they should get married.

Instructor: What were they missing?
Student: They had no ring.

Instructor: What kind of animal did they find in the wood?
Student: *They found a pig.*

Instructor: What did the pig have at the end of his nose?
Student: *He had a ring.*

Instructor: Who married the Owl and the Cat?
Student: *The turkey who lived on the hill married them.*

Instructor: Can you remember one of the foods they ate?
Student: *They ate mince and quince.*

Instructor: What kind of spoon did they use?
Student: *They ate with a runcible spoon.*

Instructor: What did they do at the end of the poem?
Student: *They danced by the light of the moon.*

You will now continue to teach the student to summarize the basic narrative thread in the passage. In order to do this, say to the student:

Instructor: What did the Pussy-Cat and the Owl want to do?
Student: *They wanted to get married.*

Instructor: What did they need before they could get married?
Student: *They needed a ring.*

Instructor: How (and where!) did they get a ring?
Student: *They sailed to a far-away land and got a ring from a pig's nose.*

Instructor: Were they able to get married?
Student: *Yes, they were married by the turkey who lives on a hill.*

Now ask the student, "Can you tell me in two or three sentences what happened in this story?" The student's answer should resemble one of the following:

"The Owl and the Pussy-Cat wanted to get married. They sailed to a far-away land and got a ring from the nose of a pig, and then they were married by a turkey."

"The Owl and the Pussy-Cat set out in a pea-green boat. They wanted to get married, but they had no ring. So they sailed to a far-away land, got a ring from a pig, and got married."

"The Owl and the Pussy-Cat were sailing on the sea when they decided to get married. They sailed to a far-away land, where a pig sold them his nose ring. Then they got married and danced by the light of the moon."

Write down the student's narration on Student Page 39 as she watches. Then, choose one of the sentences from the narration to use as a dictation exercise (Student Page 40). Follow the same dictation techniques as above.

DAY FIVE (optional): Creative Writing   *Student Pages 41–42*

Pull out Student Pages 41–42. Write the student's name and the date for her as she watches, or ask her to write the name and date independently.

> **Instructor:** Imagine that your shadow runs off to do something all alone. What does your shadow do?

Remind the student to answer you in a complete sentence. If she answers in a fragment, turn the fragment into a complete sentence, say it to her, and then ask her to repeat this sentence back to you. Write the student's answer down on the "Instructor" lines of Student Page 41 as she watches. Then have her copy the sentence onto the "Student" lines.

WEEK 7

Day One: Narration Exercise   *Student Page 43*

Focus: *Identifying the narrative thread in a passage*

Pull out Student Page 43. Ask the student to write his name and the date.

Read the following passage out loud to the student. After reading this passage, you will help the student identify the central narrative thread.

Tell the student that this passage is from a book called *Ginger Pye* by Eleanor Estes. The Pyes are a family with two children—and the older boy, Jerry, is dreaming about having a dog of his own.

> Would Gracie-the-cat be jealous if the Pyes got another pet—a dog? That was what Jerry Pye wanted to know and what he was dreaming about as he sat with Rachel, his sister, on their little upstairs veranda. Gracie had belonged to the family for eleven years. This was longer than Rachel, aged nine, or even Jerry, aged ten, had. She had been a wedding present to Mama, and she was known in the neighborhood as "the New York Cat." Jerry was trying to imagine what Gracie's feelings would be if the Pyes did get another pet—a dog.
>
> The one thing that Jerry Pye wanted more than anything else in the world right now was a dog. Ever since he had seen the new puppies over in Speedy's barn, he was not only more anxious than ever to have a dog, he was most anxious to have one of these Speedy puppies. He had the particular one picked out that he would most like to have as his own. This was not easy to do for they were all wonderful.
>
> Jerry had chosen this certain special puppy because he was convinced that he was the smartest of the new puppies. Naturally, he would love any dog he had, but imagine owning such a smart puppy as this one! When he owned him he would teach him to heel, be dead dog, sneeze, scratch his stomach when Jerry scratched his back, beg, and walk on his hind legs.
>
> —From *Ginger Pye*
> by Eleanor Estes

Ask the following questions to test the student's listening ability. Remind the student to answer in complete sentences; if he answers in a fragment, put the answer in the form of a sentence and then require the student to repeat it back to you.

Instructor: What kind of an animal is Gracie?
Student: *Gracie is a cat.*

Instructor: What is Jerry's sister named?
Student: *Her name is Rachel.*

Instructor: How old are Jerry and Rachel?
Student: *Jerry is ten, and Rachel is nine.*

Instructor: What does Jerry want more than anything else in the world?
Student: *He wants a dog.*

Instructor: Does Jerry have a dog picked out?
Student: *Yes, he has already seen a puppy that he wants.*

Instructor: Why does he want that particular puppy?
Student: *He thinks the puppy is the smartest of all the puppies.*

Instructor: Can you tell me four things that Jerry hoped to teach his puppy?
Student: *He wanted to teach the puppy to heel, play dead, sneeze, scratch his stomach, beg, and walk on his hind legs.*

You will now continue to teach the student to summarize the basic narrative thread in the passage. In order to do this, say to the student:

Instructor: What does Jerry want?
Student: *He wants a dog.*

Instructor: What problem is he afraid of?
Student: *He is afraid that the cat might be jealous.*

Instructor: What kind of dog does he want?
Student: *He wants a puppy that he has already seen.*

Instructor: What does he want to do with the puppy?
Student: *He wants to teach it to do tricks.*

Now say to the student, "Tell me about Jerry and his dog in two or three brief sentences." The student's answer should resemble one of the following:

"Jerry wanted a dog. He was afraid that their cat might be jealous, but he had already picked out a puppy. He planned to teach the puppy many tricks."

"Jerry had a cat, but now he wanted a dog. He wanted to have one of the puppies—the smartest one. He would teach it how to play dead, beg, and do other tricks."

"Jerry wanted a puppy. The puppy would be smart, so it could learn how to do tricks. But Jerry was afraid that the cat might be jealous."

Write the student's narration down on Student Page 43 while he watches.

DAY TWO: Copywork Exercise   *Student Page 44*

Focus: *Commas in a series*

Pull out Student Page 44. Ask the student to write his name and the date. The following model sentence is already printed on it:

> Jerry would teach his puppy to heel, play dead, sneeze, beg, and walk on his hind legs.

Ask the student to put his finger on each of the actions Jerry will teach his puppy to do, as you read them out loud: heel, play dead, sneeze, beg, walk on his hind legs. Ask him how many actions there are (five). Then ask him to find each comma. There is a comma after each action (except for the last). Tell the student the rule: Whenever you write things in a series (whether they are actions, nouns, adjectives, or other words), use commas to separate them.

Ask the student to look at the two other sentences on Student Page 44:

> Jerry's puppy will be smart, hungry, wiggly, and noisy.

In this sentence, the series of adjectives that describe Jerry's puppy are separated by commas.

> Jerry's pet could be a cat, dog, mouse, goldfish, or hamster.

In this sentence, the series of nouns that name Jerry's pets are separated by commas.

Now ask the student to copy the first sentence. Remember to watch him write, and to correct him at once if he begins to make errors in spelling or format.

DAY THREE: Dictation Exercise   *Student Page 45*

Pull out Student Page 45. Ask the student to write his name and the date.
Dictate the following sentence to the student:

> Jerry would teach his puppy to heel, play dead, sneeze, beg, and walk on his hind legs.

Before he begins to write, remind him that commas separate items in a series. Read the sentence twice, pausing for the silent count of three at each comma. Then ask the student to repeat the sentence back to you. If he cannot remember it, repeat the sentence together until he can.

DAY FOUR: Narration Exercise and Dictation   *Student Pages 46–47*

Focus: *Identifying the central narrative thread in a passage*

Pull out Student Pages 46–47. Ask the student to write his name and the date on Student Page 47.

Today's exercise will combine narration and dictation. Tell the student that you will read the following passage to him, ask him a few questions about it, and then help him to summarize. After you write these summary sentences down (while the student watches), you will dictate one or two of them back to him.

Read the following passage out loud to the student. Tell him that this is also from *Ginger Pye* by Eleanor Estes. Jerry has gotten his puppy—and for the first time, his puppy, Ginger, sees himself in the mirror.

> There was another dog in this house and he was in the shiny mirror! Yet, all along, Ginger had mistakenly thought he was the only dog in this house.
>
> Ginger Pye gave this new dog a friendly woof for he did not realize all in a second that this was his enemy dog that was going to torment him and stay in shiny places. The dog gave Ginger a friendly woof too, only Ginger couldn't hear it. Ginger Pye then barked loudly at the new dog and the new dog barked back at Ginger, only still he made no sound. His woofing and his barking were silent and, because of this, rather exasperating.
>
> Ginger made a dash for the dog in the mirror and the dog in the mirror made a dash for Ginger. They growled at each other, Ginger in his loud fashion and the new dog in his silent fashion. Their noses were plastered right close together, so close Ginger couldn't even see the other dog anymore. But the cowardly dog stayed inside where he was good and safe and he wouldn't come out. It was infuriating and it made Ginger Pye frantic.
>
> It was then that Ginger realized that this dog in the mirror was an enemy dog and not a friendly companion.
>
> —From *Ginger Pye*
> by Eleanor Estes

Ask the following questions to test the student's listening ability. Remind the student to answer in complete sentences; if he answers in a fragment, put the answer in the form of a sentence and then require the student to repeat it back to you.

Instructor: What does Ginger Pye see in the mirror?
Student: *He sees another dog.*

Instructor: Is there really another dog in the mirror?
Student: *No, it's just his reflection.*

Instructor: How did Ginger greet the dog?
Student: *He gave a friendly woof.*

Instructor: What was wrong with the woofing and barking of the other dog?
Student: *They were silent.*

Instructor: When Ginger made a dash for the dog in the mirror, what did the dog do?
Student: *He made a dash for Ginger.*

Instructor: Did the dog growl back when Ginger growled?
Student: *Yes, but the growl was silent.*

Instructor: What made Ginger furious and frantic?
Student: *The other dog wouldn't come out of the mirror.*

Instructor: Did Ginger decide that the dog was a friend or an enemy?
Student: *He decided that the dog was an enemy.*

You will now continue to teach the student to summarize the basic narrative thread in the passage. In order to do this, say to the student:

Instructor: What did Ginger Pye discover?
Student: *He discovered a dog in the mirror.*

Instructor: What was wrong with the dog in the mirror?
Student: *He would only bark and growl silently, and he wouldn't come out of the mirror.*

Note: If the student only gives one half of this answer, prompt him for the other half.

Instructor: What did Ginger decide?
Student: *He decided that the dog in the mirror was an enemy.*

Now ask the student, "Can you tell me in two or three sentences what happened in this story?" The student's answer should resemble one of the following:

"Ginger Pye saw another dog in the mirror. The dog wouldn't make noise or come out, so Ginger decided it was an enemy."

"Ginger Pye looked in a mirror and saw another dog. He barked at the dog, but the dog would only bark back silently. Ginger couldn't get the other dog to come out of the mirror."

"Ginger Pye found another dog in the mirror, but the dog was silent. Ginger wanted the dog to come out. When it wouldn't come out, he decided that the dog was an enemy."

Write down the student's narration on Student Page 46 as he watches. Then, choose one of the sentences from the narration to use as a dictation exercise (Student Page 47). Follow the same dictation techniques as above.

DAY FIVE (optional): Creative Writing   *Student Pages 48–49*

Pull out Student Pages 48–49. Write the student's name and the date for him as he watches, or ask him to write the name and date independently.

> **Instructor:** What animal would be your dream pet? Write a sentence with two or three reasons why you want that animal for a pet. Or, if you already have a pet, you can write a sentence with three things you like about your pet. Make sure to use commas between each part of your answer.

Remind the student to answer you in a complete sentence. If he answers in a fragment, turn the fragment into a complete sentence, say it to him, and then ask him to repeat this sentence back to you. Write the student's answer down on the "Instructor" lines of Student Page 48 as he watches. Then have him copy the sentence onto the "Student" lines.

WEEK 8

DAY ONE: Narration Exercise

Focus: *Identifying central ideas and actions*

Pull out Student Page 50. Ask the student to write her name and the date.

Read the following passage out loud to the student. After reading this passage, you will help the student identify the actions that form the "skeleton" of the plot.

Tell the student that this passage comes from Rudyard Kipling's classic story *The Jungle Book*. At the beginning of the story, the Wolf family discovers a human baby near their cave.

If the student does not know what an "atom" is, explain that an atom is a very small particle. Kipling calls the baby an "atom" because he is so small.

> The bushes rustled a little in the thicket, and Father Wolf dropped with his haunches under him, ready for his leap. Then, if you had been watching, you would have seen the most wonderful thing in the world—the wolf checked in mid-spring. He made his bound before he saw what it was he was jumping at, and then he tried to stop himself. The result was that he shot up straight into the air for four or five feet, landing almost where he left ground.
>
> "Man!" he snapped. "A man's cub. Look!"
>
> Directly in front of him, holding on by a low branch, stood a naked brown baby who could just walk—as soft and as dimpled a little atom as ever came to a wolf's cave at night. He looked up into Father Wolf's face and laughed.
>
> "Is that a man's cub?" said Mother Wolf. "I have never seen one. Bring it here."
>
> A wolf accustomed to moving his own cubs can, if necessary, mouth an egg without breaking it, and though Father Wolf's jaws closed right on the child's back not a tooth even scratched the skin as he laid it down among the cubs.
>
> "How little! How naked, and—how bold!" said Mother Wolf softly. The baby was pushing his way between the cubs to get close to the warm hide. "Ahai! He is taking his meal with the others. And so this is a man's cub. Now, was there ever a wolf that could boast of a man's cub among her children?"
>
> "I have heard now and again of such a thing, but never in our Pack or in my time," said Father Wolf. "He is altogether without hair, and I could kill him with a touch of my foot. But see, he looks up and is not afraid."
>
> —From *The Jungle Book*
> by Rudyard Kipling

Ask the following questions to test the student's listening ability. Remind the student to answer in complete sentences; if she answers in a fragment, put the answer in the form of a sentence and then require the student to repeat it back to you.

Instructor: What happened to Father Wolf's jump when he saw the baby?
Student: *He stopped in mid-jump.*

Instructor: What do the wolves call the baby?
Student: *They call him a man-cub.*

Instructor: How does Father Wolf bring the baby to Mother Wolf?
Student: *He carries the baby in his mouth.*

Instructor: When the baby is brought to Mother Wolf, what does he do?
Student: *He pushes his way in between the other cubs.*

Instructor: Is the baby afraid?
Student: *No, he is not afraid.*

You will now continue to teach the student to summarize the basic narrative thread in the passage. In order to do this, say to the student:

Instructor: What did Father Wolf see coming out of the bushes?
Student: *He saw a baby.*

Instructor: What did he do with the baby?
Student: *He brought the baby into the cave.*

Instructor: What did the baby do once he was in the cave?
Student: *He pushed his way in with the other cubs.*

Instructor: Was the baby afraid?
Student: *No, he was not afraid.*

Now say to the student, "Tell me how the wolves found the baby, and what happened next." The answer should be two or three brief sentences that resemble one of the following:

"The wolves heard a rustling in the bushes, and a baby came out. Father Wolf brought the baby in to Mother Wolf. He joined the other cubs and was not afraid."

"Father and Mother Wolf found a human baby near their cave. They brought the baby in to join their wolf cubs."

"A baby came out of the bushes near the wolves' cave. Father Wolf brought the baby into the cave, and Mother Wolf nursed it."

Write the student's narration down on Student Page 50 while she watches.

DAY TWO: Copywork Exercise   *Student Page 51*

Focus: *Commas in a series*

Pull out Student Page 51. Ask the student to write her name and the date. The following model sentence is already printed on it:

> They are evil, dirty, shameless, and they desire to be noticed by the Jungle People.

Tell the student that this sentence is about the monkeys, who live in the jungle along with the wolves. The monkeys cause trouble and throw nuts at the other animals, and the other animals refuse to take any notice of them. Point out that "Jungle People" is capitalized because Rudyard Kipling, who wrote *The Jungle Book*, is using it as though it were a proper name—like "American," "Mexican," or "Japanese."

Ask the student to put her finger on each comma. The commas separate the series of adjectives that describe the monkeys.

Now ask the student to copy the sentence. Remember to watch her write, and to correct her at once if she begins to make errors in spelling or format.

DAY THREE: Dictation Exercise   *Student Page 52*

Pull out Student Page 52. Ask the student to write her name and the date.

Dictate the following sentence to the student:

> They are evil, dirty, shameless, and they desire to be noticed by the Jungle People.

Before she begins to write, ask her if she can remember which two words in the sentence are proper names. Those should begin with capital letters! Remind her that commas separate items in a series. Read the sentence twice, pausing for the silent count of three at each comma. Then ask the student to repeat the sentence back to you. If she cannot remember it, repeat the sentence together until she can.

DAY FOUR: Narration Exercise and Dictation   *Student Pages 53–54*

Focus: *Identifying the central narrative thread in a passage*

Pull out Student Pages 53–54. Ask the student to write her name and the date on Student Page 54.

Today's exercise will combine narration and dictation. Tell the student that you will read the following passage to her, ask her a few questions about it, and then help her to summarize. After you write these summary sentences down (while the student watches), you will dictate one or two of them back to her.

Read the following passage out loud to the student. Tell her that this is also from *The Jungle Book.* Father and Mother Wolf name the baby Mowgli, and raise him with their cubs. But when Mowgli is a little older, they have to bring him to the Pack Meeting—the gathering of all the wolves—so that the pack can decide whether or not Mowgli can stay with the wolves. The leader of the pack is Akela, the oldest and wisest of the wolves. Father and Mother Wolf are afraid that Mowgli will be forced to leave the pack—and leave their family.

Now, the Law of the Jungle lays down that if there is any dispute as to the right of a cub to be accepted by the Pack, he must be spoken for by at least two members of the Pack who are not his father and mother.

"Who speaks for this cub?" said Akela. "Among the Free People who speaks?" There was no answer, and Mother Wolf got ready for what she knew would be her last fight, if things came to fighting.

Then the only other creature who is allowed at the Pack Council—Baloo, the sleepy brown bear who teaches the wolf cubs the Law of the Jungle: old Baloo, who can come and go where he pleases because he eats only nuts and roots and honey—rose up on his hind quarters and grunted.

"The man's cub—the man's cub?" he said. "*I* speak for the man's cub. I have no gift of words, but I speak the truth. Let him run with the Pack, and be entered with the others. I myself will teach him."

"We need yet another," said Akela. "Baloo has spoken, and he is our teacher for the young cubs. Who speaks besides Baloo?"

A black shadow dropped down into the circle. It was Bagheera the Black Panther, inky black all over, but with the panther markings showing up in certain lights like the pattern of watered silk. Everybody knew Bagheera, and nobody cared to cross his path; for he was as cunning as Tabaqui [the jackal], as bold as the wild buffalo, and as reckless as the wounded elephants. But he had a voice as soft as wild honey dripping from a tree, and a skin softer than down.

"O Akela, and ye the Free People," he purred, "I have no right in your assembly, but the Law of the Jungle says that if there is a doubt which is not a killing matter in regard to a new cub, the life of that cub may be bought at a price . . . .Baloo has spoken in his behalf. Now to Baloo's word I will add one bull, and a fat one, newly killed, not half a mile from here, if you will accept the man's cub according to the Law. Is it difficult?"

There was a clamor of scores of voices, saying: "What matter? He will die in the winter rains. He will scorch in the sun . . . . Let him run with the Pack. Where is the bull, Bagheera? Let him be accepted." And then came Akela's deep bay, crying: "Look well—look well, O Wolves!"

> Mowgli was still deeply interested in the pebbles, and he did not notice when the wolves came and looked at him one by one. At last they all went down the hill for the dead bull, and only Akela, Bagheera, Baloo, and Mowgli's own wolves were left.

—From *The Jungle Book*
by Rudyard Kipling

Ask the following questions to test the student's listening ability. Remind the student to answer in complete sentences; if she answers in a fragment, put the answer in the form of a sentence and then require the student to repeat it back to you.

Instructor: If a cub isn't accepted by the Pack, who is supposed to speak for him?
Student: Two members of the Pack who are not his father and mother are supposed to speak for him.

Instructor: What kind of animal is Baloo?
Student: He is a brown bear.

Instructor: What does he do for the wolf cubs?
Student: He teaches them the Law of the Jungle.

Instructor: What does Baloo do when he thinks that the Pack may not accept Mowgli?
Student: He speaks for Mowgli.

Instructor: Who else speaks for Mowgli?
Student: Bagheera the panther.

Instructor: In the story, Bagheera is compared to three animals. He is as bold as one animal, and as reckless as another. Can you remember one of the animals that he is compared to?
Student: Bagheera is as bold as a buffalo and as reckless as a wounded elphant.

Instructor: What does Bagheera offer the pack if they will accept Mowgli?
Student: He offers them a bull.

Instructor: What is Mowgli doing while the Pack argues over him?
Student: He is playing with pebbles.

You will now continue to teach the student to summarize the basic narrative thread in the passage. In order to do this, say to the student:

Instructor: Why is the Pack reluctant to accept Mowgli?
Student: Mowgli is human, not a wolf.

Instructor: What two animals speak up for Mowgli?
Student: Baloo the bear and Bagheera the panther speak up for him.

Instructor: Does the Pack finally accept Mowgli?
Student: Yes, the Pack accepts him.

Instructor: After they accept him, what do they do?
Student: *They go away to find the bull that Bagheera killed.*

Now ask the student, "Can you tell me in two or three sentences what happened in this story?" The student's answer should resemble one of the following:

> "The wolves did not want to accept Mowgli as part of the pack. Bagheera the panther and Baloo the brown bear both spoke up for him. The Pack agreed to accept him because Bagheera offered them a bull."

> "At the Pack Meeting, Bagheera and Baloo both spoke for Mowgli. When Bagheera offered the wolves a bull, they agreed to accept Mowgli."

> "The wolves accepted Mowgli because Bagheera and Baloo spoke up for him. Then they went away to find the bull Bagheera had given them. Mowgli was playing with pebbles the whole time."

Write down the student's narration on Student Page 53 as she watches. Then, choose one of the sentences from the narration to use as a dictation exercise (Student Page 54). Follow the same dictation techniques as above.

DAY FIVE (optional): Creative Writing   *Student Pages 55–56*

Pull out Student Pages 55–56. Write the student's name and the date for her as she watches, or ask her to write the name and date independently.

Instructor: What if you grew up in the jungle? What animal would raise you? What would you learn from your animal parent?

Write the student's answer down on the "Instructor" lines of Student Page 55 as she watches. Then have her copy the sentence onto the "Student" lines.

WEEK 9

DAY ONE: Narration Exercise   *Student Page 57*

Focus: *Identifying the narrative thread in a passage*

Pull out Student Page 57. Ask the student to write his name and the date.

Read the following passage out loud to the student. After reading this passage, you will help the student identify the central narrative thread.

Tell the student that this passage is from a book called *Pippi Longstocking* by Astrid Lindgren. Pippi is a little girl who lives all by herself with her monkey, Mr. Nilsson. Her two friends Tommy and Annika are fascinated by Pippi!

> That morning Pippi was busy making *pepparkakor*—a kind of Swedish cookie. She had made an enormous amount of dough and rolled it out on the kitchen floor.
>
> "Because," said Pippi to her little monkey, "what earthly use is a baking board when one plans to make at least five hundred cookies?"
>
> And there she lay on the floor, cutting out cookie hearts for dear life. "Stop climbing around in the dough, Mr. Nilsson," she said crossly just as the doorbell rang.
>
> Pippi ran and opened the door. She was white as a miller from top to toe, and when she shook hands heartily with Tommy and Annika a whole cloud of flour blew over them.
>
> "So nice you called," she said and shook her apron—so there came another cloud of flour. Tommy and Annika got so much in their throats that they could not help coughing.
>
> "What are you doing?" asked Tommy.
>
> "Well, if I say that I'm sweeping the chimney, you won't believe me, you're so clever," said Pippi. "Fact is, I'm baking. But I'll soon be done. You can sit on the woodbox for a while."
>
> Pippi could work fast, she could. Tommy and Annika sat and watched how she went through the dough, how she threw the cookies onto the cookie pans and swung the pans into the oven. They thought it was as good as a circus.
>
> "Done!" said Pippi at last and shut the oven door on the last pans with a bang.
>
> "What are we going to do now?" asked Tommy.
>
> "I don't know what you are going to do," said Pippi, "but I know I can't lie around and be lazy. I am a Thing-Finder, and when you're a Thing-Finder you don't have a minute to spare."
>
> —From *Pippi Longstocking*
> by Astrid Lindgren

Ask the following questions to test the student's listening ability. Remind the student to answer in complete sentences; if he answers in a fragment, put the answer in the form of a sentence and then require the student to repeat it back to you.

Instructor: What is a *pepparkakor*?
Student: *It is a Swedish cookie.*

Instructor: Where did Pippi roll out the dough?
Student: *She rolled it out on the kitchen floor.*

Instructor: How many cookies did she plan to make?
Student: *She planned to make at least five hundred.*

Instructor: What was the monkey, Mr. Nilsson, doing while she cut the cookies out?
Student: *He was climbing around through the dough.*

Instructor: What was Pippi covered with?
Student: *She was covered with flour.*

Instructor: What happened when she shook hands with Tommy and Annika?
Student: *They got flour all over them and in their throats.*

Instructor: What did Tommy and Annika do while Pippi finished baking?
Student: *They sat on the woodbox and watched.*

Instructor: What did Pippi decide that she would be?
Student: *She decided to be a Thing-Finder.*

You will now help the student summarize the basic narrative thread in the passage. In order to do this, say to the student:

Instructor: What was Pippi doing at the beginning of the passage?
Student: *Pippi was making cookies on the floor.*

Instructor: When Tommy and Annika came, what did they do?
Student: *They watched her make cookies.*

Instructor: What did Pippi tell them that she would be?
Student: *She said that she would be a Thing-Finder.*

Now say to the student, "Tell me what happened in the passage in two sentences." The student's answer should resemble one of the following:

"Pippi Longstocking and her monkey were making cookies. When Tommy and Annika came in, Pippi told them that she would be a Thing-Finder."

"Pippi was making cookies when Tommy and Annika came to her house. They watched her finish making cookies, and then Pippi decided to be a Thing-Finder."

"Pippi was making Swedish cookies on the floor. Tommy and Annika came over, and Pippi told them that she was a Thing-Finder."

Write the student's narration down on Student Page 57 while he watches.

DAY TWO: Copywork Exercise

Focus: *Commas in a series*

Pull out Student Page 58. Ask the student to write his name and the date. The following model sentence is already printed on it:

> The little monkey was dressed in blue pants, yellow jacket, and a white straw hat.

Tell the student that this sentence comes from *Pippi Longstocking* and describes the monkey, Mr. Nilsson. Ask the student to put his finger on each of the commas. Explain that the commas separate the series of three items of clothing that the monkey is wearing: the blue pants, the yellow jacket, and the white hat.

Now ask the student to copy the sentence. Remember to watch him write, and to correct him at once if he begins to make errors in spelling or format.

DAY THREE: Dictation Exercise

Pull out Student Page 59. Ask the student to write his name and the date.
Dictate the following sentence to the student:

> The little monkey was dressed in blue pants, yellow jacket, and a white straw hat.

Before he begins to write, remind him that commas separate items in a series. Read the sentence twice, pausing for the silent count of three at each comma. Then ask the student to repeat the sentence back to you. If he cannot remember it, repeat the sentence together until he can.

DAY FOUR: Narration Exercise and Dictation

Focus: *Identifying the central narrative thread in a passage*

Pull out Student Pages 60–61. Ask the student to write his name and the date on Student Page 61.

Today's exercise will combine narration and dictation. Tell the student that you will read the following passage to him, ask him a few questions about it, and then help him to summarize. After you write these summary sentences down (while the student watches), you will dictate one or two of them back to him.

Read the following passage out loud to the student. Tell him that this is also from *Pippi Longstocking.*

"What did you say you are?" asked Annika.

"A Thing-Finder."

"What's that?" asked Tommy.

"Somebody who hunts for things, naturally. What else could it be?" said Pippi as she swept all the flour left on the floor into a little pile.

"The whole world is full of things, and somebody has to look for them. And that's just what a Thing-Finder does," she finished.

"What kind of things?" asked Annika.

"Oh, all kinds," said Pippi. "Lumps of gold, ostrich feathers, dead rats, candy snapcrackers, little tiny screws, and things like that."

Tommy and Annika thought it sounded as if it would be fun and wanted very much to be Thing-Finders too, although Tommy did say he hoped he'd find a lump of gold and not a little tiny screw.

"We shall see what we shall see," said Pippi. "One always finds something. But we've got to hurry up and get going so that other Thing-Finders don't pick up all the lumps of gold around here before we get them."

All three Thing-Finders now set out. They decided that it would be best to begin hunting around the houses in the neighborhood, because Pippi said that although it could perfectly well happen that one might find a little screw deep in the woods, still the very best things were usually found where people were living . . . .

Tommy and Annika looked at Pippi to see just how a Thing-Finder acted. Pippi ran from one side of the road to the other, shaded her eyes with her hand, and hunted and hunted. Sometimes she crawled about on her hands and knees, stuck her hands in between the pickets of a fence, and then said in a disappointed tone, "Oh dear! I was sure I saw a lump of gold."

"May we really take everything we find?" asked Annika.

"Yes, everything that is lying on the ground," said Pippi.

Presently they came to an old man lying asleep on the lawn outside his cottage.

"There," said Pippi, "that man is lying on the ground and we have found him. We'll take him!"

—From *Pippi Longstocking*
by Astrid Lindgren

Ask the following questions to test the student's listening ability. Remind the student to answer in complete sentences; if he answers in a fragment, put the answer in the form of a sentence and then require the student to repeat it back to you.

Instructor: What do Pippi, Tommy, and Annika all decide to be?
Student: *They decide to be Thing-Finders.*

Instructor: What does a Thing-Finder do?
Student: *A Thing-Finder finds things.*

Instructor: Can you list three things that a Thing-Finder finds?
Student: *A Thing-Finder finds gold, ostrich feathers, dead rats, candy snapcrackers, and screws.*

Instructor: What are two things that Pippi does while she looks for things?
Student: *She runs from one side of the road to the other, shades her eyes, crawls on her hands and knees, and sticks her hands between fence pickets.*

Instructor: What does Pippi want to take, at the end of the passage?
Student: *She wants to take the old man lying on the ground!*

You will now continue to teach the student to summarize the basic narrative thread in the passage. In order to do this, say to the student:

Instructor: What do Pippi, Tommy, and Annika become in the story?
Student: *They all become Thing-Finders.*

Instructor: What are they allowed to take?
Student: *They can take anything they find that is lying on the ground.*

Instructor: What do they find?
Student: *They find an old man lying on the ground.*

Now ask the student, "Can you tell me in two sentences what happened in this story?" The student's answer should resemble one of the following:

> "Pippi, Tommy, and Annika became Thing-Finders. When Pippi found an old man lying on the ground, she wanted to take him."

> "Pippi, Tommy, and Annika became Thing-Finders and looked for things lying on the ground. Pippi wanted them to take an old man!"

Write down the student's narration on Student Page 60 as he watches. Then, choose one of the sentences from the narration to use as a dictation exercise (Student Page 61). Follow the same dictation techniques as above.

Day Five (optional): Creative Writing   *Student Pages 62–63*

Pull out Student Pages 62–63. Write the student's name and the date for him as he watches, or ask him to write the name and date independently.

Instructor: In the book *Pippi Longstocking*, Pippi describes herself as a "thing-finder." She likes to go around town and find things to keep. If you became a thing-finder and searched around your house, what three things might you find lying on the ground?

Write the student's answer down on the "Instructor" lines of Student Page 62 as he watches. Then have him copy the sentence onto the "Student" lines.

WEEK 10

DAY ONE: Narration Exercise   *Student Page 64*

Focus: *Identifying the central idea or theme in a passage*

Pull out Student Page 64. Ask the student to write her name and the date.

Read the following passage out loud to the student. After reading this passage, you will help the student identify the central idea.

Tell the student that this passage is from *Nurse Matilda* by Christianna Brand. Nurse Matilda is a magical nanny who can make disobedient children good. (If the child has seen the movie *Nanny McPhee*, you can tell her that the movie was based on the Nurse Matilda books.)

You may need to explain that "barley sugar" and "demerara sugar" are golden-brown kinds of sugar that are more often used in Great Britain than in the United States.

> Once upon a time there was a huge family of children; and they were terribly, terribly naughty.
>
> In those days, mothers and fathers used to have much larger families than they do now; and these families often *were* naughty. The mothers and fathers had to have all sorts of nurses and nannies and governesses . . . .
>
> This family I'm telling you about seemed to have more children, and naughtier children, than any other. There were so many of them that I shan't even tell you their names but leave you to sort them out as you go along, and add up how many there were. But even their parents had to think of them in groups—there were the Big Ones and the Middling Ones and the Little Ones; and the Baby. The baby was really a splendid character. It had fat, bent legs and its nappy was always falling down round its fat, pink knees; but it kept up with the children to the last ounce of its strength. It talked a curious language all of its own.
>
> There was also the Tiny Baby, but it was so small that it *couldn't* be naughty, so it was very dull and we needn't count it.
>
> The children had two dogs, who were dachshunds. One was a goldeny brown and he was called Brown Sugar or Barley Sugar or sometimes even Demerara Sugar, but anyway, Sugar for short. The other was tiny and black and as sleek as a little seal and she was called Spice.
>
> And the naughtiness of these children was almost past believing.
>
> —From *Nurse Matilda*
> by Christianna Brand

Ask the following questions to test the student's listening ability. Remind the student to answer in complete sentences; if she answers in a fragment, put the answer in the form of a sentence and then require the student to repeat it back to you.

Instructor: What was the problem with the huge family of children?
Student: *They were terribly naughty.*

Instructor: The parents thought about them in four groups. Can you remember three of the groups?
Student: *The parents thought of them as Big Ones, Middling Ones, Little Ones, and the Baby.*

Instructor: Could the baby talk?
Student: *Yes, but it talked its own language.*

Instructor: What about the Tiny Baby?
Student: *No, the Tiny Baby couldn't talk (or be naughty).*

Instructor: What kind of dogs did the family have?
Student: *They had two dachshunds.*

Instructor: What were their names? (You only need to list one name per dog!)
Student: *One was called Brown Sugar, Barley Sugar, or Sugar; the other was Spice.*

You will now continue to teach the student to sum up the description in the passage. In order to do this, say to the student:

Instructor: The family was so huge that the parents thought of the children in groups. What were the four groups?
Student: *They were the Big Ones, Middling Ones, Little Ones, and the Baby.*

Instructor: What was the huge family like?
Student: *The huge family was very naughty.*

Instructor: How bad was their naughtiness?
Student: *Their naughtiness was almost past believing.*

Now say to the student, "Tell me about the family of naughty children in two sentences." The student's answer should resemble one of the following.

> "The family was so large that the children had to be divided into Big Ones, Middling Ones, Little Ones, and Baby. They were unbelievably naughty."

> "The family was so huge that the parents had to divide the children into groups. They were terribly naughty."

> "The family was huge and naughty. It was so big that the children were known as Big Ones, Middling Ones, Little Ones, and Baby."

Write the student's narration down on Student Page 64 while she watches.

DAY TWO: Copywork Exercise   *Student Page 65*

Focus: *Commas in a series*

Pull out Student Page 65. Ask the student to write her name and the date. The following model sentence is already printed on it:

> I shall give you half an hour to be up, dressed, washed, teeth cleaned, pajamas folded, windows opened, and beds turned back.

This is a sentence from *Nurse Matilda.* Nurse Matilda is telling the naughty children in the big family to get up and get dressed. Do you think they'll be obedient?

Ask the student to put her finger on each of the tasks Nurse Matilda asks the children to do: be up, dressed, washed, teeth cleaned, pajamas folded, windows opened, beds turned back. Ask the student how many tasks there are (seven). Then ask her to find each comma. There is a comma after each task (except for the last). Remind the student of the rule: Whenever you write things in a series (whether they are actions, nouns, adjectives, or other words), use commas to separate them.

Now ask the student to copy the sentence. Remember to watch her write, and to correct her at once if she begins to make errors in spelling or format.

DAY THREE: Dictation Exercise   *Student Page 66*

Pull out Student Page 66. Ask the student to write her name and the date.

Dictate the following sentence to the student:

> I shall give you half an hour to be up, dressed, washed, teeth cleaned, pajamas folded, windows opened, and beds turned back.

Before she begins to write, remind her that commas separate items in a series. Read the sentence twice, pausing for the silent count of three at each comma. Then ask the student to repeat the sentence back to you. If she cannot remember it, repeat the sentence together until she can.

DAY FOUR: Narration Exercise and Dictation   *Student Pages 67–68*

Focus: *Identifying central details in a description*

Pull out Student Pages 67–68. Ask the student to write her name and the date on Student Page 68.

Today's exercise will combine narration and dictation. Tell the student that you will read the following passage to her, ask her a few questions about it, and then help her to sum up the description. After you write these summary sentences down (while the student watches), you will dictate one or two of them back to her.

Read the following passage out loud to the student. Tell her that this is also from *Nurse Matilda*. Nurse Matilda has arrived to take care of the naughty large family.

> She was very ugly—the ugliest person you ever saw in your life! Her hair was scraped into a bun, sticking straight out at the back of her head like a teapot handle; and her face was very round and wrinkly, and she had eyes like two little black boot-buttons. And her nose!—she had a nose like two potatoes. She wore a rusty black dress right up to the top of her neck and right down to her button boots, and a rusty black jacket and a rusty black bonnet, all trimmed with trembly black jet, with her teapot-handle of a bun sticking out at the back. And she carried a small brown case and a large black stick, and she had a very fierce expression indeed on her wrinkly, round, brown face.
>
> But what you noticed most of all was that she had one huge front Tooth, sticking right out like a tombstone over her lower lip. You never, in the whole of your life, ever saw such a Tooth!
>
> Mrs. Brown was quite aghast at the sight of the Tooth. Her poor, dear, darling blameless angels! She faltered: "I'm not sure that . . . Well, I mean . . . I don't really know that we need you after all," and, politely but firmly, she started to close the door.
>
> "Oh, yes, you do," said Nurse Matilda, and she tapped at the door with her big black stick.
>
> —From *Nurse Matilda*
> by Christianna Brand

Ask the following questions to test the student's listening ability. Remind the student to answer in complete sentences; if she answers in a fragment, put the answer in the form of a sentence and then require the student to repeat it back to you.

Instructor: What did Nurse Matilda's hair look like?
Student: *It looked like a teapot handle.*

Instructor: What did her face look like?
Student: *It was round and wrinkly.*

Instructor: What were her eyes like?
Student: *They were like boot-buttons.*

Instructor: What did her nose look like?
Student: *Her nose looked like two potatoes.*

Instructor: What color was she wearing?
Student: *She was wearing all black.*

Instructor: What was the strangest thing about her whole face?
Student: *She had a huge front tooth.*

Instructor: When Mrs. Brown saw her, what did she say?
Student: *She said, "We don't really need you after all."*

Instructor: What did Nurse Matilda do when Mrs. Brown tried to close the door?
Student: *She tapped on it with her big black stick.*

You will now continue to teach the student to sum up the description of Nurse Matilda. In order to do this, say to the student:

Instructor: Overall, was Nurse Matilda beautiful or ugly?
Student: *She was ugly.*

Instructor: What are two things that were ugly about her?
Student: *She had hair like a teapot handle, a round wrinkly face, eyes like buttons, a nose like potatoes, and a huge front tooth.*

Instructor: How did Mrs. Brown react to the sight of her?
Student: *Mrs. Brown tried to send her away.*

Now ask the student, "Can you tell me in two sentences what Nurse Matilda was like?" The student's answer should resemble one of the following:

"Nurse Matilda was so ugly that Mrs. Brown tried to send her away. She had a nose like two potatoes and a huge front tooth."

"Nurse Matilda had a wrinkly face and a huge front tooth. When Mrs. Brown saw how ugly she was, Mrs. Brown tried to send her away."

"Mrs. Brown tried to send Nurse Matilda away. Nurse Matilda was horribly ugly—she wore all black and had a nose like two potatoes."

Write down the student's narration on Student Page 67 as she watches. Then, choose one of the sentences from the narration to use as a dictation exercise (Student Page 68). Follow the same dictation techniques as above.

DAY FIVE (optional): Creative Writing   *Student Pages 69–70*

Pull out Student Pages 69–70. Write the student's name and the date for her as she watches, or ask her to write the name and date independently.

Instructor: Can you draw a picture of Nurse Matilda based on the description that I will read to you now? If you would rather write than draw, write a sentence about what would happen if Nurse Matilda came to live with your family. What is the first thing Nurse Matilda would teach you?

If the student chooses to answer the drawing prompt, read aloud to her the first two paragraphs of Nurse Matilda's description on page 55 of your book, from "She was very ugly" to "such a Tooth!"

If the student chooses to answer the written prompt, write her answer down on the "Instructor" lines of Student Page 70 as she watches. Then have her copy the sentence onto the "Student" lines.

WEEK 11

DAY ONE: Narration Exercise   *Student Page 71*

Focus: *Identifying central details in a description*

Pull out Student Page 71. Ask the student to write his name and the date.

Read the following passage out loud to the student. Explain to the student that this passage is from the original book *The Hundred and One Dalmatians,* written by Dodie Smith; the Disney version was a very simplified retelling of this wonderful story. This scene takes place near the beginning of the book; Mr. and Mrs. Dearly, owners of the Dalmatian dogs Pongo and Missis, are taking a walk with their dogs when they meet Mrs. Dearly's old friend Cruella de Vil.

It was a beautiful September evening, windless, very peaceful. The park and the old, cream-painted houses facing it basked in the golden light of sunset. There were many sounds but no noises. The cries of playing children and the whir of London's traffic seemed quieter than usual, as if softened by the evening's gentleness. Birds were singing their last song of the day, and farther along the Circle, at the house where a great composer lived, someone was playing the piano.

"I shall always remember this happy walk," said Mr. Dearly.

At that moment the peace was shattered by an extremely strident motor horn. A large car was coming towards them. It drew up at a big house just ahead of them, and a tall woman came out onto the front-door steps. She was wearing a tight-fighting emerald satin dress, several ropes of rubies, and an absolutely simple white mink cloak, which reached to the high heels of her ruby-red shoes. She had dark skin, black eyes with a tinge of red in them, and a very pointed nose. Her hair was parted severely down the middle and one half of it was black and the other white—rather unusual.

"Why, that's Cruella de Vil," said Mrs. Dearly. "We were at school together. She was expelled for drinking ink."

"Isn't she a bit showy?" said Mr. Dearly, and would have turned back. But the tall woman had seen Mrs. Dearly and come down the steps to meet her. So Mrs. Dearly had to introduce Mr. Dearly.

"Come and meet *my* husband," said the tall woman.

"But you were going out," said Mrs. Dearly, looking at the chauffeur who was waiting at the open door of the large car. It was painted black and white, in stripes—rather noticeable.

—From *The Hundred and One Dalmatians*
by Dodie Smith

Ask the following questions to test the student's listening ability. Remind the student to answer in complete sentences; if he answers in a fragment, put the answer in the form of a sentence and then require him to repeat it back to you.

If the student cannot remember the details, reread the section of the passage that answers the question.

Instructor: In what month does the story take place?
Student: *The story happens in September.*

Instructor: In the first part of the story, four different sounds are mentioned. Can you remember two of them?
Student: *Playing children were making noise; traffic was whirring; birds were singing; someone was playing the piano.*

Instructor: What kind of noise shattered the peace?
Student: *The noise of a motor horn shattered the peace.*

Instructor: Can you remember two of the four things that Cruella de Vil was wearing?
Student: *She was wearing an emerald satin dress, rubies, a mink cloak, and ruby red shoes.*

Instructor: What was unusual about Cruella's hair?
Student: *It was half black and half white.*

Instructor: How about her eyes?
Student: *They had a red tinge.*

Instructor: Why was Cruella expelled from school?
Student: *She drank ink.*

Instructor: What did Cruella's car look like?
Student: *Her car had black and white stripes.*

Now ask the student, "Can you describe the most important things about Cruella de Vil in one or two sentences?" The description should mention at least one of the odd things about her—the color of her hair, and the red tint in her eyes. Encourage the student to list *only* details that are in the passages, and not details that he may have seen in a movie version. If the student points out that "de Vil" sounds like "devil," that is acceptable (since it can be deduced from the passage).

Acceptable answers might sound like one of the following:

"Cruella de Vil was a very tall woman in a mink cloak. She had red eyes, and her hair was half black and half white."

"Cruella de Vil had a pointed nose and black-and-white hair. She was wearing a satin dress and rubies."

"Cruella de Vil had red shoes and red eyes. Her hair was black and white, and so was her car."

Write down the student's narration on Student Page 71 as he watches.

DAY TWO: Copywork Exercise   *Student Page 72*

Focus: Ending punctuation marks for statements, questions, and exclamations

Pull out Student Page 72. Ask the student to write his name and the date. The following model sentences are already printed on it:

The soup was dark purple. And what did it taste of? Pepper!

Tell the student that these sentences come from a little later in the book *The Hundred and One Dalmatians*; Cruella de Vil has invited the two Dearlys for dinner, but all the food tastes like pepper.

Remind the student that the copied sentences should look exactly like the original. Point out that there are three kinds of ending punctuation here—a period following the statement, a question mark following the question, and an exclamation point following the one-word exclamatory answer to the question. "Pepper!" is not a complete sentence; answering a question is one of the instances in which it is correct to use a fragment in writing.

Now ask the student to copy the sentence. Remember to watch him write, and to correct him at once if he begins to make errors in spelling or format.

DAY THREE: Dictation Exercise   *Student Page 73*

Pull out Student Page 73. Ask the student to write his name and the date.

Dictate the following sentences to the student twice:

The soup was dark purple. And what did it taste of? Pepper!

Ask him if he can remember the punctuation without looking at it. When you read the sentences, use a flat tone for the first statement, a questioning voice for the second question, and an excited voice for "Pepper!" If the student begins to write the wrong ending punctuation, gently correct him.

DAY FOUR: Narration Exercise and Dictation   *Student Pages 74–75*

Focus: Identifying the central narrative thread of a passage

Pull out Student Pages 74–75. Ask the student to write his name and the date on Student Page 75.

Before reading this passage to the student, tell him that Missis and Pongo have already had their puppies. Cruella de Vil comes to see them while the puppies are playing in the "area"—the little fenced courtyard just outside the door to their house. Nanny Butler, who is Mr. Dearly's old nurse, and Nanny Cook, who is Mrs. Dearly's old nurse, are watching the puppies, when they see Cruella de Vil approaching. Lucky, the most adventuresome puppy, has a horseshoe pattern of spots on his back; that's where he gets his nickname.

> Cruella opened the gate and walked down the steps, saying how pretty the puppies were. Lucky, always the ringleader, came running towards her and nibbled at the fur round the tops of her boots. She picked him up and placed him against her cloak, as if he were something to be worn.
>
> "Such a pretty horseshoe," she said, looking at the spots on his back. "But they all have pretty markings. Are they old enough to leave their mother yet?"
>
> "Very nearly," said Nanny Butler. "But they won't have to. Mr. and Mrs. Dearly are going to keep them *all*." (Sometimes the Nannies wondered just how this was going to be managed.)
>
> "How nice!" said Cruella, and began going up the steps, still holding Lucky against her cloak. Pongo, Missis, and Perdita all barked sharply, and Lucky reached up and nipped Cruella's ear. She gave a scream and dropped him. Nanny Butler was quick enough to catch him in her apron.
>
> "That woman!" said Nanny Cook, who had just come out into the area. "She's enough to frighten the spots off a pup. What's the matter, Lucky?"
>
> For Lucky had dashed into the laundry and was gulping down water. Cruella's ear had tasted of pepper.

—From *The Hundred and One Dalmatians*
by Dodie Smith

Ask the following questions to test the student's listening ability. Remind the student to answer in complete sentences; if he answers in a fragment, put the answer in the form of a sentence and then require the student to repeat it back to you.

Instructor: Which puppy ran forward to greet Cruella?
Student: *Lucky ran to greet her.*

Instructor: What markings did Lucky have on his back?
Student: *He had a horseshoe on his back.*

Instructor: When Cruella picked Lucky up, where did she hold him?
Student: *She held him against her cloak as if she wanted to wear him.*

Instructor: What are the names of the two nannies in the passage?
Student: *They are Nanny Cook and Nanny Butler.*

Instructor: How did Lucky get out of Cruella's arms?
Student: *He nipped her ear.*

Instructor: What did she taste like?
Student: *She tasted like pepper.*

Instructor: What do you think Cruella was trying to do with Lucky?
Student: *She was trying to kidnap him. (Prompt the student for this answer if necessary.)*

You will now continue to teach the student to summarize the basic narrative thread in the passage. In order to do this, say to the student:

Instructor: What were the puppies doing when Cruella arrived?
Student: *They were playing in the "area."*

Instructor: What did she do then?
Student: *She picked Lucky up.*

Instructor: Did she put him down right away?
Student: *No.*

Instructor: What did she do instead?
Student: *She walked away with him.*

Instructor: How did Lucky get free?
Student: *Lucky nipped Cruella's ear.*

Now ask the student, "Can you tell me in two sentences what happened in this story?" The student's answer should resemble one of the following (three BRIEF sentences are also acceptable):

"Cruella de Vil saw the puppies playing. She picked Lucky up and tried to take him away. He nipped her ear and got away from her."

"Cruella de Vil tried to steal Lucky, but he bit her ear and got away. Her ear tasted like pepper."

"Cruella de Vil came to see whether the puppies were ready to leave their mother. She tried to take Lucky, but he escaped from her."

Write down the student's narration on Student Page 74, but do not allow him to see the sentences. Choose one of the sentences from the narration to use as a dictation exercise. Be sure to indicate any unusual punctuation with your voice; give any necessary spelling help. When the student has finished writing the dictation sentence on Student Page 75, show him your written original and allow him to compare the two.

DAY FIVE (optional): Creative Writing   *Student Pages 76–77*

Pull out Student Pages 76–77. Write the student's name and the date for him as he watches, or ask him to write the name and date independently.

For creative writing activities for weeks 11–27, student responses to the prompt should be one sentence of roughly 12–14 words. If your student wants to narrate sentences longer than 14 words, encourage him to break his answers up into two shorter sentences.

Instructor: Listen as I read the description of Cruella De Vil and her car from an earlier lesson. Using the description you just heard, complete the illustration on Student Page 76. You will need crayons or something to color with! If you like, write a sentence describing something expensive you would buy if you were as rich as Cruella De Vil.

Read aloud to the student the description of Cruella and her car from page 58 of your book, starting with "At that moment" and ending with "rather unusual." You may also include the description of the car's colors from the last two lines of the passage.

If the student chooses to answer the written prompt, write his answer down on the "Instructor" lines of Student Page 77 as he watches. Then have him copy the sentence onto the "Student" lines.

WEEK 12

DAY ONE: Narration Exercise   *Student Page 78*

Focus: *Summarizing the central narrative thread in a story*

Pull out Student Page 78. Ask the student to write her name and the date.

Read the following passage out loud to the student. Tell the student that this story is from *Pilgrim's Progress*, which was written several hundred years ago by John Bunyan. In the story, a pilgrim named Christian is trying to get to the Celestial City, but he keeps running into difficulties. In this passage, he is travelling with another pilgrim, named Pliable.

You may need to explain that a "pilgrim" is someone who is on a journey.

Now I saw in my dream, that just as they had ended this talk, they drew near to a very miry swamp that was in the midst of the plain, and because they were not paying attention, they both fell suddenly into the bog. The name of the swamp was Despair. Here they wallowed for a time, all covered over with dirt. Then Christian, because of the burden that was on his back, began to sink into the mire.

Pliable said, "Neighbor Christian, where are you now?"

"Truly," said Christian, "I do not know."

At that, Pliable began to be offended. Angrily, he said to his friend, "Is this the happiness you have told me about all this time? If we have such ill luck at our first setting out, what may we expect to happen before the journey ends? If I get out of this swamp alive, you can go and find the beautiful country alone." And with that he gave a desperate struggle or two, and got out of the mire, on that side of the swamp which was next to his own house. So away he went, and Christian saw him no more.

Christian was left to tumble around in the Swamp of Despair alone. But he still tried to struggle to that side of the swamp which was further away from his own house, and next to the Wicket Gate. He got to the side, but he could not get out because of the burden that was upon his back.

But then I saw in my dream that a man came to him, whose name was Help, and said, "What are you doing in there?"

"Sir," said Christian, "I was told to go this way by a man named Evangelist, who directed me towards that Wicket Gate in the distance, so that I may escape the wrath to come. As I was going, I fell in there."

Help said, "But why did you not look for the steps?"

Christian said, "Fear followed me so hard, that I ran away, and fell in."

"Then give me your hand," Help said. So Christian held out his hand, and Help drew him out, and set him on sound ground, and told him to go on his way.

—From *Pilgrim's Progress*
by John Bunyan

Ask the following questions to test the student's listening ability. Remind the student to answer in complete sentences; if she answers in a fragment, put the answer in the form of a sentence and then require her to repeat it back to you.

Instructor: What happened to Christian and Pliable while they were walking?
Student: *They fell into a swamp.*

Instructor: What was the swamp called?
Student: *It was called the Swamp of Despair.*

Instructor: Why did Christian start to sink?
Student: *He had a burden on his back.*

Instructor: What did Pliable do, when he found himself in the swamp?
Student: *He got out of the swamp and went away.*

Instructor: Did Christian see him again?
Student: *No, Christian did not see him.*

Instructor: Why couldn't Christian climb out of the swamp?
Student: *The burden on his back kept him from climbing out.*

Instructor: Who came to the swamp and asked him what he was doing?
Student: *The man named Help came to the swamp.*

Instructor: What did Help do for Christian?
Student: *He pulled Christian out of the swamp.*

You will now continue to teach the student to summarize the basic narrative thread in the passage. In order to do this, say to the student:

Instructor: What happened to Christian and Pliable?
Student: *They fell into the Swamp of Despair.*

Instructor: Were they able to get out?
Student: *Pliable was able to get out, but Christian couldn't get out because of the burden on his back.*

Note: If the student does not give the entire answer, prompt her by asking, "Why couldn't Christian get out?"

Instructor: How did Christian finally get out?
Student: *The man named Help pulled him out.*

Now ask the student, "Can you tell me in two or three short sentences what happened in this story?" The student's answer should resemble one of the following:

"Christian and Pliable fell into the Swamp of Despair. Pliable was able to get out, but Christian couldn't get out because of the burden on his back. Finally a man named Help came along and pulled him out."

"Christian and Pliable were going to the Celestial City when they fell into the Swamp of Despair. Pliable got out, but Christian couldn't until a man named Help helped him."

"Christian and Pliable were walking when they fell into the Swamp of Despair. Pliable got out of the swamp and went home. Christian couldn't get out until Help came along and gave him a hand."

Write down the student's narration on Student Page 78 as she watches.

DAY TWO: Copywork Exercise   *Student Page 79*

Focus: *Helping verbs*

Pull out Student Page 79. Ask the student to write her name and the date. The following model sentences are already printed on it:

> **The man was wearing rags. He was holding a book in his hand, and he was carrying a great burden upon his back.**

Tell the student that these lines are from the beginning of the story *Pilgrim's Progress*. They describe Christian, just before he set off to find the Celestial City.

Tell the student to put her finger on the words "was wearing." "Wearing" is an action verb. "Was" is a helping verb. If the sentence just said "The man wearing rags," it wouldn't sound right. The helping verb helps the main verb to sound right.

Now tell the student to put her finger on the words "was holding." "Holding" is an action verb. "Was" is the helping verb.

Ask the student if she can find the last helping verb in the sentence (*was* carrying).

Now ask the student to copy the sentence. Remember to watch her write, and to correct her at once if he begins to make errors in spelling or format.

DAY THREE: Dictation Exercise   *Student Page 80*

Pull out Student Page 80. Ask the student to write her name and the date.

Dictate the following sentences to the student twice:

> **The man was wearing rags. He was holding a book in his hand, and he was carrying a great burden upon his back.**

Remind the student that there is both a period and a comma in the selection. As you dictate, pause for a silent count of five when you reach the period; pause for a count of three when you reach the comma.

Ask the student to repeat the sentences back to you. If she cannot remember them, repeat them together until she can. If she begins to make a mistake, gently stop and correct her.

DAY FOUR: Narration Exercise and Dictation

Focus: *Identifying the central narrative thread in a passage*

Pull out Student Pages 81–82. Ask the student to write her name and the date on Student Page 82.

Today's exercise will combine narration and dictation. Read the following passage out loud to the student. Tell the student that this passage also comes from *Pilgrim's Progress.* Another pilgrim has joined Christian as he travels towards the Celestial City, and together they have come to a town called Vanity.

> Then I saw in my dream that, when they had left the Wilderness, they saw a town in front of them. The name of that town is Vanity, and at the town is a fair, called Vanity Fair. Vanity Fair has been in this town since ancient times, and at this fair all sorts of goods are sold—houses, lands, countries, kingdoms, silver, gold, pearls, precious stones, lives, souls, and delights of all sorts. And also at this Fair there are jugglers, cheats, games, plays, and fools of all sorts.
>
> The way to the Celestial City lies just through this town, where the Fair is kept, and anyone who wants to go to the city, and yet not go through this town, must go out of the world.
>
> When the pilgrims entered Vanity Fair, all of the people turned to stare at them. For one thing, they were wearing clothes that were different from anyone else's; and their speech was different as well. But what most amused all the merchants was that these pilgrims did not even look at all the wares that were for sale. If the merchants called upon them to buy, they would put their fingers in their ears, and look upwards towards heaven.
>
> One merchant called out to them in mockery, "What will you buy?" And they, looking gravely at him, said, "We buy only the Truth."
>
> —From *Pilgrim's Progress*
> by John Bunyan

Ask the following questions to test the student's listening ability. Remind the student to answer in complete sentences; if she answers in a fragment, put the answer in the form of a sentence and then require the student to repeat it back to you.

Instructor: What is the fair at Vanity called?
Student: *It is called Vanity Fair.*

Instructor: Can you remember three things that are sold at the fair?
Student: *Houses, lands, countries, kingdoms, silver, gold, pearls, precious stones, lives, and souls are sold at the fair.*

Instructor: Why do the pilgrims have to go through the town of Vanity?
Student: *The only way to get to the Celestial City is through Vanity.*

Instructor: There were three reasons why the people stared at the pilgrims. Can you remember two of them?
Student: *Their clothes were different, their speech was different, and they did not look at the things that were for sale.*

Instructor: When the merchants asked them to buy, what did the pilgrims do?
Student: *They put their fingers in their ears and looked up to heaven.*

Instructor: What did the pilgrims say that they would buy?
Student: *They said that they would only buy the Truth.*

You will now continue to teach the student to summarize the basic narrative thread in the passage. In order to do this, say to the student:

Instructor: What did the pilgrims go through?
Student: *They went through Vanity Fair.*

Instructor: Why did they have to go through Vanity Fair?
Student: *They had to go through it to get to the Celestial City.*

Instructor: What two things did the merchants do when they saw the pilgrims?
Student: *They stared at them and asked them to buy.*

Instructor: Did the pilgrims buy anything at Vanity Fair?
Student: *No, they put their fingers in their ears and looked up to heaven.*

Now ask the student, "Can you tell me in two or three sentences what happened in this story?" The student's answer should resemble one of the following:

> "The pilgrims had to go through Vanity Fair to get to the Celestial City. All the merchants stared at them and wanted them to buy things. The pilgrims only put their fingers in their ears."

> "When the pilgrims went through Vanity Fair, the merchants stared at them. They wanted the pilgrims to buy their goods, but the pilgrims put their fingers in their ears instead."

Write down the student's narration on Student Page 81, but do not allow her to see the sentences. Choose one of the sentences from the narration to use as a dictation exercise. Be sure to indicate any unusual punctuation with your voice; give any necessary spelling help. When the student has finished writing the dictation sentence on Student Page 82, show her your written original and allow her to compare the two.

DAY FIVE (optional): Creative Writing   *Student Pages 83–84*

Pull out Student Pages 83–84. Write the student's name and the date for her as she watches, or ask her to write the name and date independently.

Instructor: In *Pilgrim's Progress*, Christian goes on a long journey. His travel companion, Pliable, becomes discouraged and abandons him. If you had to go on a long journey, who is one person you would like to take with you? What is something about that person that would make you want to have them along on your journey?

Write the student's answer down on the "Instructor" lines of Student Page 83 as she watches. Then have her copy the sentence onto the "Student" lines.

WEEK 13

DAY ONE: Narration Exercise   *Student Page 85*

Focus: *Identifying central details in a description*

Pull out Student Page 85. Ask the student to write his name and the date.

   Read the following passage out loud to the student. Explain to the student that this passage is from *The Borrowers* by Mary Norton. The Borrowers are tiny people who live under the floorboards of houses. Everything that they have is borrowed from the "big people" who live in the house. Pod is the father, and Homily is the mother; Arrietty is their daughter. Eggletina is a cousin that Arrietty has never met.

> There were yards of dark and dusty passageway, with wooden doors between the joists and metal gates against the mice. Pod used all kinds of things for these gates—a flat leaf of a folding cheese-grater, the hinged lid of a small cash-box, squares of pierced zinc from an old meat-safe, a wire fly-swatter . . . . "Not that I'm afraid of mice," Homily would say, "but I can't abide the smell." In vain Arrietty had begged for a little mouse of her own, a little blind mouse to bring up by hand—"like Eggletina had had." But Homily would bang with the pan lids and exclaim: "And look what happened to Eggletina!" "What," Arrietty would ask, "what did happen to Eggletina?" But no one would ever say.
>
> It was only Pod who knew the way through the intersecting passages to the hole under the clock. And only Pod could open the gates. There were complicated clasps made of hair-pins and safety pins of which Pod alone knew the secret. His wife and child led more sheltered lives in homelike apartments under the kitchen, far removed from the risks and dangers of the dreaded house above. But there was a grating in the brick wall of the house, just below the floor level of the kitchen above, through which Arrietty could see the garden—a piece of graveled path and a bank where crocus bloomed in spring; where blossom drifted from an unseen tree; and where later an azalea bush would flower; and where birds came—and pecked and flirted and sometimes fought. "The hours you waste on them birds," Homily would say, "and when there's a little job to be done you can never find the time. I was brought up in a house," Homily went on, "where there wasn't no grating, and we were all the happier for it. Now go off and get me the potato . . . .And when I say 'potato' I don't mean the whole potato. Take the scissor, can't you, and cut off a slice."

> —From *The Borrowers*
> by Mary Norton

Ask the following questions to test the student's listening ability. Remind the student to answer in complete sentences; if he answers in a fragment, put the answer in the form of a sentence and then require him to repeat it back to you.

If the student cannot remember the details, reread the section of the passage that answers the question.

Instructor: Why were there metal gates in the passageway?
Student: *The gates were to keep the mice out.*

Instructor: Can you remember two things that Pod made the gates from?
Student: *He used part of a cheese-grater, the lid of a cash-box, parts of a meat-safe, and a fly-swatter.*

Instructor: What were the clasps (or locks) of the gates made from?
Student: *They were made from hair pins and safety pins.*

Instructor: Who could open the locks?
Student: *Pod was the only one who could open the locks.*

Instructor: What room did the Borrowers live underneath?
Student: *They lived underneath the kitchen floorboards.*

Instructor: What could Arrietty see through the grating?
Student: *She could see the garden.*

Instructor: Can you tell me two things that she could see *in* the garden?
Student: *She could see the graveled path, a bank, crocuses, tree blossoms, an azalea bush, and birds.*

Now ask the student, "Can you describe the place where the Borrower family lived in two or three sentences?" The description should mention the gates and something that Arrietty can see through the grating.

Acceptable answers might sound like one of the following:

"The Borrowers lived under the kitchen. Gates and locks made of metal pieces and safety pins kept the mice away. Arrietty could see a garden with flowers and birds in it through the grating."

"Arrietty and her parents lived behind gates made of old pieces of metal. They lived under the floor, but Arrietty could see the garden through a grating. The garden had a gravel path, flowers, and trees."

"The Borrowers lived under the floor, and gates made of metal protected them from the mice. Arrietty, the little girl, could see the garden through a grating. The garden had birds, trees, and flowers in it."

Write the student's narration down on Student Page 85 while he watches.

DAY TWO: Copywork Exercise   *Student Page 86*

Focus: *Contractions*

Pull out Student Page 86. Ask the student to write his name and the date. The following model sentences are already printed on it:

> I don't mean the whole potato. Take the scissor, can't you, and cut off a slice.

Ask him to put his finger on the word "don't." This word is a *contraction*. It is the words "do" and "not" put together, with the "o" in "not" left out. The apostrophe shows where the missing letter goes. To "contract" something means that you make it shorter. Leaving the "o" out makes the two words shorter, so we call this a "contraction."

Ask the student to put his finger on the word "can't." This is a contraction of "cannot." What letters have been left out?

Now ask the student to copy the sentence. Remember to watch him write, and to correct him at once if he begins to make errors in spelling or format.

DAY THREE: Dictation Exercise   *Student Page 87*

Pull out Student Page 87. Ask the student to write his name and the date.

Dictate the following sentences to the student twice:

> I don't mean the whole potato. Take the scissor, can't you, and cut off a slice.

Tell the student that there are two periods and two commas in these sentences. When you dictate, pause for a count of five at the periods and for a count of three at each comma.

Before the student writes, ask him to tell you which two words are contractions. Watch him as he writes, and correct him if he begins to put the apostrophe in the wrong place. If necessary, remind him that the apostrophe goes where the missing letters belong.

DAY FOUR: Narration Exercise and Dictation   *Student Pages 88–89*

Focus: *Identifying central details in a description*

Pull out Student Pages 88–89. Ask the student to write his name and the date on Student Page 89.

Today's exercise will combine narration and dictation. Read the following passage out loud to the student. Tell the student that this is also from *The Borrowers*. Arrietty is lying in her bed, listening to her parents have an argument. She doesn't know what the argument is about, but she knows that they are trying to make a difficult decision! Uncle Hendreary is another Borrower. You may need to explain that "emigrate" means "to go away from your native land."

Arrietty had not been asleep. She had been lying under her knitted coverlet staring up at the ceiling. It was an interesting ceiling. Pod had built Arrietty's bedroom out of two cigar boxes, and on the ceiling lovely painted ladies dressed in swirls of chiffon blew long trumpets against a background of blue sky; below there were feathery palm trees and small white houses set about a square. It was a glamour scene, above all by candlelight, but tonight Arrietty had stared without seeing. The wood of a cigar box is thin and Arrietty, lying straight and still under the quilt, had heard the rise and fall of worried voices . . . .

So when Homily appeared beside her bed, she wrapped herself obediently in her quilt and, padding in her bare feet along the dusty passage, she joined her parents in the warmth of the kitchen. Crouched on her little stool she sat clasping her knees, shivering a little, and looking from one face to another.

Homily came beside her and, kneeling on the floor, she placed an arm round Arrietty's skinny shoulders. "Arrietty," she said gravely, "you know about upstairs?"

"What about it?" asked Arrietty.

"You know there are two giants?"

"Yes," said Arrietty, "Great-Aunt Sophy and Mrs. Driver."

"That's right," said Homily . . . "You know about Uncle Hendreary? . . . He emigrated . . . because he was 'seen'. . . . [The maid] dusted him, they say, with a feather duster, and he stood so still, alongside a cupid, that she might never have noticed him if he hadn't sneezed. She was new, you see, and didn't know the ornaments. We heard her screeching right here under the kitchen."

—From *The Borrowers*
by Mary Norton

Ask the following questions to test the student's listening ability. Remind the student to answer in complete sentences; if he answers in a fragment, put the answer in the form of a sentence and then require him to repeat it back to you.

Instructor: What was Arrietty's bedroom built out of?
Student: *It was made from two cigar boxes.*

Instructor: What were the lovely ladies painted on the ceiling doing?
Student: *They were blowing trumpets.*

Instructor: What was painted underneath the blue sky?
Student: *There were feathery palm trees and small white houses.*

Instructor: What were the walls like—thick or thin?
Student: *The walls were thin.*

Instructor: What did the Borrowers call the people who lived upstairs?
Student: *The Borrowers called them "giants."*

Instructor: Why did Uncle Hendreary have to emigrate?
Student: *He was seen by the maid.*

Instructor: What did Uncle Hendreary do when the maid dusted him?
Student: *He sneezed!*

Now ask the student, "Can you describe Arrietty's bedroom in one or two sentences?" The description should mention something about the cigar boxes or the wood, and also something about the painted scenes.

Acceptable answers might sound like one of the following:

"Arrietty's bedroom was made from cigar boxes. Two ladies were painted on the ceiling, blowing trumpets."

"Arrietty's bedroom had very thin walls because it was made from cigar boxes. White houses and palm trees were painted on the walls, and ladies blowing trumpets were on the ceiling."

"Arrietty lived in a bedroom made of cigar boxes, with painted scenes of houses and palm trees on the walls."

Write down the student's narration on Student Page 88, but do not allow him to see the sentences. Choose one of the sentences from the narration to use as a dictation exercise. Be sure to indicate any unusual punctuation with your voice; give any necessary spelling help. When the student has finished writing the dictation sentence on Student Page 89, show him your written original and allow him to compare the two.

Day Five (optional): Creative Writing   *Student Page 90*

Pull out Student Page 90. Write the student's name and the date for him as he watches, or ask him to write the name and date independently.

Instructor: Complete the story below by adding 1–2 sentences:

"Once upon a time I woke up and realized that I had shrunk to be just three inches tall . . ."

Remind the student to answer you in a complete sentence. If he answers in a fragment, turn the fragment into a complete sentence, say it to him, and then ask him to repeat this sentence back to you. Write the student's answer down on the "Instructor" lines of Student Page 90 as he watches. Then have him copy the sentence onto the "Student" lines.

WEEK 14

DAY ONE: Narration Exercise

Focus: *Identifying central details in a description*

Pull out Student Page 91. Ask the student to write her name and the date.

Read the following passage out loud to the student. This passage (slightly abridged and adapted from the original) comes from *The Boxcar Children* by Gertrude Chandler Warner. In the story, four siblings are sent to live with their grandfather after both their parents die. They decide to run away to live on their own instead. When it begins to rain, they find a boxcar abandoned in a forest and take shelter in it. In this passage the rain has just stopped and the four children are peeking out of the boxcar to look at their surroundings for the first time.

If the student asks, tell her that a boxcar is a kind of train car that looks like one big rectangular box with a sliding door on the side. They are used for carrying all kinds of non-living cargo.

Presently the thunder grew fainter, and rumbled away down the valley, and the rain spent itself. Only the drip from the trees on the top of the car could be heard. Then Henry ventured to open the door.

He knelt on his hands and knees and thrust his head out.

The warm sunlight was filtering through the trees, making golden pools of light here and there. The beautiful trees, pines and white birches and oaks, grew thickly around and the ground was carpeted with flowers and wonderful ferns more than a yard high. But most miraculous of all was a miniature waterfall, small but perfect, where the same little brown brook fell gracefully over some ledges, and danced away down the glen.

In an instant Jess and Violet were looking over Henry's shoulder at the pretty sight.

"Henry!" said Jess sharply. "Let's live here!"

"Live here?" repeated Henry dully.

"Yes! Why not?" replied Jess. "Nobody uses this car, and it's dry and warm. We're quite far away. And yet we are near enough to a town so we can buy things."

"And we're near water," added Violet.

Jess hugged her sister. "So we are, little mouse," she said—"the most important thing of all."

*   *   *

When the meal was over, and exactly half of each bottle of milk remained, Jess said, "We are going to sleep on *beds* tonight, and just as soon as we get our beds made, we are all going to be washed."

"First, let's gather armfuls of dry pine needles," ordered Jess. "Get those on top that have been lying in the sunshine." Jess started to scoop up piles of the fragrant needles. Soon a pile as high as her head stood just under the freight-car door.

"I think we have enough," she said at last. Taking the scissors from Violet's workbag, she cut the laundry bag carefully into two pieces, saving the cord for a clothesline. One of the big squares was laid across Benny's hay and tucked under. That was the softest bed of all.

"I'll sleep next to Benny," said Henry, "with my head up by the door. Then I can hear what is going on." A big pile of pine needles was loaded into the freight car for Henry's bed, and covered with the other half of the laundry bag.

The remainder of the needles Jess piled into the farthest corner of the car for herself and Violet. "We'll all sleep on one side, so we can call it the bedroom."

"What'll be the other side?" inquired Benny.

"The other side?" repeated Jess. "Let me think! I guess that'll be the sitting room, and perhaps some of the time the kitchen."

"On rainy days, maybe the dining room," added Henry with a wink.

"Couldn't it be the parlor?" begged Benny.

"Certainly, the parlor! We forgot that," agreed Jess, returning the wink. She was covering the last two soft beds with the two aprons.

"Looks like home already, Jess," said Henry, smiling.

Ask the following questions to test the student's listening ability. Remind the student to answer in complete sentences; if she answers in a fragment, put the answer in the form of a sentence and then require her to repeat it back to you.

If the student cannot remember the details, reread the section of the passage that answers the question.

Instructor: What was the most miraculous thing the children saw when they looked around the forest for the first time?
Student: *The most miraculous thing they saw was a miniature waterfall.*

Instructor: What reasons did Jess and Violet give to convince their brother that the boxcar was a good place for them to live? (list at least two)
Student: *Some reasons they gave were that nobody was living in it, it was dry, it was warm, it was close enough to town to get food, and there was water nearby.*

Instructor: After finishing eating, what did Jess ask her siblings to collect? What did she want to make?
Student: *She asked them to collect pine needles to turn into beds for her and her siblings.*

Instructor: What did Jess do with the pieces of cloth she cut from the laundry bag?
Student: *She laid them across the pine needles to make soft beds for Benny and Henry.*

Instructor: Where did Henry say he would put his pine needle bed?
Student: *Henry said he would put his bed by Benny, with his head close to the door.*

Instructor: What room names do the children give the empty side of their boxcar, the side without the pine needles? (list at least one)
Student: *The children call the other side of the boxcar the sitting room, the kitchen, the dining room, and the parlor.*

Now ask the student, "Can you tell me in two or three sentences what the siblings' new home looked like? Make sure you tell me what the children did to the boxcar to make it their home." Acceptable answers might sound like one of the following:

"The children live in an empty boxcar in the forest. They put piles of pine needles inside the boxcar to sleep on."

"The siblings found a boxcar in a beautiful forest and decided to make it their home. They picked up pine needles to make beds on one side of the car and called it the bedroom. They left the other side empty but gave it names like "the dining room," "the kitchen," and "the parlor.""

"The children found an empty boxcar in a beautiful forest by a miniature waterfall. They made it their own by adding beds out of pine needles and giving names to different parts of the car."

Write the student's narration down on Student Page 91 while she watches.

DAY TWO: Copywork Exercise

Student Page 92

Focus: *Contractions*

Pull out Student Page 92. Ask the student to write her name and the date. The following model sentences are already printed on it:

> "Oh, don't you worry," Jess said. "We'll have a surprise for you when you come back. You just wait and see!"

Tell the student that these sentences are from *The Boxcar Children*. After the four siblings find a train car and decide to make it their new home, they realize that they need food. So the oldest brother, Henry, reluctantly decides to leave his siblings and go to town. His younger sister assures him that they will be alright while he is gone.

Ask your student to put her finger on the word "don't." What two words form this *contraction*? ("Do" and "not"). Ask her to put her finger on the word "we'll." Tell her that this word is a contraction of "we will." Which letters have been left out? (The letter "o" in "don't" and the letters"wi" in "will").

Now ask the student to copy the sentences. Remember to watch her write, and to correct her at once if she begins to make errors in spelling or format.

DAY THREE: Dictation Exercise   *Student Page 93*

Pull out Student Page 93. Ask the student to write her name and the date.

Dictate the following sentences to the student twice:

> "What's the matter?" demanded Henry. "Isn't the woods a good place to sleep? We can't sleep on the road."

Remind the student that there are two sentences in this exercise. You will pause at the end of the first sentence, which ends with a period. The next word should begin with a capital letter.

Before the student writes, remind her that there are three contractions in the sentences. "What's" stands for "what is." "Isn't" stands for "is not." "Can't" stands for "can not." In each sentence, the apostrophe comes where the letters have been left out.

Watch the student as she writes, and correct her if she begins to put the apostrophes in the wrong places (or if she makes other errors).

DAY FOUR: Narration Exercise and Dictation   *Student Pages 94–95*

Focus: *Identifying the central narrative thread in a story*

Pull out Student Pages 94–95. Ask the student to write her name and the date on Student Page 95.

Today's exercise will combine narration and dictation. Read the following passage out loud to the student. Tell the student that this passage is also from *The Boxcar Children*. After their older brother leaves to find food in town, the three youngest children are left alone in the boxcar. They hear a noise and worry that someone might discover them:

> "Keep still!" whispered Jess.
>
> Benny obeyed. The three children were as motionless as stone images, huddled inside the freight car. Jess opened her mouth in order to breathe at all, her heart was thumping so wildly. She watched like a cat through the open door, in the direction of the rustling noise. And in a moment the trembling bushes parted, and out crawled a dog. He was an Airedale and was pulling himself along on three legs, whimpering softly.
>
> Jess drew a long breath of relief, and said to the children, "It's all right. Only a dog. But he seems to be hurt."
>
> At the sound of her voice the dog lifted his eyes and wagged his tail feebly. He held up his front foot.
>
> "Poor doggie," murmured Jess soothingly, as she clambered out of the car. "Let Jess see your poor lame foot." She approached the dog carefully, for

she remembered that her mother had always told her never to touch a strange dog unless he wagged his tail.

But this dog's tail was wagging, certainly, so Jess bent over without fear to look at the paw. An exclamation of pity escaped her when she saw it, for a stiff, sharp thorn had been driven completely through one of the cushions of the dog's foot, and around it the blood had dried.

"I guess I can fix that," said Jess briskly. "But taking the thorn out is going to hurt you, old fellow."

The dog looked up at her as she laid his paw down, and licked her hand.

"Come here, Violet and Benny," directed Jess.

She took the animal gently in her lap and turned him on his side. She patted his head and stroked his nose with one finger, and offered him the rest of her breadcrust, which she had put in her apron pocket. The dog snapped it up as if he were nearly starved. Then she held the soft paw firmly with her left hand, and pulled steadily on the thorn with her right hand. The dog did not utter a sound. He lay motionless in her lap, until the thorn suddenly let go and lay in Jess' hand.

"Good, good!" cried Violet.

"Wet my handkerchief," Jess ordered briskly.

Violet did so, dipping it in the running brook. Jess wrapped the cool, wet folds around the hot paw, and gently squeezed it against the wound, the dog meanwhile trying to lick her hands.

"We'll s'prise Henry, won't we?" laughed Benny delightedly. "Now we got a dog!"

Ask the following questions to test the student's listening ability. Remind the student to answer in complete sentences; if she answers in a fragment, put the answer in the form of a sentence and then require her to repeat it back to you.

Instructor: What did Benny, Violet, and Jess do when they heard the rustling noise outside the boxcar?
Student: *They sat perfectly still.*

Instructor: How did Jess react to seeing the dog? Was she scared or relieved?
Student: *Jess was relieved that it was just a dog.*

Instructor: What did Jess check before touching the strange dog (because her mother always told her to)?
Student: *Jess checked to make sure that the dog wagged his tail.*

Instructor: What was wrong with the dog?
Student: *The dog had a thorn stuck in his foot.*

Instructor: What did Jess do to the dog?
Student: *She gave it bread and then pulled the thorn out of his foot.*

You will now continue to teach the student to summarize the basic narrative thread in the passage. In order to do this, say to the student:

Instructor: Who comes to the boxcar and surprises the children after their brother leaves?
Student: *A dog comes to the boxcar and surprises the children.*

Instructor: What do they do when they find out the dog is hurt?
Student: *They feed him and pull a thorn from his foot.*

Now ask the student, "Can you tell me in one or two sentences what happened in this story?" The student's answer should resemble one of the following:

"The children find a hurt dog and decide to take care of him."

"After their brother left for town, the younger children met a friendly dog. The dog was hurt, so they took him in, removed the thorn from his foot, and took care of his wound."

Write down the student's narration on Student Page 94, but do not allow her to see the sentences. Choose one of the sentences from the narration to use as a dictation exercise. Be sure to indicate any unusual punctuation with your voice; give any necessary spelling help. When the student has finished writing the dictation sentence on Student Page 95, show her your written original and allow her to compare the two.

DAY FIVE (optional): Creative Writing   *Student Pages 96–97*

Pull out Student Pages 96–97. Write the student's name and the date for her as she watches, or ask her to write the name and date independently.

Instructor: In *The Boxcar Children* four siblings tried to live all by themselves, with no adults. If you got to live in your house for a day, with no adults around, what is the first thing you think you should do? What is the first thing you would want to do? Are they the same, or are they different?

Write the student's answer down on the "Instructor" lines of Student Page 96 as she watches. Then have her copy the sentence onto the "Student" lines.

WEEK 15

DAY ONE: Narration Exercise

Focus: *Identifying central details in a description*

Pull out Student Page 98. Ask the student to write his name and the date.

Read the following passage out loud to the student. Tell the student that this is the beginning of the book *Mrs. Frisby and the Rats of NIMH* by Robert O'Brien.

> Mrs. Frisby, the head of a family of field mice, lived in an underground house in the vegetable garden of a farmer named Mr. Fitzgibbon. It was a winter house, such as some field mice move to when food becomes too scarce, and the living too hard in the woods and pastures. In the soft earth of a bean, potato, black-eyed pea, and asparagus patch there is plenty of food left over for mice after the human crop has been gathered.
>
> Mrs. Frisby and her family were especially lucky in the house itself. It was a slightly damaged cinder block, the hollow kind with two oval holes through it; it had somehow been abandoned in the garden during the summer and lay almost completely buried, with only a bit of one corner showing above ground, which is how Mrs. Frisby had discovered it. It lay on its side in such a way that the solid parts of the block formed a roof and a floor, both waterproof, and the hollows made two spacious rooms. Lined with bits of leaves, grass, cloth, cotton fluff, feathers and other soft things Mrs. Frisby and her children had collected, the house stayed dry, warm, and comfortable all winter. A tunnel to the surface-earth of the garden, dug so that it was slightly larger than a mouse and slightly smaller than a cat's foreleg, provided access, air, and even a fair amount of light to the living room. The bedroom, formed by the second oval, was warm but dark, even at midday. A short tunnel through the earth behind the block connected the two rooms.
>
> Although she was a widow (her husband had died only the preceding summer), Mrs. Frisby was able, through luck and hard work, to keep her family—there were four children—happy and well fed. January and February were the hardest months; the sharp, hard cold that began in December lasted until March, and by February the beans and black-eyes had been picked over (with help from the birds), the asparagus roots were frozen into stone, and the potatoes had been thawed and refrozen so many times they had acquired a slimy texture and a rancid taste. Still, the Frisbys made the best of what there was, and one way or another they kept from being hungry.
>
> Then one day at the very end of February, Mrs. Frisby's younger son, Timothy, fell sick.
>
> —From *Mrs. Frisby and the Rats of NIMH*
> by Robert C. O'Brien

Ask the following questions to test the student's listening ability. Remind the student to answer in complete sentences; if he answers in a fragment, put the answer in the form of a sentence and then require him to repeat it back to you.

If the student cannot remember the details, reread the section of the passage that answers the question.

Instructor: What kind of house did Mrs. Frisby live in?
Student: She lived in an underground house.

Instructor: What kind of garden was the house in?
Student: It was in a vegetable garden.

Instructor: Why do mice move to a winter house?
Student: They move because food is too scarce and living is too hard in woods and pastures.

Instructor: Can you remember two kinds of food that were in the vegetable garden?
Student: There were beans, potatoes, black-eyed peas, and asparagus.

Instructor: What was the house made out of?
Student: It was made out of a cinder block.

Instructor: What were the rooms of the house lined with? Try to remember three of the soft things that Mrs. Frisby and her children used to line the rooms.
Student: They were lined with leaves, grass, cloth, cotton fluff, and feathers.

Instructor: The tunnel to the surface was dug to be slightly larger than what?
Student: It was slightly larger than a mouse.

Instructor: What was it slightly smaller than?
Student: It was slightly smaller than a cat's foreleg.

Instructor: How many children did Mrs. Frisby have?
Student: She had four children.

Instructor: What were the hardest months?
Student: January and February were the hardest months.

Instructor: Why did the potatoes taste slimy?
Student: They had been thawed and refrozen.

Now ask the student, "Can you tell me what Mrs. Frisby's house was like in three sentences?" The description should include *where* the house was (either "underground" or "in the vegetable garden").

Acceptable answers might sound like one of the following:

> "Mrs. Frisby had an underground house in the garden. It was made out of a cinder block, and it had two rooms. The rooms were lined with leaves, grass, cotton, and feathers."

"Mrs. Frisby and her four children lived in a cinder block under the ground. They moved into it during the winter because it was hard to find food. There were asparagus, beans, and potatoes in the garden where the house was."

"The mice lived in two rooms under the garden. They lined the rooms with soft things—leaves, grass, cotton, and cloth. They got food out of the garden, even though the potatoes and the asparagus had been frozen."

Write the student's narration down on Student Page 98 while he watches.

DAY TWO: Copywork Exercise   *Student Page 99*

Focus: *Adjectives*

Pull out Student Page 99. Ask the student to write his name and the date. The following model sentence is already printed on it:

> She wished she knew where to find a bit of green lettuce, or a small egg, or a taste of cheese, or a corn muffin.

Tell the student that this is what Mrs. Frisby is thinking as she looks at the same old dry winter food that her family has been eating for months. She is ready to eat some good spring food instead!

In the phrases "winter food" and "spring food," both "winter" and "spring" are *adjectives*. Adjectives are words that describe nouns. What kind of food is it? "Winter" food or "spring" food.

Ask the student to put his finger on the phrase "green lettuce." Which one of these words is the name of a thing? "Lettuce." "Lettuce" is a noun, because it is the name of a thing. What kind of lettuce is it? "Green" lettuce. "Green" is the adjective that describes "lettuce."

Ask the student to put his finger on the phrase "small egg." Which one of these words is the name of a thing? "Egg." "Egg" is a noun because it is the name of a thing. What kind of egg is it? A "small" egg. "Small" is the adjective that describes "egg."

Ask the student to put his finger on the phrase "corn muffin." Which one of these words is the name of a thing? "Muffin." "Muffin" is a noun because it is the name of a thing. What kind of muffin is it? A "corn" muffin. "Corn" is the adjective that describes "muffin."

> **Note:** If the student asks, tell him that "corn" can also be the name of a thing—the grain that grows in fields. In this sentence, though, it describes "muffin," so it is an adjective.

Now ask the student to copy the sentence. Remember to watch him write, and to correct him at once if he begins to make errors in spelling or format.

DAY THREE: Dictation Exercise   *Student Page 100*

Pull out Student Page 100. Ask the student to write his name and the date.
Dictate the following sentence to the student twice:

> She wished she knew where to find a bit of green lettuce, or a small
> egg, or a taste of cheese, or a corn muffin.

Tell the student that there are three commas in this sentence. When you dictate, pause for a count of three at each comma.

Before the student writes, ask him which word in the phrase "green lettuce" is the adjective. ("Green.") How about in the phrase "small egg" ("small") or "corn muffin" ("corn")?

Watch the student as he writes, and correct him if he begins to make a mistake.

DAY FOUR: Narration Exercise and Dictation   *Student Pages 101–102*

Focus: *Identifying the central narrative thread in a passage*

Pull out Student Pages 101–102. Ask the student to write his name and the date on Student Page 102.

Today's exercise will combine narration and dictation. Read the following passage out loud to the student. Tell the student that this passage is also from *Mrs. Frisby and the Rats of NIMH*. Mrs. Frisby is setting off to find food for her family—and help for her young son Timothy, who is sick.

> That day began with a dry, bright, icy morning. Mrs. Frisby woke up early, as she always did. She and her family slept close together in a bed of down, fluff, and bits of cloth that they had gathered, warm as a ball of fur.
>
> She stood up carefully so as not to awaken the children, and walked quietly through the short tunnel to the living room. Here it was not so warm, but not really cold either. She could see from the light filtering down the entrance tunnel that the sun was up, and bright. She looked at the food in her pantry, a hollowed-out space lined with small stones in the earth behind the living room. There was plenty of food for breakfast, and lunch and dinner, too, for that matter; but still the sight depressed her, for it was the same tiresome fare they had been eating every day, every meal, for the last month. She wished she knew where to find a bit of green lettuce, or a small egg, or a taste of cheese, or a corn muffin. There were eggs in plenty not far off, in the hen house. But hens and hens' eggs are too big for a field mouse to cope with; and besides, between the garden and the henhouse there was a wide sward of shrubs and grass, some of it grown up quite tall. Cat territory.

She climbed up the tunnel, emerging whiskers first, and looked around warily. The air was sharp, and there was white frost thick on the ground and on the dead leaves at the edge of the wood across the garden patch.

Mrs. Frisby set off over the gently furrowed earth, and when she reached the fence, she turned right, skirting the border of the forest, searching with her bright round eyes for a bit of carrot, a frozen parsnip, or something green. But there was nothing green at that time of year but the needles on the pine trees and the leaves on the holly, neither of which a mouse—or any other animal, for that matter—could reach.

—From *Mrs. Frisby and the Rats of NIMH*
by Robert C. O'Brien

Ask the following questions to test the student's listening ability. Remind the student to answer in complete sentences; if he answers in a fragment, put the answer in the form of a sentence and then require him to repeat it back to you.

Instructor: Was the morning warm or cold?
Student: It was cold (icy).

Instructor: Can you remember one thing that the family's bed was made of?
Student: It was made of down, fluff, and cloth.

Instructor: How did Mrs. Frisby know that the sun was up?
Student: She could see light in the tunnel.

Instructor: Why was Mrs. Frisby depressed by the food in her pantry?
Student: It was the same food they had been eating for a month.

Instructor: Why was it hard for a mouse to get a hen's egg? (There are actually two reasons.)
Student: Eggs were too big for mice to carry; also, there were cats in the grass around the henhouse.

Instructor: (If the student does not give you the second part of the answer) What kind of animal prowled around in the grass between the garden and the henhouse?
Student: Cats prowled around in the grass.

Instructor: Can you remember two things that Mrs. Frisby was looking for as she crept along the edge of the forest?
Student: She was looking for a carrot, a parsnip, or something green.

Instructor: Did she find anything?
Student: No, she did not.

You will now continue to teach the student to summarize the basic narrative thread in the passage. In order to do this, say to the student:

Instructor: What happened right at the beginning of the story?
Student: Mrs. Frisby got up early in the morning.

Instructor: What did Mrs. Frisby go outside to do?
Student: *She went outside to find some food.*

Instructor: Did she find any food?
Student: *No, she did not.*

Now ask the student, "Can you tell me in one or two sentences what happened in this story?" The student's answer should resemble one of the following:

"Mrs. Frisby got up in the morning and went outside to find food for her children. There was nothing outside to eat."

"Mrs. Frisby got up on a cold morning and went outside to find something to eat. She was tired of the food they had been eating for a month, and she wanted to find something green."

"Mrs. Frisby was tired of the food her family had been eating, so she went outside to try to find something else."

Write down the student's narration on Student Page 101, but do not allow him to see the sentences. Choose one of the sentences from the narration to use as a dictation exercise. Be sure to indicate any unusual punctuation with your voice; give any necessary spelling help. When the student has finished writing the dictation sentence on Student Page 102, show him your written original and allow him to compare the two.

DAY FIVE (optional): Creative Writing   *Student Pages 103–104*

Pull out Student Pages 103–104. Write the student's name and the date for him as he watches, or ask him to write the name and date independently.

Instructor: Look in your refrigerator or pantry and pick three different foods. Then, think of three different adjectives to describe each food! You can describe how it looks (color, size, shape), how it tastes (salty, sweet, tart), and its texture (mushy, crunchy, crisp). Try to find different adjectives than the ones we've used here.

Remind the student to answer you in a complete sentence. If he answers in a fragment, turn the fragment into a complete sentence, say it to him, and then ask him to repeat this sentence back to you. Write the student's answer down on the "Instructor" lines of Student Page 103 as he watches. Then have him copy the sentence onto the "Student" lines.

WEEK 16

DAY ONE: Narration Exercise

Focus: *Identifying the central narrative thread in a story*

Pull out Student Page 105. Ask the student to write her name and the date.

Read the following passage out loud to the student. Tell the student that this is a traditional fairy tale. Something in the world of the fairy tale is very different than in today's world. Can you figure out what it is?

> Once upon a time there lived a young man in a dirty, tumble-down cottage, not very far from the splendid palace where the king and queen dwelt. He had only six copper pennies to his name, and although he worked hard in his garden to grow fruit and vegetables, he grew hungry and hungrier. Finally he decided to set out into the world to find work that would earn him enough money to buy bread.
>
> He set out into the forest, not knowing where he was going. As he walked, his stomach ached from hunger. Finally, seeing a small hut in front of him, he knocked at the door and asked if they could give him some milk.
>
> The old woman who opened it begged him to come in, adding kindly, that if he wanted a night's lodging he might have it without its costing him anything.
>
> Two women and three men were at supper when he entered, and silently made room for him to sit down by them. At first he was so hungry that he could only pay attention to his food. But once he had eaten he began to look about him, and was surprised to see an animal sitting by the fire different from anything he had ever noticed before. It was grey in color, and not very big; but its eyes were large and very bright, and it seemed to be singing in an odd way, quite unlike any animal in the forest.
>
> "What is the name of that strange little creature?" he asked. And they answered, "We call it a cat."
>
> "I should like to buy it," said the young man. "It would be company for me."
>
> And they told him that he might have it for six copper pennies, if he cared to give so much. Now, this was all the money the young man had in the world, but he was strangely anxious to buy the cat. So he took out his precious coins and handed them over. The next morning he bade them farewell, with the cat lying snugly in his cloak.
>
> For the whole day they wandered through meadows and forests, till in the evening they reached a house. The young fellow knocked at the door and asked the old man who opened it if he could rest there that night, adding that he had no money to pay for it.

"Then I must give it to you," answered the man, and led him into a room where two women and two men were sitting at supper. One of the women was the old man's wife, the other his daughter. He placed the cat on the mantel shelf, and they all crowded round to examine this strange beast, and the cat rubbed itself against them, and held out its paw, and sang to them; and the women were delighted, and gave it everything that a cat could eat, and a great deal more besides.

—Adapted from "The Young Man and the Cat"
from *The Crimson Fairy Book*
by Andrew Lang

Ask the following questions to test the student's listening ability. Remind the student to answer in complete sentences; if she answers in a fragment, put the answer in the form of a sentence and then require her to repeat it back to you.

Instructor: What kind of cottage did the young man live in?
Student: *It was a dirty, tumble-down cottage.*

Instructor: How many copper pennies did he have?
Student: *He had six copper pennies.*

Instructor: How many women and how many men were in the small cottage?
Student: *There were two women and three men in the cottage.*

Instructor: What color was the strange animal sitting by the fire?
Student: *It was grey.*

Instructor: What odd thing was it doing?
Student: *It was making a singing noise.*

Instructor: What was this animal?
Student: *It was a cat.*

Instructor: What was the cat really doing when it was "singing"?
Student: *It was purring.*

Instructor: After the young man spent another day wandering, what did he come to?
Student: *He came to a house.*

Instructor: What did the women in the house think of the cat?
Student: *They were delighted by the cat.*

You will now continue to teach the student to summarize the basic narrative thread in the passage. In order to do this, say to the student:

Instructor: Why did the young man set out into the world?
Student: *He wanted to find work.*

Instructor: What strange animal did he find?
Student: *He found a cat.*

Instructor: How did he get the cat?
Student: *He paid all his money for it.*

Instructor: When he left the first cottage, what happened?
Student: *He wandered for a day and then came to another house.*

Now ask the student, "Can you tell me in two or three sentences what happened in this story?" The student's answer should resemble one of the following:

"A poor young man set out to find work. When he stopped at a cottage for the night, he found a cat. He bought the cat and took it with him."

"A man had no money, so he went out to find work. He stopped at a cottage and found a strange animal he had never seen before. The animal was a cat."

"A poor man went to find work, but instead he found a cat. He had never seen a cat before, so he took it with him."

Write down the student's narration on Student Page 105 as she watches.

DAY TWO: Copywork Exercise   *Student Page 106*

Focus: *Predicate adjectives*

Pull out Student Page 106. Ask the student to write her name and the date. The following model sentences are already printed on it:

> The strange animal was grey. Its eyes were large and bright, and it
> seemed to be singing in an odd way.

These sentences describe the cat that the young man bought. Tell the student that there are two adjectives in the first sentence. "Strange" modifies, or describes, "animal." It is an adjective that tells you more about the noun "animal."

Now ask the student to put her finger on the word "grey." "Grey" is also an adjective. It describes "animal," just like the adjective "strange." But this adjective doesn't come right next to the noun it modifies. Instead, it comes after the verb ("was"). We call it a "predicate adjective."

In the second sentence, there are two more predicate adjectives. Ask the student to put her finger on the verb "were." Now, have her move her finger to the adjective "large." This adjective comes after the verb. What does it describe? ("Eyes.") This is also a predicate adjective.

Can the student find the other predicate adjective that describes "eyes"? ("Bright.")

Note: If the student asks, explain that "its" does not stand for "it is," so it does not have an apostrophe (it's). "Its" is the possessive form of the pronoun "it."

Watch the student as she copies the sentences, and correct her if she begins to make a mistake.

DAY THREE: Dictation Exercise   *Student Page 107*

Pull out Student Page 107. Ask the student to write her name and the date.
    Dictate the following sentences to the student twice:

> The strange animal was grey. Its eyes were large and bright, and it seemed to be singing in an odd way.

Remind the student that there are two periods and one comma in the sentences. When you dictate, pause for a count of five at the first period, and for a count of three at the comma. Watch the student as she writes, and correct her if she begins to make a mistake.

DAY FOUR: Narration Exercise and Dictation   *Student Pages 108–109*

Focus: *Identifying the central narrative thread in a passage*

Pull out Student Pages 108–109. Ask the student to write her name and the date on Student Page 109.
    Today's exercise will combine narration and dictation. Read the following passage out loud to the student. Tell the student that this is the second half of the fairy tale that she began reading earlier in the week. The young man and his cat have just come to the house of an old man and his family, who are giving him shelter for the night.

> After hearing the youth's story, and how he had nothing in the world left him except his cat, the old man advised him to go to the palace, which was only a few miles distant, and take counsel of the king, who was kind to everyone, and would certainly be his friend. The young man thanked him, and said he would gladly take his advice; and early next morning he set out for the royal palace.
>   He sent a message to the king to beg for an audience, and received a reply that he was to go into the great hall, where he would find his Majesty.
>   The king was at dinner with his court when the young man entered, and he signed to him to come near. The youth bowed low, and then gazed in surprise at the crowd of little black creatures who were running about

the floor, and even on the table itself. Indeed, they were so bold that they snatched pieces of food from the King's own plate, and if he drove them away, tried to bite his hands, so that he could not eat his food, and his courtiers fared no better.

"What sort of animals are these?" asked the youth of one of the ladies sitting near him.

"They are called rats," answered the king, who had overheard the question, "and for years we have tried some way of putting an end to them, but it is impossible. They come into our very beds."

At this moment something was seen flying through the air. The cat was on the table, and with two or three shakes a number of rats were lying dead round him. Then a great scuffling of feet was heard, and in a few minutes the hall was clear.

For some minutes the King and his courtiers only looked at each other in astonishment. "What kind of animal is that which can work magic of this sort?" asked he. And the young man told him that it was called a cat, and that he had bought it for six copper pennies.

And the King answered: "Because of the luck you have brought me, in freeing my palace from the plague which has tormented me for many years, I will give you the choice of two things. Either you shall be my Prime Minister, or else you shall marry my daughter and reign after me. Say, which shall it be?"

"The princess and the kingdom," said the young man.

And so it was.

—Adapted from "The Young Man and the Cat"
from *The Crimson Fairy Book*
by Andrew Lang

Ask the following questions to test the student's listening ability. Remind the student to answer in complete sentences; if she answers in a fragment, put the answer in the form of a sentence and then require her to repeat it back to you.

Instructor: Where did the old man tell the young man that he should go?
Student: *He told the young man to go to the palace.*

Instructor: What was the king doing when the young man entered?
Student: *He was having dinner.*

Instructor: What was running around the floor?
Student: *Rats were running around on the floor.*

Instructor: What else were the rats doing?
Student: *They were eating food right from the plates on the table.*

Instructor: When the cat saw the rats, what did it do?
Student: *It jumped on the table and killed the rats.*

Instructor: What two choices did the king give the young man in return for bringing his cat?
Student: *He told the young man that he could be Prime Minister, or he could marry the princess.*

Instructor: Which did the young man choose?
Student: *He chose to marry the princess.*

You will now continue to teach the student to summarize the basic narrative thread in the passage. In order to do this, say to the student:

Instructor: What did the young man do at the beginning of this reading?
Student: *He went to the palace.*

Instructor: What problem did the palace have?
Student: *It was filled with rats.*

Instructor: How did the young man solve the problem?
Student: *His cat killed the rats.*

Instructor: What did he get to do as a reward?
Student: *He got to marry the princess.*

Now ask the student, "Can you tell me in two or three sentences what happened in this story?" The student's answer should resemble one of the following:

> "The young man and his cat went to the palace. It was filled with rats which were eating the food on the table. The cat killed the rats, so the king allowed the young man to marry the princess."

> "The young man went to the palace, which was filled with rats. His cat killed the rats. The king told him that he could marry the princess or become Prime Minister, so he chose to marry the princess."

> "The young man and his cat went to the palace. The cat killed the rats that were eating the king's food, so the king told the young man that he could marry the princess."

Write down the student's narration on Student Page 108, but do not allow her to see the sentences. Choose one of the sentences from the narration to use as a dictation exercise. Be sure to indicate any unusual punctuation with your voice; give any necessary spelling help. When the student has finished writing the dictation sentence on Student Page 109, show her your written original and allow her to compare the two.

DAY FIVE (optional): Creative Writing   *Student Pages 110–111*

Pull out Student Pages 110–111. Write the student's name and the date for her as she watches, or ask her to write the name and date independently.

Instructor: In the story, the rats were ruining the king's life. Imagine that you are a king or queen with one really big problem. What is the problem that you can't solve? If you're enjoying this assignment, here's an extra credit suggestion: Who arrives in your kingdom to solve the problem for you?

Write the student's answer down on the "Instructor" lines of Student Page 110 as she watches. Then have her copy the sentence onto the "Student" lines.

WEEK 17

DAY ONE: Narration Exercise   *Student Page 112*

Focus: *Identifying the central narrative thread in a poem*

Pull out Student Page 112. Ask the student to write his name and the date.

Read the following poem out loud to the student. Tell the student that this is the beginning of "The Pied Piper of Hamelin" by Robert Browning. It is an old poem—and a very famous one.

Hamelin Town, Brunswick, Hanover, and the River Weser are all in Germany. Salted sprats are small fish that are preserved in salt (a little bit like sardines). "Noddy" is an old name for a fool. Ermine is a kind of fur. The Corporation is like the city council—they are the business men who decide how to solve the city's problems. A guilder is an old kind of coin.

> Hamelin Town's in Brunswick,
> By famous Hanover city;
> The river Weser, deep and wide,
> Washes its wall on the southern side;
> A pleasanter spot you never spied;
> But, when begins my ditty,
> Almost five hundred years ago,
> To see the townsfolk suffer so
> From vermin, was a pity.
>
> Rats!
> They fought the dogs and killed the cats,
> And bit the babies in the cradles,
> And ate the cheeses out of the vats.
> And licked the soup from the cooks' own ladles,
> Split open the kegs of salted sprats,
> Made nests inside men's Sunday hats,
> And even spoiled the women's chats,
> By drowning their speaking
> With shrieking and squeaking
> In fifty different sharps and flats.
>
> At last the people in a body
> To the Town Hall came flocking:
> "'Tis clear," cried they, "our Mayor's a noddy;
> And as for our Corporation—shocking
> To think we buy gowns lined with ermine
> For dolts that can't or won't determine

What's best to rid us of our vermin!
You hope, because you're old and obese,
To find in the furry civic robe ease?
Rouse up, sirs! Give your brains a racking
To find the remedy we're lacking,
Or, sure as fate, we'll send you packing!"
At this the Mayor and Corporation
Quaked with a mighty consternation.

An hour they sat in council,
At length the Mayor broke silence:
"For a guilder I'd my ermine gown sell;
I wish I were a mile hence!
It's easy to bid one rack one's brain—
I'm sure my poor head aches again,
I've scratched it so, and all in vain
Oh for a trap, a trap, a trap!"
Just as he said this, what should hap
At the chamber door but a gentle tap?
"Bless us," cried the Mayor, "what's that?". . .

—From "The Pied Piper of Hamelin"
by Robert Browning

Ask the following questions to test the student's listening ability. Remind the student to answer in complete sentences; if he answers in a fragment, put the answer in the form of a sentence and then require him to repeat it back to you.

Instructor: What problem did the townsfolk have?
Student: *The town was filled with rats.*

Instructor: Can you list four bad things that the rats did?
Student: *They fought the dogs, killed the cats, bit the babies, ate cheese and soup and sprats, made nests in hats, and squeaked loudly.*

Instructor: How did the townspeople feel about the Mayor and the Corporation?
Student: *They were angry OR They thought the Mayor was a fool OR They wanted the Mayor and the Corporation to get rid of the rats.*

Instructor: What did the Mayor wish for?
Student: *He wished for a trap.*

Instructor: What did he hear then?
Student: *He heard a tap on the door.*

You will now continue to teach the student to summarize the basic narrative thread in the passage. In order to do this, say to the student:

Instructor: What was the problem at the beginning of the poem?
Student: *There were rats everywhere.*

Instructor: What were two or three bad things that the rats did?
Student: *They fought the dogs, killed the cats, bit the babies, ate cheese and soup and sprats, made nests in hats, and squeaked loudly.*

Instructor: Could the Mayor and the Corporation think of a solution?
Student: *No, they could not!*

Now ask the student, "Can you tell me in two or three sentences what happened in this part of the poem?" The student's answer should resemble one of the following:

"The people of Hamelin had a problem. There were too many rats!
They ate the food, bit the babies, and squeaked so loudly that the women couldn't talk."

"The town was filled with rats. They fought the dogs, killed the cats, and bit the babies.
The Mayor and the town council couldn't figure out how to get rid of them."

"There were so many rats in Hamelin that the people asked the Mayor and the
Corporation to get rid of them. Even though the rats were eating all the food and
killing the cats, the Mayor didn't know what to do."

Write down the student's narration on Student Page 112 while he watches.

Day Two: Copywork Exercise   *Student Page 113*

Focus: *Interjections*

Pull out Student Page 113. Ask the student to write his name and the date. The following
model sentences are already printed on it:

> Rats! They fought the dogs and killed the cats. Oh, how I wish we had
> a trap!

Ask the student to read you the first word. Then ask him to put his finger on the word
"Oh." Tell him that both of these words are interjections. An interjection is a word that
expresses sudden or strong feeling.

These sentences show that there are two different ways to write an interjection. What
kind of punctuation mark comes after the first interjection? An exclamation point—showing
that "Rats!" should be spoken with great energy (and alarm). What kind of punctuation
mark comes after the second exclamation? A comma—showing that this is a softer, sadder
interjection. Interjections can be separated from the sentences around them either by
exclamation points or by commas.

Now ask the student to copy the sentences. Remember to watch him write, and to correct him at once if he begins to make errors.

DAY THREE: Dictation Exercise   *Student Page 114*

Pull out Student Page 114. Ask the student to write his name and the date.
Dictate the following sentences to the student twice:

> Rats! They fought the dogs and killed the cats. Oh, how I wish we had a trap!

Remind the student that there are two interjections in the sentences. One has an exclamation point after it; the other has a comma after it. There is also a period. Tell the student to listen for each punctuation mark. When you read, say the word "Rats!" with strong emotion, and then pause for a count of five. When you reach the period, pause for a count of five. When you say "Oh . . . " drag the word out wistfully, and then pause at the comma for a count of three.

Watch the student as he writes, and correct him if he begins to make a mistake.

DAY FOUR: Narration Exercise and Dictation   *Student Pages 115–116*

Focus: *Identifying the central narrative thread in a poem*

Pull out Student Pages 115–116. Ask the student to write his name and the date on Student Page 116.

Today's exercise will combine narration and dictation. Read the following passage out loud to the student. Tell the student that this poem continues the story of the Pied Piper from earlier in the week. "Pied" means "made out of two colors"—the piper is wearing two different colors on his coat. "Vesture" is an old word for clothing. An "adept" is someone who is very good at what he does.

> "Come in!"—the Mayor cried, looking bigger:
> And in did come the strangest figure!
> His queer long coat from heel to head
> Was half of yellow and half of red,
> And he himself was tall and thin,
> With sharp blue eyes, each like a pin,
> And light loose hair, yet swarthy skin
> No tuft on cheek nor beard on chin,
> But lips where smile went out and in;
> There was no guessing his kith and kin:

And nobody could enough admire
The tall man and his quaint attire.
Quoth one: "It's as my great-grandsire,
Starting up at the Trump of Doom's tone,
Had walked this way from his painted tombstone!"

He advanced to the council-table:
And, "Please your honours," said he, "I'm able,
By means of a secret charm, to draw
All creatures living beneath the sun,
That creep or swim or fly or run,
After me so as you never saw!
And I chiefly use my charm
On creatures that do people harm,
The mole and toad and newt and viper;
And people call me the Pied Piper."
(And here they noticed round his neck
A scarf of red and yellow stripe,
To match with his coat of the self-same cheque;

And at the scarf's end hung a pipe;
And his fingers they noticed were ever straying
As if impatient to be playing
Upon his pipe, as low it dangled
Over his vesture so old-fangled.) . . . .

[He said,] "If I can rid your town of rats
Will you give me a thousand guilders?"
"One? fifty thousand!"—was the exclamation
Of the astonished Mayor and Corporation.

Into the street the Piper stept,
Smiling first a little smile,
As if he knew what magic slept
In his quiet pipe the while;
Then, like a musical adept,
To blow the pipe his lips he wrinkled,
And green and blue his sharp eyes twinkled,
Like a candle-flame where salt is sprinkled;
And ere three shrill notes the pipe uttered,
You heard as if an army muttered;

And the muttering grew to a grumbling;
And the grumbling grew to a mighty rumbling;
And out of the houses the rats came tumbling.
Great rats, small rats, lean rats, brawny rats,
Brown rats, black rats, grey rats, tawny rats,
Grave old plodders, gay young friskers,
Fathers, mothers, uncles, cousins,
Cocking tails and pricking whiskers,
Families by tens and dozens,
Brothers, sisters, husbands, wives—
Followed the Piper for their lives.
From street to street he piped advancing,
And step for step they followed dancing,
Until they came to the river Weser
Wherein all plunged and perished!

—From "The Pied Piper of Hamelin"
by Robert Browning

Ask the following questions to test the student's listening ability. Remind the student to answer in complete sentences; if he answers in a fragment, put the answer in the form of a sentence and then require him to repeat it back to you.

Instructor: What two colors are the Piper's coat?
Student: The coat is red and yellow.

Instructor: What color are his eyes?
Student: His eyes are blue.

Instructor: What kinds of creatures can the Pied Piper call?
Student: He can call anything that does people harm.

Instructor: What instrument does he play?
Student: He plays a pipe.

Instructor: What does he offer to do?
Student: He offers to get rid of all the rats.

Instructor: When he played his pipe, what did the rats do?
Student: They followed him (dancing).

Instructor: Can you remember five kinds of rats, from the list of rats that answered the Piper?
Student: There were great rats, small rats, lean rats, brawny rats, brown rats, black rats, grey rats, tawny rats, old rats, young rats, fathers, mothers, uncles, cousins, brothers, sisters, husbands, and wives.

Instructor: What happened to the rats at the end of the poem selection?
Student: They plunged into the river.

You will now continue to teach the student to summarize the basic narrative thread in the poem. In order to do this, say to the student:

Instructor: What did the Piper offer to do?
Student: *He offered to get rid of the rats.*

Instructor: How did he get rid of the rats?
Student: *He played his pipe, and they followed him.*

Instructor: What happened to the rats?
Student: *They fell into the river.*

Now ask the student, "Can you tell me in two or three sentences what happened in this story?" The student's answer should resemble one of the following:

"The Pied Piper promised that he could get rid of the rats. He played his pipe, and the rats followed him to the river and plunged in."

"While the Mayor and the Corporation were still talking, the Pied Piper knocked on the door. He told them that he could get rid of the rats, if they would pay him. They promised to pay him, and he led all the rats to the river."

"The Pied Piper told the Mayor that he could get rid of the rats by playing his pipe. The Mayor agreed to pay him fifty thousand guilders. The Piper played his pipe to the rats, and they followed him through the town to the river."

Write down the student's narration on Student Page 115, but do not allow him to see the sentences. Choose one of the sentences from the narration to use as a dictation exercise. Be sure to indicate any unusual punctuation with your voice; give any necessary spelling help. When the student has finished writing the dictation sentence on Student Page 116, show him your written original and allow him to compare the two.

DAY FIVE (optional): Creative Writing   *Student Pages 117–118*

Pull out Student Pages 117–118. Write the student's name and the date for him as he watches, or ask him to write the name and date independently.

Instructor: Imagine you had a superpower. Which power would you want? What is the first thing you would do if you had that power? Here's a limitation, though: you can't fly or see through objects. (Too many superheroes can already do that!)

Remind the student to answer you in a complete sentence. If he answers in a fragment, turn the fragment into a complete sentence, say it to him, and then ask him to repeat this sentence back to you. Write the student's answer down on the "Instructor" lines of Student Page 117 as he watches. Then have him copy the sentence onto the "Student" lines.

WEEK 18

DAY ONE: Narration Exercise   *Student Page 119*

Focus: *Identifying the central narrative thread in a passage*

Pull out Student Page 119. Ask the student to write her name and the date.

Read the following passage out loud to the student. Tell the student that this is the first part of James Baldwin's story "The Midnight Ride," from the book *Fifty Famous People*. The story is about the Revolutionary War hero Paul Revere. It takes place in 1775.

> The midnight ride of Paul Revere happened a long time ago when this country was ruled by the king of England.
>
> There were thousands of English soldiers in Boston. The king had sent them there to make the people obey his unjust laws. These soldiers guarded the streets of the town; they would not let any one go out or come in without their leave.
>
> The people did not like this. They said, "We have a right to be free men, but the king treats us as slaves. He makes us pay taxes and gives us nothing in return. He sends soldiers among us to take away our liberty."
>
> The whole country was stirred up. Brave men left their homes and hurried toward Boston.
>
> They said, "We do not wish to fight against the king, but we are free men, and he must not send soldiers to oppress us. If the people of Boston must fight for their liberty, we will help them."
>
> These men were not afraid of the king's soldiers. Some of them camped in Charlestown, a village near Boston. From the hills of Charlestown they could watch and see what the king's soldiers were doing.
>
> They wished to be ready to defend themselves, if the soldiers should try to do them harm. For this reason they had bought some powder and stored it at Concord, nearly twenty miles away. When the king's soldiers heard about this powder, they made up their minds to go out and get it for themselves.
>
> Among the watchers at Charlestown was a brave young man named Paul Revere. He was ready to serve his country in any way that he could. One day a friend of his who lived in Boston came to see him. He came very quietly and secretly, to escape the soldiers.
>
> "I have something to tell you," he said. "Some of the king's soldiers are going to Concord to get the powder that is there. They are getting ready to start this very night."
>
> "Indeed!" said Paul Revere. "They shall get no powder, if I can help it. I will stir up all the farmers between here and Concord, and those fellows will have a hot time of it. But you must help me."
>
> "I will do all that I can," said his friend.

> "Well, then," said Paul Revere, "you must go back to Boston and watch. Watch, and as soon as the soldiers are ready to start, hang a lantern in the tower of the old North Church. If they are to cross the river, hang two. I will be here, ready. As soon as I see the light, I will mount my horse and ride out to give the alarm."

—From "The Midnight Ride"
from *Fifty Famous People*
by James Baldwin

Ask the following questions to test the student's listening ability. Remind the student to answer in complete sentences.

Instructor: What kind of soldiers were in Boston?
Student: English soldiers were in Boston.

Instructor: Why had the king sent them to Boston?
Student: He sent them to force the people to obey his laws.

Instructor: What did the people say that they had a right to be?
Student: They had the right to be free.

Instructor: What nearby village did men gather in so that they could see what the soldiers were doing?
Student: They gathered in Charlestown.

Instructor: What had the men stored in Concord, so that they could defend themselves?
Student: They stored powder (gunpowder) in Concord.

Instructor: Paul Revere's friend came to tell him some news. What was the news?
Student: The soldiers were going to go to Concord and get the powder.

Instructor: How was Paul Revere's friend going to tell him that the soldiers were getting ready to leave Boston and make their way towards Concord?
Student: He would hang a lantern in the tower of the old North Church.

Instructor: Who would see the lantern?
Student: Paul Revere would see the lantern.

Instructor: How many lanterns would the friend hang if the soldiers were going to march to Concord by land?
Student: He would hang one lantern.

Instructor: How many would he hang if the soldiers were going to cross the river?
Student: He would hang two.

You will now continue to teach the student to summarize the basic narrative thread in the passage. In order to do this, say to the student:

Instructor: What problem did the people in and around Boston have?
Student: Soldiers were forcing them to obey the king's laws.

Instructor: What did they gather together in Concord?
Student: *They gathered powder in Concord.*

Instructor: What did the soldiers plan to do?
Student: *They planned to go and get the powder.*

Instructor: How would Paul Revere find out that the soldiers were getting ready to march to Concord?
Student: *His friend would put a lantern in the church tower.*

Now ask the student, "Can you tell me in three or four sentences what happened in this part of the story?" The student's answer should resemble one of the following:

"The people of Boston were unhappy because of the soldiers that the king of England had sent. They gathered gunpowder and kept it at Concord so they could fight back. The soldiers wanted the powder. Paul Revere and his friend decided that the friend would warn Paul with a lantern when the soldiers started to march to Concord."

"The king of England sent soldiers to Boston. The people of Boston didn't want the soldiers there, so they stored powder in Concord. They wanted to fight against the soldiers. Paul Revere and his friend planned to warn the people as soon as the soldiers tried to take the powder."

"The people of Boston wanted to get rid of the English soldiers. They stored powder at Concord, but the soldiers found out about it. Paul Revere asked his friend to warn him with a lantern when the soldiers started to march to Concord."

Write down the student's narration on Student Page 119 while she watches.

Day Two: Copywork Exercise   *Student Page 120*

Focus: Conjunctions

Pull out Student Page 120. Ask the student to write her name and the date. The following model sentences are already printed on it:

> I will stir up all the farmers between here and Concord, and those fellows will have a hot time of it. But you must help me.

These are Paul Revere's words to his friend. In these two sentences, there are three conjunctions. A conjunction is a word that joins words or groups of words together. The three most common conjunctions are *and, but, or. Nor, for,* and *yet* are also conjunctions, but you won't see them as often.

The first conjunction in these sentences is "and." It joins "here" and "Concord"—two different places, connected together by the conjunction "and." Can you find the next conjuction? ("And.") This conjuction joins two groups of words—it connects "I will stir up all the farmers between here and Concord" with "those fellows will have a hot time of it."

Can you find the last conjunction? ("But.") Does it join words or groups of words? (It joins the groups of words "Those fellows will have a hot time of it" with "you must help me.")

Now ask the student to copy the sentences. Remember to watch her write, and to correct her at once if she begins to make errors.

DAY THREE: Dictation Exercise   *Student Page 121*

Pull out Student Page 121. Ask the student to write her name and the date.

Dictate the following sentences to the student twice:

> I will stir up all the farmers between here and Concord, and those
> fellows will have a hot time of it. But you must help me.

Pause at the comma for a count of three, and at the period for a count of five. If necessary, remind the student that Concord is the proper name of a town and should begin with a capital letter.

Watch the student as she writes, and correct her at once if she begins to make errors.

DAY FOUR: Narration Exercise and Dictation   *Student Pages 122–123*

Focus: *Identifying the central narrative thread in a passage*

Pull out Student Pages 122–123. Ask the student to write her name and the date on Student Page 123.

Today's exercise will combine narration and dictation. Read the following passage out loud to the student. Tell the student that this is the rest of the story of Paul Revere's ride.

> When night came, Paul Revere was at the riverside with his horse. He looked over toward Boston. He knew where the old North Church stood, but he could not see much in the darkness.
>
> Hour after hour he stood and watched. The town seemed very still; but now and then he could hear the beating of a drum or the shouting of some soldier.
>
> The moon rose, and by its light he could see the dim form of the church tower, far away. He heard the clock strike ten. He waited and watched. The clock struck eleven. He was beginning to feel tired. Perhaps the soldiers had given up their plan.
>
> He walked up and down the river bank, leading his horse behind him; but he kept his eyes turned always toward the dim, dark spot which he knew

was the old North Church. All at once a light flashed out from the tower. "Ah! there it is!" he cried. The soldiers had started.

He spoke to his horse. He put his foot in the stirrup. He was ready to mount.

Then another light flashed clear and bright by the side of the first one. The soldiers would cross the river.

Paul Revere sprang into the saddle. Like a bird let loose, his horse leaped forward. Away they went. Away they went through the village street and out upon the country road. "Up! up!" shouted Paul Revere. "The soldiers are coming! Up! up! and defend yourselves!"

The cry awoke the farmers; they sprang from their beds and looked out. They could not see the speeding horse, but they heard the clatter of its hoofs far down the road, and they understood the cry, "Up! up! And defend yourselves!"

"It is the alarm! The redcoats are coming," they said to each other. Then they took their guns, their axes, anything they could find, and hurried out.

So, through the night, Paul Revere rode toward Concord. At every farmhouse and every village he repeated his call. The alarm quickly spread. Guns were fired. Bells were rung. The people for miles around were roused as though a fire were raging.

The king's soldiers were surprised to find everybody awake along the road. They were angry because their plans had been discovered. When they reached Concord, they burned the courthouse there. At Lexington, not far from Concord, there was a sharp fight in which several men were killed. This, in history, is called the Battle of Lexington. It was the beginning of the war called the Revolutionary War.

But the king's soldiers did not find the gunpowder.

—From "The Midnight Ride"
from *Fifty Famous People*
by James Baldwin

Ask the following questions to test the student's listening ability. Remind the student to answer in complete sentences.

Instructor: Where did Paul Revere and his horse stand, waiting for news of the soldiers?
Student: They stood at the riverside.

Instructor: What was the first thing that he saw coming from the old North Church tower?
Student: He saw one light flash out.

Instructor: What happened next?
Student: A second light flashed out.

Instructor: What did this mean?
Student: It meant that the soldiers would cross the river.

Instructor: What did he shout as he rode through the streets?
Student: *He shouted, "Up, up! Defend yourselves! The soldiers are coming!"*

Instructor: When the farmers heard the cry, what did they do?
Student: *They got up and took guns, axes, or anything they could find.*

Instructor: While Paul Revere was calling out his message, what other two things did the people do to spread the alarm?
Student: *They fired guns and rang bells.*

Instructor: Were the soldiers able to find the gunpowder?
Student: *No, they were not.*

Instructor: What did they do when they reached Concord?
Student: *They burned the courthouse.*

Instructor: Where did they fight a battle?
Student: *They fought a battle at Lexington.*

Instructor: What was this the battle the beginning of?
Student: *The Battle of Lexington was the beginning of the Revolutionary War.*

You will now continue to teach the student to summarize the basic narrative thread in the passage. In order to do this, say to the student:

Instructor: What did Paul Revere see?
Student: *He saw two lights flash out in the tower.*

Instructor: What did he do then?
Student: *He rode through the villages warning people that the soldiers were coming.*

Instructor: What did the people do when they heard his warning?
Student: *They got up and found weapons.*

Instructor: Did they keep the soldiers from taking the gunpowder?
Student: *Yes, they did.*

Now ask the student, "Can you tell me in three or four sentences what happened in this story?" The student's answer should resemble one of the following:

"Paul Revere saw two lights in the old North Church tower. He rode through the villages, warning people that the soldiers were coming. The people armed themselves and kept the soldiers from taking their gunpowder."

"When Paul Revere saw the two lights in the tower, he rode through the country. He called out, 'The soldiers are coming!' People got up and found weapons. When the soldiers came, they found the people armed and ready to fight, so they could not get the gunpowder."

"Paul Revere rode through the countryside, warning people that the soldiers were coming. The people found weapons and prevented the soldiers from taking the gunpowder. The soldiers burned the courthouse at Concord and fought with the people at Lexington. This was the beginning of the Revolutionary War."

Write down the student's narration on Student Page 122, but do not allow her to see the sentences. Choose one or two of the sentences from the narration to use as a dictation exercise. Be sure to indicate any unusual punctuation with your voice; give any necessary spelling help. When the student has finished writing the dictation sentence on Student Page 123, show her your written original and allow her to compare the two.

DAY FIVE (optional): Creative Writing   *Student Pages 124–125*

Pull out Student Pages 124–125. Write the student's name and the date for her as she watches, or ask her to write the name and date independently.

Instructor: Paul Revere had to ride through villages to warn people that British soldiers were coming. If you were sent out to send an important message, what mode of transportation would you take? A car, a horse, a plane, a helicopter? How would that mode of transportation help you spread the word fast?

Write the student's answer down on the "Instructor" lines of Student Page 124 as she watches. Then have her copy the sentence onto the "Student" lines.

WEEK 19

DAY ONE: Narration Exercise   *Student Page 126*

Focus: *Identifying the central actions in a scene*

Pull out Student Page 126. Ask the student to write his name and the date.

Read the following passage out loud to the student. Tell the student that the following passage is from a book called *Five Children and It* by Edith Nesbit. Five children have been sent to live in the English countryside near the sea while their mother is away. They are looked after by a nanny named Martha, but for most of every day, they have to entertain themselves. One day, they are out digging in the sand near the sea when they discover a sand-fairy—a magical prehistoric creature called the Psammead who can grant wishes. Unfortunately, their wishes don't usually turn out as they expect.

In the day before this scene, the five children wished for boundless wealth—and the fairy gave them old-fashioned pieces of gold that no one would take for money. They have decided that they are going to talk the problem over at breakfast and decide what to wish for next, but they have to feed their baby brother breakfast while they're talking. Cyril is the oldest brother; "Panther" is the children's nickname for Anthea, the oldest sister; and the baby's nickname is "the Lamb."

> There was no chance of talking things over before breakfast, because everyone overslept itself, as it happened, and it needed a vigorous and determined struggle to get dressed so as to be only ten minutes late for breakfast. During this meal some efforts were made to deal with the question of the Psammead in an impartial spirit, but it is very difficult to discuss anything thoroughly and at the same time to attend faithfully to your baby brother's breakfast needs. The Baby was particularly lively that morning. He not only wriggled his body through the bar of his high chair, and hung by his head, choking and purple, but he seized a tablespoon with desperate suddenness, hit Cyril heavily on the head with it, and then cried because it was taken away from him. He put his fat fist in his bread-and-milk, and demanded "nam [jam]," which was only allowed for tea. He sang, he put his feet on the table—he clamoured to "go walky." The conversation was something like this—
>
> "Look here—about that Sand-fairy—Look out!—he'll have the milk over."
>
> Milk removed to a safe distance.
>
> "Yes—about that Fairy—No, Lamb dear, give Panther the narky poon."
>
> Then Cyril tried. "Nothing we've had yet has turned out—He nearly had the mustard that time!"

"I wonder whether we'd better wish—Hullo!—you've done it now, my boy!" And in a flash of glass and pink baby-paws, the bowl of golden carp in the middle of the table rolled on its side and poured a flood of mixed water and gold-fish into the Baby's lap and into the laps of the others.

Everyone was almost as much upset as the gold-fish; the Lamb only remaining calm. When the pool on the floor had been mopped up, and the leaping, gasping gold-fish had been collected and put back in the water, the Baby was taken away to be entirely re-dressed by Martha, and most of the others had to change completely.

—From *Five Children and It*
by Edith Nesbit

Ask the following questions to test the student's listening ability. If the student cannot remember, reread the section of the passage that answers the question.

Instructor: Why did the children have trouble talking to each other about the sand-fairy?
Student: *The Baby kept distracting them.*

Instructor: What happened when the Baby tried to wiggle out of his high chair?
Student: *He got caught by the head and turned purple.*

Instructor: What did he do with the tablespoon?
Student: *He hit Cyril with it.*

Instructor: What did he do when the tablespoon was taken away?
Student: *He cried.*

Instructor: What did he knock over?
Student: *He knocked over the fishbowl in the center of the table.*

Instructor: What did the other children have to do then?
Student: *They had to change their clothes completely.*

Instructor: Can you list two more annoying things the Baby did at breakfast?
Student: *He put his fist in his bread and milk; he sang; he put his feet on the table; he asked to go for a walk; he asked for jam.*

Now ask the student, "Can you describe three annoying things the Baby did at breakfast—two small things and one large thing?" The "large thing" should be the knocking over of the fishbowl. The other two actions can be any of the details highlighted in the comprehension questions. The narration can be three brief sentences, or two longer sentences.

The student's answer should resemble one of the following:

"The baby knocked over the fishbowl. He tried to wiggle out of his high chair and got his head caught. And he hit Cyril with a tablespoon and cried when it was taken away."

"The baby put his fists in the food, sang, and put his feet on the table. Finally, he knocked over the fishbowl and got water all over the table and himself."

"The baby tried to get out of his high chair and caught his head in it. He interrupted the conversation, asked for jam, and hit Cyril with a tablespoon. Then he knocked over the fishbowl and soaked himself with water."

Write down the student's narration on Student Page 126 as he watches.

DAY TWO: Copywork Exercise   *Student Page 127*

Focus: *Direct quotations*

Pull out Student Page 127. The following model sentences are already printed on it:

> "Good morning," it said. "I did that quite easily! Everyone wants him now."

Explain to the student that, after breakfast, the children were setting out to find the sand-fairy when Martha, the nanny, ordered them to take the Baby with them. They objected that they didn't want him, but Martha said, "Not want him indeed! Everybody wants him, the duck!"

So the children took him to the sandy place where the fairy lived, but he got sand in his eyes, threw sand at Anthea, and knocked over their drinks. The younger brother, Robert, was so upset that he shouted, "I only wish everybody did want him . . . . we might get some peace in our lives!" But the sand-fairy had appeared, without their realizing it, and was sitting behind them. It had granted their wish—now, everyone was going to want the baby.

Point out that quotation marks surround the exact words spoken by the sand-fairy; that there is a comma between the first part of the sand-fairy's speech and the words that tell you who said it (*it said*—this is called a *dialogue tag*); that there is a period after *it said*; that the second part of the sand-fairy's speech is an exclamation and ends with an exclamation point; and that the last period of the speech goes *inside* the closing quotation mark.

Now ask the student to copy the sentences. Watch him write, and correct him if he begins to make an error.

DAY THREE: Dictation Exercise   *Student Page 128*

Pull out Student Page 128. Ask the student to write his name and the date.
Dictate the following sentences to the student twice:

> "Good morning," it said. "I did that quite easily! Everyone wants him now."

Be certain to use a different voice for the sand-fairy's actual words. Before the student begins to write, remind him that quotation marks surround the actual words which the sand-fairy spoke. Ask him what punctuation mark separates "Good morning" from "it said": if he cannot remember, remind him that it is a comma! Remind him that there is an exclamation point in the second sentence (and be sure to speak this sentence with extra enthusiasm). Finally, remind him that the last period goes *inside* the closing quotation mark.

Watch the student as he writes, and correct him at once if he begins to make errors.

DAY FOUR: Narration Exercise and Dictation   *Student Pages 129–130*

Focus: *Identifying the central narrative thread in a story*

Pull out Student Pages 129–130. Ask the student to write his name and the date on Student Page 130.

Today's exercise will combine narration and dictation. Read the following passage out loud to the student. Tell the student that this passage comes right after the sand-fairy has granted Robert's wish. Now, everyone the children meet will want the baby. They decide they should go home immediately!

> At the gate into the road the party stopped to shift the Lamb from Cyril's back to Robert's. And as they paused a very smart open carriage came in sight, with a coachman and a groom on the box, and inside the carriage a lady—very grand indeed, with a dress all white lace and red ribbons and a parasol all red and white—and a white fluffy dog on her lap with a red ribbon round its neck. She looked at the children, and particularly at the Baby, and she smiled at him. The children were used to this, for the Lamb was, as all the servants said, a "very taking child." So they waved their hands politely to the lady and expected her to drive on. But she did not. Instead she made the coachman stop. And she beckoned to Cyril, and when he went up to the carriage she said, "What a dear darling duck of a baby! Oh, I *should* so like to adopt it! Do you think its mother would mind?"
>
> "She'd mind very much indeed," said Anthea shortly.
>
> "Oh, but I should bring it up in luxury, you know. I am Lady Chittenden. You must have seen my photograph in the illustrated papers. They call me a Beauty, you know, but of course that's all nonsense. Anyway"—
>
> She opened the carriage door and jumped out. She had the wonderfullest red high-heeled shoes with silver buckles. "Let me hold him a minute," she said. And she took the Lamb and held him very awkwardly, as if she was not used to babies.
>
> Then suddenly she jumped into the carriage with the Lamb in her arms and slammed the door, and said, "Drive on!"
>
> The Lamb roared, the little white dog barked, and the coachman hesitated.

> "Drive on, I tell you!" cried the lady; and the coachman did, for, as he said afterwards, it was as much as his place was worth not to.
>
> The four children looked at each other, and then with one accord they rushed after the carriage and held on behind. Down the dusty road went the smart carriage, and after it, at double-quick time, ran the twinkling legs of the Lamb's brothers and sisters.

—From *Five Children and It*
by Edith Nesbit

Ask the following questions to test the student's listening ability. Remind the student to answer in complete sentences.

Instructor: What were the children doing while they were standing at the gate?
Student: They were moving the Baby from one back to another—he was riding piggyback.

Instructor: Why did the children expect the lady dressed in white to "move on" after she smiled at the Baby?
Student: They were used to people smiling at the Baby.

Instructor: What did the lady ask the children?
Student: She asked whether she could adopt the Baby.

Instructor: What did the lady do then?
Student: She got out of her carriage to hold the Baby.

Instructor: Did she seem comfortable with babies?
Student: No, she held him awkwardly.

Instructor: Why do you think she wanted the Baby?
Student: The sand-fairy's magic made her want the baby. (Prompt the student for this answer if necessary.)

Instructor: What did the lady do as soon as she had the Baby in her arms?
Student: She jumped in her carriage and told her coachman to drive away.

Instructor: What did the children do?
Student: They ran after her.

You will now continue to teach the student to summarize the basic narrative thread in the passage. In order to do this, say to the student:

Instructor: What were the children doing when the lady drove by?
Student: They were standing at the gate, giving the Baby a piggyback.

Instructor: What did the lady do when she got out of the carriage?
Student: She took the Baby and drove away. (If the student only answers with "She took the Baby," ask, "What then?")

Instructor: What did the children do?
Student: They ran after her.

Now ask the student, "Can you tell me in two sentences what happened in this story? Make sure to tell me why the lady wanted the Baby." The student's answer should resemble one of the following:

> "The fairy's magic made everyone want the Baby. A lady in a carriage grabbed him and took him away, but the children ran after her."

> "After the sand-fairy granted a wish, everyone wanted the Baby. The children were standing at a gate when a lady in a carriage stopped and smiled at the Baby. She held him, and then she jumped in her carriage and drove away."

> "A lady in a carriage stole the Baby because she wanted him. She was actually awkward with babies, but the sand-fairy's magic was affecting her."

Write down the student's narration on Student Page 129, but do not allow him to see the sentences. Choose one or two of the sentences from the narration to use as a dictation exercise (Student Page 130). Be sure to indicate any unusual punctuation with your voice; give any necessary spelling help.

DAY FIVE (optional): Creative Writing   *Student Pages 131–132*

Pull out Student Pages 131–132. Write the student's name and the date for him as he watches, or ask him to write the name and date independently.

> **Instructor:** If you met a sand-fairy who could grant you one wish, what would you ask for?

Remind the student to answer you in a complete sentence. If he answers in a fragment, turn the fragment into a complete sentence, say it to him, and then ask him to repeat this sentence back to you. Write the student's answer down on the "Instructor" lines of Student Page 131 as he watches. Then have him copy the sentence onto the "Student" lines.

WEEK 20

DAY ONE: Narration Exercise   *Student Page 133*

Focus: *Identifying the narrative thread in a story*

Pull out Student Page 133. Ask the student to write her name and the date.

Read the following passage out loud to the student. This is a retelling of a very old story about Alexander the Great, who lived 356–323 BC—about 2300 years ago.

> One of the most famous of the Greeks was a Macedonian named Alexander the Great, who made himself master of a large part of the world. He had a splendid horse, which he always rode when he went to battle. He won this horse when he was a boy, by his wisdom and boldness.
>
> This is how he won it. The horse was sent as a present to King Philip, father of the young prince Alexander. The king went to a wide plain to try it, and his son and all his great men went with him.
>
> But it was soon found that the horse was very wild. It kicked and reared so that no man could mount its back. The king was angry that so wild an animal should be sent to him and gave orders for it to be taken back at once.
>
> The prince was vexed to hear this. "It is a pity to lose such a fine horse, because no man is brave enough to mount it," he said.
>
> The king thought his son spoke without thinking.
>
> "Your words are bold," said he, "but are you bold enough to mount the horse yourself?"
>
> The young prince went up to the restless animal. He took the bridle and turned its head toward the sun. He did so, because he had seen that the horse was afraid of its black shadow, which kept moving upon the ground before its eyes.
>
> With its face to the sun, the horse could no longer see the shadow which now fell on the ground behind it. It soon became quiet. Then the prince stroked it and patted it gently, and by and by, he sprang quickly upon its back.
>
> The horse at once set off at a gallop over the plain, with the boy bravely holding on. The king and his men were in great fear, for they thought the prince would be thrown to the ground and killed. But they need not have been afraid.
>
> Soon the horse grew tired of its gallop and began to trot. Then Alexander turned and gently rode it back. The men shouted, and the king took his son in his arms and shed tears of joy.
>
> The horse was given to the young prince. It loved its master and would kneel down for him to mount, but it would let no other person get upon its back.
>
> —From "Alexander the Great and His Horse"
> from *Tales from Far and Near*
> by Arthur Guy Terry

Ask the following questions to test the student's listening ability. Remind the student to answer in complete sentences.

Instructor: What nation did Alexander the Great come from?
Student: He came from Greece (or Macedonia).

Instructor: What was Alexander's father named?
Student: His name was King Philip.

Instructor: What was wrong with the horse that King Philip had been sent?
Student: It was so wild that no one could ride it.

Instructor: When Alexander said that it would be a pity to send the horse back, what did King Philip say to him?
Student: He said, "Are you bold enough to mount the horse yourself?"

Instructor: What direction did Alexander turn the horse's head?
Student: He turned it towards the sun.

Instructor: Why did he do this?
Student: He saw that the horse was afraid of its shadow.

Instructor: If the horse was facing the sun, where do you think the shadow was?
Student: It was behind the horse (where he could not see it).

Instructor: Did Alexander's solution work?
Student: Yes, he was able to ride the horse.

Instructor: What did the horse do so that Alexander could mount?
Student: He would kneel down.

You will now ask the student to summarize the basic narrative thread in the passage.

For the next few weeks, you will begin to train the student to summarize without depending on your leading questions. In order to do this, ask the student, "Can you tell me in two or three sentences what happened in this story?" The student's answer should resemble one of the following:

"Alexander's father was given a horse, but the horse was too wild to ride. Alexander saw that the horse was afraid of its shadow. When he turned the horse towards the sun, he was able to get on and ride it."

"Alexander saw that the horse was afraid of its shadow. When he turned the horse's head to the sun, the horse could no longer see the shadow. Alexander was able to ride it, although no one else could."

"Alexander's horse was wild because it was afraid of its shadow. Alexander tamed it by turning its head towards the sun."

If the student is unable to produce a narrative summary, *then* ask her the following questions:

Instructor: What was the problem with the horse?
Student: *It was afraid of its shadow OR It was too wild to ride.*

Note: If the student gives the second answer, then ask, "Why was the horse acting so wildly?" The answer should then be, *It was afraid of its shadow.*

Instructor: How did Alexander solve the problem?
Student: *He turned the horse so that it couldn't see its shadow.*

Instructor: What did he do then?
Student: *He was able to ride the horse.*

Then ask the student to narrate again. Write down the student's narration on Student Page 133 as she watches.

DAY TWO: Copywork Exercise   *Student Page 134*

Focus: *Direct quotations*

Pull out Student Page 134. The following model sentence is already printed on it:

> "Your words are bold," the king said to Alexander, "but are you bold
> enough to mount the horse yourself?"

As the student examines the sentences remind her of the rules about direct quotations. The exact words a person says are surrounded by quotation marks, so the king's words have quotation marks around them. "The king said to Alexander" is not part of the direct quotation, though. So we put a comma and quotation marks after "bold" to show that "the king said to Alexander" is *interrupting* a direct quotation. Because the sentence that the king says then continues after "Alexander," we put another comma after Alexander, and then add another quotation mark to show that the king's direct words are starting again.

The quotation ends with a question mark, and that question mark comes *inside* the final quotation marks.

Watch the student copy the sentence, and correct her if she begins to make a mistake.

DAY THREE: Dictation Exercise   *Student Page 135*

Pull out Student Page 135. Ask the student to write her name and the date.

Dictate the following sentence to the student twice:

"Your words are bold," the king said to Alexander, "but are you bold
enough to mount the horse yourself?"

Be certain to use a different voice for the king's actual words. Before the student begins
to write, remind her that quotation marks surround the actual words which the king spoke.
Ask her what punctuation mark comes after "bold," and what punctuation mark comes after
"Alexander." When you read, indicate both commas by pausing for a count of three. Also be
sure to indicate the question mark at the end of the sentence with your voice.

Watch the student as she writes, and correct her at once if she begins to make errors.

DAY FOUR: Narration Exercise and Dictation   *Student Pages 136–137*

Focus: Identifying the central narrative thread in a story

Pull out Student Pages 136–137. Ask the student to write her name and the date on Student
Page 137.

Today's exercise will combine narration and dictation. Read the following passage out loud
to the student. Tell the student that this is another story about Alexander the Great.

> Alexander had many opportunities to ride his warhorse into battle. His
> father Philip had conquered Greece, but Alexander had even larger goals in
> mind. He wanted to rule Persia. The Persians had given up trying to conquer
> Greece, but their empire was still the largest in the world. It stretched all the
> way from Asia Minor to India. And Alexander wanted it.
>
> When Alexander met the Persian army in Asia Minor, he used his
> cavalry—soldiers riding on horseback—to push the Persians back. Asia
> Minor was now his. But could he conquer the rest of the Persian Empire?
>
> According to one story, Alexander stopped at a city in Asia Minor
> and saw there, in the city's center, a chariot tied to its axle with a huge,
> complicated knot of rope, larger than a man's head. "What is this?" he asked.
>
> "That is the Gordian Knot," the people told him. "We have a legend
> about it. The man who loosens that knot will rule all the rest of Asia. But it
> is impossible to untie the knot. Hundreds of men have tried, and no one has
> ever succeeded!"
>
> Alexander studied the knot carefully. Then he took out his sword and
> sliced the knot in half.
>
> "There," he said. "I have loosened the knot."
>
> No one had ever thought of doing that before. But the prophecy of the
> knot came true. Alexander conquered all the rest of Asia. He went south into
> Egypt and was crowned the pharaoh of Egypt. And then he came back up
> into Mesopotamia and took over the rest of the Persian Empire.

> Now Alexander was king of more land than anyone else had ever ruled. He was truly "Alexander the Great"—the ruler of the largest empire the world had ever seen.

—From *The Story of the World, Volume One*
by Susan Wise Bauer

Ask the following questions to test the student's listening ability. Remind the student to answer in complete sentences.

Instructor: What large empire did Alexander want to conquer?
Student: He wanted to conquer Persia.

Instructor: What is "cavalry"?
Student: Cavalry is soldiers riding on horseback.

Instructor: What was strange about the chariot and the axle that Alexander saw?
Student: The chariot was tied to the axle with a huge, complicated knot.

Instructor: What was the knot called?
Student: It was called the Gordian Knot.

Instructor: According to the prophecy, what would happen to the man who untied the knot?
Student: He would rule all of Asia.

Instructor: Had anyone ever untied the knot?
Student: No, no man had ever been able to untie it.

Instructor: How did Alexander loosen the knot?
Student: He cut the knot with his sword.

Instructor: Did the prophecy come true for Alexander?
Student: Yes, he became ruler of all Asia.

Instructor: Alexander also conquered Persia. What other country that he conquered is mentioned in the story?
Student: He conquered Egypt.

You will now ask the student to summarize the basic narrative thread in the passage.

For the next few weeks, you will begin to train the student to summarize without depending on your leading questions. In order to do this, ask the student, "Can you tell me in two or three sentences what happened in this story?" The student's answer should resemble one of the following:

"Alexander the Great found the Gordian Knot. Instead of untying it, he cut it with his sword."

"The Gordian Knot tied a chariot to its axle. A prophecy said that the man who untied it would rule all of Asia. Instead of untying it, Alexander cut it with his sword."

"Alexander the Great saw a chariot and axle tied together with a huge knot. A man told him that the one who untied it would be ruler of all Asia. Alexander cut it with his sword, and the prophecy came true."

If the student is unable to produce a narrative summary, *then* ask her the following questions:

Instructor: What problem did Alexander have to solve?
Student: *He had to figure out how to untie the knot.*

Instructor: What solution did he decide on?
Student: *He cut the knot with his sword.*

Instructor: What happened afterwards?
Student: *He conquered Asia, Persia, and Egypt.*

Then ask the student to narrate again.

Write down the student's narration on Student Page 136, but do not allow her to see the sentences. Choose one or two of the sentences from the narration to use as a dictation exercise (Student Page 137). Be sure to indicate any unusual punctuation with your voice; give any necessary spelling help.

DAY FIVE (optional): Creative Writing   *Student Pages 138–139*

Pull out Student Pages 138–139. Write the student's name and the date for her as she watches, or ask her to write the name and date independently.

Instructor: Alexander the Great conquered lots of territory and named cities after himself. If you got to name a city, what would you call it? Add your city's name to the top of your Student Page. If you like, draw a picture or describe your city to me with words.

If you're enjoying this assignment, here's an extra credit suggestion: What would be one law or rule that everyone in your city would have to follow?

Remind the student to answer you in complete sentences. If she answers in fragments, turn the fragment into a complete sentence, say it to her, and then ask her to repeat this sentence back to you. Write the student's answer down on the "Instructor" lines of Student Page 139 as she watches. Then have her copy the sentence onto the "Student" lines.

WEEK 21

DAY ONE: Narration Exercise   *Student Page 140*

Focus: *Identifying the central narrative thread in a passage*

Pull out Student Page 140. Ask the student to write his name and the date.

Read the following passage out loud to the student. This is another story from *Nurse Matilda*, the book about the naughty children and the nanny who comes to straighten them out. We read two passages from this book a few weeks ago.

In this story, the children are having their breakfast. Nurse Matilda has told them to say "please," but instead of saying please, they grab and stuff themselves with more and more food. Here is what happens next.

So they went on gobbling: snatching bread and butter from under one another's noses, scooping out the last of the jam without caring who else wanted it, holding out their mugs for more, without a "Please" or "thank you" . . .

Nurse Matilda sat at the top of the table, her big black stick in her hand.

Down went the porridge, down went the eggs, down went the bread and butter and jam.

And more bread and butter and jam.

And *more* bread and butter and jam and *more* bread and butter and jam and MORE and MORE and MORE bread and butter and jam . . .

"Here," said the children with their mouths full, "that's enough!" only their mouths were so full that what they said sounded like "Assawuff," and Nurse Matilda only looked politely puzzled and said, "Did you ask for more porridge?" and to every child's utter horror, there before it was a plate of porridge all over again, spinning dizzily with its golden signature in its sea of milk. And their hands seized up their spoons and down went the porridge, stuff, stuff, stodge, stodge, on top of all that bread and butter. And suddenly all those upside-down eggshells really *were* full, new eggs; and up and down flashed their egg-spoons chocking down egg on top of porridge; and on top of the egg came more and more of that dreadful bread and butter and jam . . . And then the porridge started all over again . . .

The children puffed and blew, their cheeks bulged, their eyes goggled. They felt that at any moment they would blow up and burst. They longed to cry out for mercy. They would even have said "Please" if they had thought of it. They would have done anything if only they could have stopped eating.

—From *Nurse Matilda*
by Christianna Brand

Ask the following questions to test the student's listening ability. Remind the student to answer in complete sentences.

Instructor: Tell me four foods that the children were eating at breakfast.
Student: They were eating bread and butter, jam, eggs, and porridge.

Instructor: What happened to the empty plates of porridge?
Student: They were suddenly filled up again.

Instructor: Did the children eat the new plates of porridge?
Student: Yes, they did.

Instructor: Did they want to?
Student: No, they didn't!

Instructor: What happened to all the empty eggshells?
Student: They were filled with eggs.

Instructor: What did the children want to do, more than anything else?
Student: They wanted to stop eating.

Instructor: Tell me in your own words—how did Nurse Matilda punish the children for grabbing food and not saying please?
Student: She made them eat and eat and eat without stopping.

You will now ask the student to summarize the basic narrative thread in the passage.

You will continue to train the student to summarize without depending on your leading questions. In order to do this, ask the student, "Can you tell me in three sentences what happened in this story?" The student's answer should resemble one of the following:

"The children would not say please. They grabbed their food and stuffed it down. So Nurse Matilda made them eat and eat and eat without stopping."

"The children were grabbing for more and more and more food. While they ate, more and more food appeared on the table. They could not stop eating it."

"The children were greedy and wouldn't say please. So Nurse Matilda made more and more porridge and eggs and bread and butter appear on the table. They couldn't stop eating it, even though they were full."

If the student is unable to produce a narrative summary, *then* ask him the following questions:

Instructor: What were the children doing wrong?
Student: They were grabbing food and not saying please.

Instructor: What did Nurse Matilda make them do?
Student: She made them eat and eat without stopping.

Then ask the student to narrate again. Write down the student's narration on Student Page 140 as he watches.

DAY TWO: Copywork Exercise   *Student Page 141*

Focus: *Direct quotations*

Pull out Student Page 141. The following model sentence is already printed on it:

> Nurse Matilda only looked politely puzzled and said, "Did you ask for more porridge?"

As the student examines the sentence, remind him of the rules about direct quotations. The exact words a person says are surrounded by quotation marks, so Nurse Matilda's actual words—"Did you ask for more porridge?"—have quotation marks on either side of them.

Point out that there is a comma after "said." Commas usually come before direct quotations. The quotation is a question, so it ends with a question mark. The question mark goes inside the closing quotation mark.

Watch the student copy the sentence, and correct him if he begins to make a mistake.

DAY THREE: Dictation Exercise   *Student Page 142*

Pull out Student Page 142. Ask the student to write his name and the date.

Dictate the following sentence to the student twice:

> Nurse Matilda only looked politely puzzled and said, "Did you ask for more porridge?"

Be sure to use a different voice for Nurse Matilda's actual words. Before the student begins to write, remind him that quotation marks surround the actual words that Nurse Matilda says. Remind him that the quotation is separated from the rest of the sentence by a comma. Ask him what punctuation mark ends the sentence, and whether it goes inside or outside the closing quotation mark. (Inside.)

Watch the student as he writes, and correct him at once if he begins to make errors.

DAY FOUR: Narration Exercise and Dictation   *Student Pages 143–144*

Focus: *Identifying the central narrative thread in a story*

Pull out Student Pages 143–144. Ask the student to write his name and the date on Student Page 144.

Today's exercise will combine narration and dictation. Read the following passage out loud to the student. Tell the student that this story happens in England during the Middle Ages.

The great desire of good King John was that every man, woman and child in his dominions should be able to obtain justice without delay. He hung a bell in one of the city towers, and issued a proclamation to say that when this was rung a judge would immediately proceed to the public square and administer justice in his name.

In the course of time, however, the bell-rope wore thin, and some ingenious citizen fastened a wisp of hay to it, that this might serve as a handle. One day in the height of summer, when most of the citizens were taking their noonday rest, their naps were disturbed by the violent pealing of the bell.

"Surely some great injustice has been done," they cried, hastening to the square. To their amazement they found a poor old horse, lame and half blind, with bones that nearly broke through his skin. He was trying with pathetic eagerness to eat the wisp of hay. In struggling to do this, he had rung the bell.

The judge who had run to the square to hear the case shouted, "To whom does this wretched horse belong?"

"Sir, he belongs to a rich nobleman," said an old man. "Time was that he bore his master to battle, more than once saving his life by his courage and fleetness. When the horse became old and feeble, he was turned adrift, since his master had no further use for him; and now the poor creature picks up what food he can in highways and byways."

On hearing this the judge's face grew dark with anger. "Bring his master before me," he thundered, and when the amazed nobleman appeared, he questioned him sternly.

"Is it true," he demanded, "that you left this, your faithful servant, to starve, since he could no longer serve you? For the rest of his life you shall care for the poor beast as he deserves."

This decision was greeted with loud applause by the town folk. "Our bell gains justice not only for men," they said to each other, "but for animals too in their time of need."

> —From "The Horse That Aroused the Town"
> from *Junior Classics: Animal and Nature Stories*
> by Lillian M. Gask,
> abridged by Susan Wise Bauer

Ask the following questions to test the student's listening ability. Remind the student to answer in complete sentences.

Instructor: What happened when a man, woman, or child rang the bell?
Student: *A judge would go to the square to hear their complaint.*

Instructor: Why did someone fasten hay to the bell rope?
Student: *The rope was growing thin.*

Instructor: How did the horse ring the bell by accident?
Student: *He was eating the hay.*

Instructor: What did the horse look like?
Student: He was lame, half blind, and thin.

Instructor: To whom did the horse belong?
Student: He belonged to a rich nobleman.

Instructor: Why did the nobleman turn the horse loose?
Student: The horse grew old and feeble and was of no use.

Instructor: Was this a just or an unjust action?
Student: This was very unjust.

Instructor: What did the judge order the nobleman to do?
Student: He ordered the nobleman to feed and care for the horse for the rest of his life.

You will now ask the student to summarize the basic narrative thread in the passage.

You will continue to train the student to summarize without depending on your leading questions. In order to do this, ask the student, "Can you tell me in four sentences what happened in this story?" The student's answer should resemble one of the following:

"A king hung a bell that anyone could ring if they needed justice. The bell rope had a piece of hay tied to it. An old, starving horse pulled the bell rope by accident, and a judge came to find out what was wrong. He ordered the horse's owner to feed and take care of it."

"A cruel nobleman set his horse loose because it was not useful to him any more. The horse wandered around, trying to find food. When he saw the hay on the bell rope, he ate it and made the bell ring. A judge came to the square and forced the nobleman to take care of his horse."

"A king wanted his people to have justice, so he hung up a bell. When someone wanted justice, he would ring the bell, and a judge would come hear his story. One day a horse whose master had thrown him out pulled on the bell and rang it. The judge ordered the horse's master to take the horse back and care for it."

If the student is unable to produce a narrative summary, *then* ask him the following questions:

Instructor: How did the king arrange for his subjects to get justice?
Student: If they rang the bell, a judge would come and hear their problems.

Instructor: What problem did the horse have?
Student: His master threw him out, and he was old and starving.

Instructor: What happened when the horse rang the bell?
Student: The judge ordered the nobleman to take care of his horse for the rest of his life.

Then ask the student to narrate again.

Write down the student's narration on Student Page 143, but do not allow him to see the sentences. Choose one or two of the sentences from the narration to use as a dictation exercise (Student Page 144). Be sure to indicate any unusual punctuation with your voice; give any necessary spelling help.

DAY FIVE (optional): Creative Writing   *Student Pages 145–146*

Pull out Student Pages 145–146. Write the student's name and the date for him as he watches, or ask him to write the name and date independently.

Instructor: If you could make a grocery list and your parents had to buy everything on it, what are three things that you would put on the list?

Remind the student to answer you in a complete sentence or sentences. If he answers in fragments, turn the fragments into complete sentences, say them to him, and then ask him to repeat the sentences back to you. Write the student's answer down on the "Instructor" lines of Student Page 145 as he watches. Then have him copy the sentences onto the "Student" lines.

WEEK 22

Day One: Narration Exercise

Focus: *Identifying the central narrative thread in a passage*

Pull out Student Page 147. Ask the student to write her name and the date.

Read the following passage out loud to the student. This is the beginning of a traditional tale from India.

> There was once a little nervous hare who was always afraid that something dreadful was going to happen to her. She was always saying: "Suppose the earth were to fall in, what would happen to me?" And she said this so often that at last she thought it really was about to happen. One day, when she had been saying over and over again, "Suppose the earth were to fall in, what would happen to me?" she heard a slight noise: it really was only a heavy fruit which had fallen upon a rustling leaf, but the little hare was so nervous she was ready to believe anything, and she said in a frightened tone: "The earth *is* falling in." She ran away as fast as she could go, and presently she met an old brother hare, who said: "Where are you running to, Mistress Hare?"
>
> And the little hare said: "I have no time to stop and tell you anything. The earth is falling in, and I am running away."
>
> "The earth is falling in, is it?" said the old brother hare, in a tone of much astonishment; and he repeated this to *his* brother hare, and *he* to *his* brother hare, and *he* to *his* brother hare, until at last there were a hundred thousand brother hares, all shouting: "The earth is falling in." Now presently the bigger animals began to take the cry up. First the deer, and then the sheep, and then the wild boar, and then the buffalo, and then the camel, and then the tiger, and then the elephant.
>
> —From "The Hare That Ran Away"
> from *Eastern Stories and Legends*
> by Marie L. Shedlock

Ask the following questions to test the student's listening ability. Remind the student to answer in complete sentences.

Instructor: What was the hare afraid of?
Student: *She was afraid that the earth would fall in OR She was afraid that something dreadful would happen.*

Instructor: What did the hare hear, while she was worrying about the earth falling in?
Student: *She heard a fruit fall on a rustling leaf.*

Instructor: What did she think was happening?
Student: *She thought the earth was falling in.*

Instructor: Whom did she tell about this?
Student: She told old brother hare.

Instructor: Who else learned about this?
Student: All of the hares, and then the bigger animals too.

Instructor: Can you remember three kinds of animals, besides hares, that began to say that the earth was falling in?
Student: Deer, sheep, wild boar, buffalo, camels, tigers, and the elephant all began to say that the earth was falling in.

You will now ask the student to summarize the basic narrative thread in the passage.

You will continue to train the student to summarize without depending on your leading questions. In order to do this, ask the student, "Can you tell me in two or three sentences what happened in this story?" The student's answer should resemble one of the following:

> "The hare was afraid that the earth was falling in. When she heard a rustle, she told the older brother hare that the earth was falling in. He told the other hares and the story spread to all the animals."

> "The hare heard a fruit fall on the ground, and she thought the earth was falling in. She told brother hare, and he told the other hares. Then the bigger animals, like deer, sheep, camels, and tigers, began to say that the earth was falling in."

> "When the hare heard a fruit fall, she was sure that the earth was falling in. She told her brother hare, who told the other hares, and soon the story spread to all the other animals."

If the student is unable to produce a narrative summary, *then* ask her the following questions:

Instructor: What was the hare afraid of?
Student: She was afraid of the earth falling in.

Instructor: Why did she think that the earth was falling in?
Student: She heard a fruit fall and rustle a leaf.

Instructor: Who else started to say that the earth was falling in?
Student: The other hares and all the bigger animals began to say that the earth was falling in.

Then ask the student to narrate again. Write down the student's narration on Student Page 147 as she watches.

DAY TWO: Copywork Exercise   *Student Page 148*

Focus: Indirect and direct quotations

Pull out Student Page 148. Ask the student to write her name and the date. The following model sentences are already printed on it:

> The little hare told the other brother hare that the earth was falling in.
>
> The little hare told the other brother hare, "The earth is falling in!"

Ask the student to tell you what is different about the two sentences. The first sentence contains an indirect quotation—it tells you what the little hare said, but it does not use her exact words. The second sentence contains a direct quotation—the exact words that the little hare spoke.

Notice that indirect quotations do not use quotation marks. Quotation marks are only used for direct quotations.

Also point out that the direct quote ends with an exclamation point because the little hare is feeling strong emotion! The exclamation point goes inside the closing quotation mark.

Watch the student as she writes, and correct her at once if she begins to make a mistake.

DAY THREE: Dictation Exercise   *Student Page 149*

Pull out Student Page 149. Ask the student to write her name and the date.

Dictate the following sentences to the student twice:

> The little hare told the other brother hare that the earth was falling in.
>
> The little hare told the other brother hare, "The earth is falling in!"

Remind the student that one of these sentences contains an indirect quote, while one contains a direct quote. Only the sentence with the direct quote uses quotation marks. When you read the sentences, be sure to indicate with your voice the exact words that the little hare speaks.

Remind the student that a comma comes before the direct quote, and that the closing exclamation mark goes inside the closing quotation marks.

Watch the student as she writes, and correct her at once if she begins to make an error.

DAY FOUR: Narration Exercise and Dictation   *Student Pages 150–151*

Focus: *Identifying the central narrative thread in a story*

Pull out Student Pages 150–151. Ask the student to write her name and the date on Student Page 151.

Today's exercise will combine narration and dictation. Read the following passage out loud to the student. Tell the student that this is the second half of the story about the little hare who was afraid the earth would fall in.

Now the wise lion heard all this noise and wondered at it. "There are no signs," he said, "of the earth falling in. They must have heard something." And then he stopped them all short and said: "What is this you are saying?"

And the elephant said: "I remarked that the earth was falling in."

"How do you know this?" asked the lion.

"Why, now I come to think of it, it was the tiger that remarked it to me."

And the tiger said, "*I* had it from the camel," and the camel said, "*I* had it from the buffalo." And the buffalo from the wild boar, and the wild boar from the sheep, and the sheep from the deer, and the deer from the hares, and the hares said: "Oh! *We* heard it from *that* little hare."

And the lion said: "Little hare, *what* made you say that the earth was falling in?"

And the little hare said: "I *saw* it."

"You saw it?" said the lion. "Where?"

"Yonder, by the tree."

"Well," said the lion, "come with me and I will show you how—"

"No, no," said the hare, "I would not go near that tree for anything, I'm *so* nervous."

"But," said the lion, "I am going to take you on my back." And he took her on his back, and begged the animals to stay where they were until they returned. Then he showed the little hare how the fruit had fallen upon the leaf, making the noise that had frightened her, and she said: "Yes, I see—the earth is *not* falling in." And the lion said: "Shall we go back and tell the other animals?" And they went back. The little hare stood before the animals and said: "The earth is *not* falling in." And all the animals began to repeat this to one another, and they dispersed gradually, and you heard the words more and more softly.

"The earth is *not* falling in," over and over again, until the sound died away altogether.

—From "The Hare That Ran Away"
from *Eastern Stories and Legends*
by Marie L. Shedlock

Ask the following questions to test the student's listening ability. Remind the student to answer in complete sentences.

Instructor: Which wise animal decided to find out whether the story was true?
Student: The lion wanted to find out whether the story was true.

Instructor: Which animal told the elephant that the earth was falling in?
Student: The tiger told him.

Instructor: Who told the tiger?
Student: The camel told the tiger.

Instructor: Who told the camel?
Student: The buffalo told the camel.

Instructor: The lion finally traced the story back to the source. What animal was the source of the story?
Student: The little hare was the source of the story.

Instructor: How did the lion convince the little hare that the earth was not falling in?
Student: He took the hare to see where the fruit had fallen to the ground.

Instructor: What did the little hare tell all the other animals?
Student: The little hare told all the animals that the earth was not falling in.

You will now ask the student to summarize the basic narrative thread in the passage.

You will continue to train the student to summarize without depending on your leading questions. In order to do this, ask the student, "Can you tell me in three sentences what happened in this story?" The student's answer should resemble one of the following:

"The lion started to wonder whether the earth was really falling in. He asked the other animals where the rumor came from, and found that the little hare had started it. So he took the hare back to see where the fruit had fallen on the ground."

"The lion knew that the earth wasn't falling in. He found out that the story had come from the little hare, so he showed the hare where the fruit had fallen on the ground. Then the hare told all the other animals that the earth wasn't falling in."

"The lion found out that the little hare had started the story about the earth falling in. He showed the little hare that the noise was just a fruit falling on a leaf. The little hare told the other animals that she was wrong, and the animals all repeated the news to each other."

If the student is unable to produce a narrative summary, *then* ask her the following questions:

Instructor: What did the lion find out?
Student: He found out that the earth was not falling in.

Instructor: How did he convince the little hare that the earth was not falling in?
Student: He took the little hare to see where the fruit fell on a leaf.

Instructor: How did all of the other animals find out that the earth was *not* falling in?
Student: *The little hare told them, and they told each other.*

Then ask the student to narrate again.

Write down the student's narration on Student Page 150, but do not allow her to see the sentences. Choose one or two of the sentences from the narration to use as a dictation exercise (Student Page 151). Be sure to indicate any unusual punctuation with your voice; give any necessary spelling help.

Day Five (optional): Creative Writing　　　　　　　*Student Pages 152–153*

Pull out Student Pages 152–153. Write the student's name and the date for her as she watches, or ask her to write the name and date independently.

Instructor: Finish the story below by adding 1–2 sentences:

"Once upon a time I woke up and my hands had turned into feet!"

Remind the student to answer you in a complete sentence or sentences. If she answers in fragments, turn the fragments into complete sentences, say them to her, and then ask her to repeat the sentences back to you. Write the student's answer down on the "Instructor" lines of Student Page 152 as she watches. Then have her copy the sentences onto the "Student" lines.

WEEK 23

DAY ONE: Narration Exercise

Focus: *Identifying contrasts in a description*

Pull out Student Page 154. Ask the student to write his name and the date.

Read the following passage out loud to the student. This story is from *Little Women* by Louisa May Alcott. The March family has four girls—the oldest is Meg; the second oldest is Jo; the third is Beth; and the youngest is Amy. Their father is away fighting in the Civil War. Hannah is their housekeeper.

At the beginning of the book, the girls are getting ready to celebrate Christmas. They have been waiting eagerly for their mother to get home from running her errands so that they can eat their Christmas breakfast together. But when their mother comes home, she tells them what she has just seen:

"Not far away from here lies a poor woman with a little newborn baby. Six children are huddled into one bed to keep from freezing, for they have no fire. There is nothing to eat over there; and the oldest boy came to tell me they were suffering hunger and cold. My girls, will you give them your breakfast as a Christmas present?"

They were all unusually hungry, having waited nearly an hour, and for a minute no one spoke; only a minute, for Jo exclaimed impetuously:

"I'm so glad you came before we began!"

"May I go and help carry the things to the poor little children?" asked Beth eagerly.

"*I* shall take the cream and the muffins," added Amy, heroically giving up the articles she most liked.

Meg was already covering the buckwheats, and piling the bread into one big plate.

"I thought you'd do it," said Mrs. March, smiling as if satisfied. "You shall all go and help me, and when we come back we will have bread and milk for breakfast, and make it up at dinnertime."

They were soon ready, and the procession set out. Fortunately it was early, and they went through back streets, so few people saw them, and no one laughed at the queer party.

A poor, bare, miserable room it was, with broken windows, no fire, ragged bedclothes, a sick mother, wailing baby, and a group of pale, hungry children cuddled under one old quilt, trying to keep warm . . . . In a few minutes it really did seem as if kind spirits had been at work there. Hannah, who had carried wood, made a fire, and stopped up the broken panes with old hats and her own cloak. Mrs. March gave the mother tea and gruel, and comforted her with promises of help, while she dressed the little baby as tenderly as if it had been her own. The girls, meantime, spread the table, set the children round the fire, and fed them like so many hungry birds . . . . That was a very happy breakfast, though they didn't get any of it; and when they went away, leaving comfort behind, I think there were not in all the city four merrier people than the hungry little girls who gave away their breakfasts and contented themselves with bread and milk on Christmas morning.

—From *Little Women*
by Louisa May Alcott

Ask the following questions to test the student's listening ability. Remind the student to answer in complete sentences.

Instructor: The poor family has a mother and a newborn baby. How many other children are there?
Student: There are six other children.

Instructor: Do they have anything to eat?
Student: No, they do not.

Instructor: List three things that the March girls had on their breakfast table.
Student: They had cream, muffins, buckwheats (pancakes), and bread.

Instructor: Tell me two things you remember about the room where the poor family lived.
Student: It had broken windows, no fire, and ragged bedclothes (blankets).

Instructor: What two things did Hannah do to make the room better?
Student: She stuffed her cloak and old hats into the holes in the window, and she made a fire.

Instructor: What two things did Mrs. March do?
Student: She fed the mother and dressed the baby.

Instructor: What did the girls do?
Student: They fed the children breakfast around the fire.

Now say to the student, "In three or four sentences, can you tell me what the poor family's room was like before the Marches came, and what it was like after the Marches arrived?" The student's narration should resemble one of the following:

"The poor family had no fire. Six children were in one bed. The windows were broken. When the Marches came, they brought food, built a fire, and stopped up the holes in the windows."

"The mother and the baby were in one bed, and six children were in another. There was no fire and no food. When the March family came, they brought tea and muffins and bread. They also made a fire and stopped up the holes in the windows."

"The family's room was cold because there was no fire and the windows were broken. They also had no food. The March family brought food for everyone, made a fire, and stuffed cloaks and hats into the holes in the windows."

Write the student's narration down on Student Page 154 as he watches.

DAY TWO: Copywork Exercise   *Student Page 155*

Focus: *Direct and indirect quotations*

Pull out Student Page 155. Ask the student to write his name and the date. The following model sentences are already printed on it:

> "I shall take the cream and the muffins," added Amy, heroically giving up the articles she most liked.

> Amy said that she would bring the cream and the muffins, heroically giving up the articles she most liked.

Ask the student to read Amy's exact words in the first sentence out loud. Tell him to find those same words in the second sentence. Notice that in the second sentence, there are no quotation marks. That's because the second sentence doesn't use Amy's exact words.

Tell the student to choose one of the sentences to copy. (You will use the other sentence for dictation.) Watch the student copy the sentence, and correct him if he begins to make a mistake.

DAY THREE: Dictation Exercise   *Student Page 156*

Pull out Student Page 156. Ask the student to write his name and the date.

Choose whichever of the following sentences the student did *not* use for copywork. Dictate it to the student twice.

> "I shall take the cream and the muffins," added Amy, heroically giving up the articles she most liked.

> Amy said that she would bring the cream and the muffins, heroically giving up the articles she most liked.

If you choose the first sentence, be sure to use a different voice for Amy's exact words. In both sentences, pause for a count of three when you reach each comma.

Watch the student as he writes, and correct him at once if he begins to make errors.

DAY FOUR: Narration Exercise and Dictation   *Student Pages 157–158*

Focus: *Identifying the central narrative thread in a passage*

Pull out Student Pages 157–158. Ask the student to write his name and the date on Student Page 158.

Today's exercise will combine narration and dictation. Read the following passage out loud to the student. Tell the student that this story is from the biography (life story) of Louisa May Alcott, the author of *Little Women*. Louisa's family wasn't much like the March family. This story shows you one important difference between some of her relatives, and the family she invented in *Little Women*.

In this story, Louisa has gone to stay with older cousins for a visit.

There were no other children in the house; but none the less young Louisa had a glorious time for a few days, playing with the pet animals, inspecting the spice mill and being made much of by every one in the family. Small as she was, she did observe that the grown-up members of the household began to seem a little worn, while she herself became suddenly desperately bored and very homesick. She was finally left to her own devices with the inevitable result that she got into trouble.

In a very short time, she found some dirty children who seemed to her ideal playmates, after the stiff adult companions who had been trying so hard to amuse her. She played with her friends for a long time in the barn. Finding that they were poorly fed and hungry, she ran in haste to the pantry, by chance unguarded at that moment, and helped herself to figs for them and cakes. She made several journeys back and forth and then suddenly was discovered. Her exhausted hostess could endure no more, gave Louisa a tremendous scolding, and sent her up to the attic to think over her outrageous behavior. Poor little Louisa! She had not the faintest idea that in "feeding the poor" she was doing anything other than what was right. They always fed the poor at her house, no matter how little there was with which to feed anybody. She sat on a trunk, not crying, but thinking dark, hard thoughts, furious with anger, bewildered, ashamed, knowing that she was disgraced but not understanding why.

. . . There came in one of the young men of the family, Christopher, who had been so good to her ever since she came. He said a very little in brief explanation to make Louisa see that she had done wrong in taking things without permission, and then he held her on his knee while she leaned her face against his shoulder and broke into a storm of weeping. He did not make stupid attempts to comfort her, but let her cry her fill, until in sheer exhaustion she went to sleep. She awoke an hour afterward, frightened for an instant to find herself in the twilight of the big garret, then reassured to discover that she was still upon his knee, within the circle of his comforting arm. He took her downstairs. . . . That good, wise Christopher she remembered long with infinite gratitude.

—From *Invincible Louisa*
by Cornelia Meigs

Ask the following questions to test the student's listening ability. Remind the student to answer in complete sentences.

Instructor: What kinds of things did young Louisa play, during her visit?
Student: *She played with the pet animals and inspected the spice mills, and also found children to play with.*

Instructor: What did she get her new friends after they had played in the barn?
Student: *She got them figs and cakes from the pantry.*

Instructor: Why do you think her hostess (the cousin she was staying with) was upset by Louisa taking the food?
Student: *Louisa took it without permission.*

Instructor: Who comforted Lousia?
Student: *Christopher, one of the young men in the family, comforted her.*

You will now ask the student to summarize the basic narrative thread in the passage.

You will continue to train the student to summarize without depending on your leading questions. In order to do this, ask the student, "Can you tell me in two or three sentences what happened in this story?" The student's answer should resemble one of the following:

"Louisa was visiting cousins when she found some hungry children to play with. She went and got them food from the pantry, but her cousin was angry because Louisa took the food without permission."

"Louisa was visiting cousins, but she got bored. Finally she found children to play with. They were hungry, so she got them food—but she didn't ask permission."

"Louisa found playmates in the barn. They were hungry, so she got them food. Her cousin was very angry because she didn't ask permission, but in Louisa's family, they always fed the poor."

If the student is unable to produce a narrative summary, *then* ask the following questions:

Instructor: What did Louisa do that angered her cousin?
Student: *She took food without permission.*

Instructor: Why did she take the food?
Student: *She wanted to feed hungry children.*

Instructor: Why did she think that it was all right to take the food?
Student: *At home, her family fed the poor and hungry.*

Then ask the student to narrate again.

Write down the student's narration on Student Page 157, but do not allow him to see the sentences. Choose one or two of the sentences from the narration to use as a dictation exercise (Student Page 158). Be sure to indicate any unusual punctuation with your voice; give any necessary spelling help.

DAY FIVE (optional): Creative Writing   *Student Pages 159–160*

Pull out Student Pages 159–160. Write the student's name and the date for him as he watches, or ask him to write the name and date independently.

> **Instructor:** In the story *Little Women*, four sisters choose to give away their Christmas breakfast to poorer neighbors. Imagine that you give away something you really want to someone else. What do you give away? (It doesn't have to be real–you can make it up!) And who receives your gift? (They can be real or imaginary.)

Remind the student to answer you in a complete sentence or sentences. If he answers in fragments, turn the fragments into complete sentences, say them to him, and then ask him to repeat the sentences back to you. Write the student's answer down on the "Instructor" lines of Student Page 159 as he watches. Then have him copy the sentences onto the "Student" lines.

WEEK 24

DAY ONE: Narration Exercise   *Student Page 161*

Focus: *Identifying contrasts in a description*

Pull out Student Page 161. Ask the student to write her name and the date.

Read the following passage out loud to the student. This story is from *The Plant That Ate Dirty Socks* by Nancy McArthur. Michael and Norman are two brothers who share a room. They also have houseplants—and one of the plants has a very odd habit.

> Michael was the world's messiest kid. His brother Norman, three years younger, was a neatness nut.
>
> This would not have been such a big problem except that they shared the same room.
>
> Norman's side looked like a picture in a magazine.
>
> Michael's side looked like a junk heap.
>
> There were clothes crumpled on the floor, socks and comic books under the bed, model kits with pieces scattered all over, baseball cards, rocks, bird feathers, pine cones, and heaps of books and papers. And that was just the top layer.
>
> When Norman was supposed to make his bed, he just did it. When Michael was forced to make his bed, first he had to find it.
>
> Mom kept saying about forty-two times a week, "Pick that up. Put this away. Throw that out."
>
> Dad kept saying, "Where does all this stuff come from? Is it multiplying at night when we're asleep?"
>
> Norman kept complaining, "Your junk is oozing across the middle into my side of the room!"
>
> "I'm going to build a wall," he yelled, "to defend myself from all that messiness!"
>
> Michael yelled back, "I'll build a wall so I won't have to look at all that neatness!"
>
> "No walls," said Mom. "How about drawing a line?"
>
> They measured to find the exact middle. Then they made the line with tape right across the rug.
>
> Norman had fun kicking Michael's things back across the line if they were sticking over even just a tiny bit.
>
> When Michael had any clear space, he told Norman, "Your neatness is oozing over on my side! Ugh!"
>
> —From *The Plant That Ate Dirty Socks*
> by Nancy McArthur

Ask the following questions to test the student's listening ability. Remind the student to answer in complete sentences.

Instructor: What are the two brothers named?
Student: Their names are Michael and Norman.

Instructor: Which one is the messy brother?
Student: Michael is the messy brother.

Instructor: What did Norman's side of the room look like?
Student: It looked like a picture in a magazine.

Instructor: What did Michael's side of the room look like?
Student: It looked like a junk heap.

Instructor: Can you tell me three things that were scattered around on Michael's floor?
Student: There were clothes, socks, model kits, baseball cards, rocks, bird feathers, pine cones, books, and papers.

Instructor: What did Norman tell his brother about his junk?
Student: He told him that it was oozing over onto Norman's side of the room.

Instructor: How did the two boys divide the room?
Student: They made a line with tape across the rug.

Instructor: What did Norman do if Michael's stuff stuck over the tape?
Student: He kicked it back across the line.

Now say to the student, "In two or three sentences, can you tell me what Norman's side of the room was like, and then what Michael's side of the room was like? Begin by telling me how the sides were divided." The student's narration should resemble one of the following:

"Norman and Michael divided their room with tape on the floor. Norman's side of the room was neat and tidy. Michael's was covered with clothes, socks, bird feathers, pine cones, and other things."

"Norman and Michael used tape to divide their room. Norman's side of the room looked like a magazine picture, but Michael's looked like a junk heap."

"The two brothers put tape on their rug to divide the room in half. Norman's side of the room was neat, and his bed was made. Michael's side of the room was messy and covered with things like books, papers, and clothes."

Write the narration down on Student Page 161 as the student watches.

DAY TWO: Copywork Exercise   *Student Page 162*

Focus: *Direct quotations, interjections*

Pull out Student Page 162. Ask the student to write her name and the date. The following model sentences are already printed on it:

> When Michael had any clear space, he told Norman, "Your neatness is oozing over on my side! Ugh!"

Remind the student that a comma comes before a direct quote, and that the words of the direct quote are surrounded by quotation marks. Ask the student if she can find the interjection in the sentences. Remember: an interjection is a word that shows sudden or strong feeling. (The interjection is "Ugh!") Remind the student that the quotation mark should go inside the closing quotation marks.

Watch the student copy the sentences, and correct her if she begins to make a mistake.

DAY THREE: Dictation Exercise   *Student Page 163*

Pull out Student Page 163. Ask the student to write her name and the date.

Dictate the following sentences to the student twice:

> When Michael had any clear space, he told Norman, "Your neatness is oozing over on my side! Ugh!"

Be sure to use a different voice for Michael's exact words. Pause for a count of three at each comma. When you reach the exclamation points, indicate them by using an excited voice; also pause for a count of five at each exclamation point.

Watch the student as she writes, and correct her at once if she begins to make errors.

DAY FOUR: Narration Exercise and Dictation   *Student Pages 164–165*

Focus: *Identifying the central narrative thread in a passage*

Pull out Student Pages 164–165. Ask the student to write her name and the date on Student Page 165.

Today's exercise will combine narration and dictation. Read the following passage out loud to the student. Tell the student that this passage also comes from *The Plant That Ate Dirty Socks.* Michael and Norman have noticed that dirty socks keep disappearing from their room in the dark. They decide that they must solve the mystery of the disappearing socks.

Michael took off his socks, tied the strings to them, and put them where the others had vanished. Then he got into bed, lay there with his arms straight out, and told Norman to tie the strings to his wrists.

Norman got his Super Splasher Water Blaster and favorite disguise from his detective kit and climbed into bed.

"You don't need a disguise in the dark," said Michael.

"I always detect better when I'm wearing one," replied Norman. He turned out the light and put on his disguise.

"Ready?" asked Michael.

"Ready," said Norman.

They had left the door ajar so a little light came in from the hall. They could barely see the white socks on the floor.

They lay there in the dark waiting. Nothing happened. They waited some more. Norman was lying on his side staring at the socks.

Suddenly one moved!

"It's moving!" he shouted and began squirting wildly with his Water Blaster.

"Oh, no!" yelled Michael.

"I saw it!" Norman insisted excitedly. "It was creeping fast across the floor! Then it jumped up in the air and fell down! There it goes again!" he yelled, bouncing up and down on his bed and squirting more water in every direction.

"No," said Michael. "My nose started to itch. I forgot and reached *up* to scratch it."

Their parents ran in and turned on the light.

There was Michael with strings and socks dangling. Water was dripping off his hair and the end of his nose.

Norman was waving a giant water pistol and wearing glasses with an attached rubber nose and moustache.

Water was dripping off the plants, soaking into the rug and bed, and running down the walls.

"I know," said Mom, "that there has to be a logical explanation for all this, but it better be a good one, or else."

—From *The Plant That Ate Dirty Socks*
by Nancy McArthur

Ask the following questions to test the student's listening ability. Remind the student to answer in complete sentences.

Instructor: What did Michael do with his socks once he had taken them off?
Student: *He tied strings to them.*

Instructor: What did he tie the other ends of the strings to?
Student: *He tied them to his wrists.*

Instructor: What two things did Norman get to help him detect?
Student: *He got a disguise and a Super Splasher Water Blaster.*

Instructor: Norman got all excited because something happened. What happened?
Student: *He saw one of the socks move.*

Instructor: Why did the sock move?
Student: *Michael scratched his nose.*

Instructor: When the parents came into the room, what did Michael look like?
Student: *He was tied to his socks with string, and water was dripping off his hair and his nose.*

Instructor: What did Norman look like?
Student: *He was waving a water pistol and wearing glasses, a rubber nose, and a moustache.*

You will now ask the student to summarize the basic narrative thread in the passage.

You will continue to train the student to summarize without depending on your leading questions. In order to do this, ask the student, "Can you tell me in three or four sentences what happened in this story?" The student's answer should resemble one of the following:

"Norman and Michael wanted to figure out why their socks were disappearing. They tied strings to the socks and to Michael's hands and turned the lights off. Norman got all excited when the socks moved. But Michael had just scratched his nose."

"Norman and Michael tied strings to Michael's socks and attached the strings to Michael's hands. Then they turned off the lights. Norman put on a disguise and got in bed with a water pistol. When he saw the socks move, he started shooting with the pistol."

"The brothers wanted to find out why socks were disappearing. They tied strings to Michael's wrists and to the socks and turned off the lights. But Michael forgot about the strings and scratched his nose."

If the student is unable to produce a narrative summary, *then* ask the following questions.

Instructor: What did Norman and Michael want to figure out?
Student: *They wanted to know why the socks were disappearing.*

Instructor: What was their plan?
Student: *They tied strings to the socks and to Michael's wrists.*

Instructor: What happened when Michael scratched his nose?
Student: *The socks moved and Norman shot him with the water pistol.*

Then ask the student to narrate again.

Write down the student's narration on Student Page 164, but do not allow her to see the sentences. Choose one or two of the sentences from the narration to use as a dictation exercise

(Student Page 165). Be sure to indicate any unusual punctuation with your voice; give any necessary spelling help.

DAY FIVE (optional): Creative Writing   *Student Pages 166–167*

Pull out Student Pages 166–167. Write the student's name and the date for her as she watches, or ask her to write the name and date independently.

> **Instructor:** In *The Plant That Ate Dirty Socks* two brothers share a room. One of the brothers is a messy person and the other brother is a neat person. Imagine that you are the messy person. What do you do that irritates your neatnik roommate? Or, imagine that you are the neat person. What does your messy roommate leave around the room that annoys you?

Remind the student to answer you in a complete sentence or sentences. If she answers in fragments, turn the fragments into complete sentences, say them to her, and then ask her to repeat the sentences back to you. Write the student's answer down on the "Instructor" lines of Student Page 166 as she watches. Then have her copy the sentences onto the "Student" lines.

WEEK 25

DAY ONE: Narration Exercise   *Student Page 168*

Focus: *Identifying the central thread in a narrative*

Pull out Student Page 168. Ask the student to write his name and the date.

Read the following passage out loud to the student. Tell the student that this is from the story "The Elephant's Child" by Rudyard Kipling. "The Elephant's Child" is one of the *Just So Stories*—stories that give an imaginary reason for why something is the way it is. "The Elephant's Child" explains why the elephant has a long trunk.

When Kipling wrote these stories, he made up some of his own words, just for fun. He says that the Elephant's Child has "'satiable curtiosity," which means "insatiable curiosity"—curiosity that can't be satisfied.

The "precession of the Equinoxes" is an astronomical term (having to do with stars and planets). It has to do with the earth's rotation. (Note to instructor: The precession of the equinoxes is a complicated phenomenon; if the student is interested, you can do further research using the encyclopedia.)

> In the High and Far-Off Times the Elephant, O Best Beloved, had no trunk. He had only a blackish, bulgy nose, as big as a boot, that he could wriggle about from side to side; but he couldn't pick up things with it. But there was one Elephant—a new Elephant—an Elephant's Child—who was full of 'satiable curtiosity, and that means he asked ever so many questions. *And* he lived in Africa, and he filled all Africa with his 'satiable curtiosities. He asked his tall aunt, the Ostrich, why her tail-feathers grew just so, and his tall aunt the Ostrich spanked him with her hard, hard claw. He asked his tall uncle, the Giraffe, what made his skin spotty, and his tall uncle, the Giraffe, spanked him with his hard, hard hoof. And still he was full of 'satiable curtiosity! He asked his broad aunt, the Hippopotamus, why her eyes were red, and his broad aunt, the Hippopotamus, spanked him with her broad, broad hoof; and he asked his hairy uncle, the Baboon, why melons tasted just so, and his hairy uncle, the Baboon, spanked him with his hairy, hairy paw. And *still* he was full of 'satiable curtiosity! He asked questions about everything that he saw, or heard, or felt, or smelt, or touched, and all his uncles and his aunts spanked him. And still he was full of 'satiable curtiosity!
>
> One fine morning in the middle of the Precession of the Equinoxes this 'satiable Elephant's Child asked a fine question that he had never asked before. He asked, "What does the Crocodile have for dinner?" Then everybody said, "Hush" in a loud and dreadful tone, and they spanked him immediately and directly, without stopping, for a long time.
>
> By and by, when that was finished, he came upon Kolokolo Bird sitting in the middle of a wait-a-bit thorn-bush, and he said, "My father has

spanked me, and my mother has spanked me; all my aunts and uncles have spanked me for my 'satiable curtiosity, and *still* I want to know what the Crocodile has for dinner!"

Then Kolokolo Bird said, with a mournful cry, "Go to the banks of the great grey-green, greasy Limpopo River, all set about with fever-trees, and find out."

—From "The Elephant's Child"
by Rudyard Kipling

Ask the following questions to test the student's listening ability. Remind the student to answer in complete sentences.

Instructor: What was the Elephant's Child's nose like?
Student: *It was blackish, bulgy, and as big as a boot.*

Instructor: Where did the Elephant's Child live?
Student: *He lived in Africa.*

Instructor: What did the Elephant's Child ask his uncle, the Giraffe?
Student: *He asked why the Giraffe's skin was spotty.*

Instructor: What did he ask the Hippopotamus?
Student: *He asked why the Hippopotamus had red eyes.*

Instructor: What did all the animals do when the Elephant's Child asked questions?
Student: *They spanked him.*

Instructor: What question did the Elephant's Child ask about the Crocodile?
Student: *He asked what the Crocodile has for dinner.*

Instructor: The Kolokolo Bird told him to go to the river and find out. Do you remember the name of the river?
Student: *The river is the Limpopo River.*

Instructor: Do you remember two of the adjectives that described the river?
Student: *It was the great grey-green, greasy Limpopo River.*

You will now ask the student to summarize the basic narrative thread in the passage.

You will continue to train the student to summarize without depending on your leading questions. In order to do this, ask the student, "Can you tell me in three or four sentences what happened in this story?" The student's answer should resemble one of the following (you should feel free to remind the student of the unfamiliar names if he cannot remember them):

"The Elephant's Child asked all of the animals questions. Finally he asked them what the Crocodile had for dinner. They wouldn't tell him, but the Kolokolo Bird told him to go to the Limpopo River to find out."

"The Elephant's Child had insatiable curiosity. He asked all of the animals questions, and they spanked him. Then he asked them what the crocodile had for dinner. They wouldn't tell him, but the Kolokolo Bird told him to go to the river and find out."

"The Elephant's Child had a bulgy nose and insatiable curiosity. He asked his relatives what the Crocodile ate for dinner. They spanked him instead of telling him the answer, but he still wanted to know. So a bird told him to go to the Limpopo River to find out."

If the student is unable to produce a narrative summary, *then* ask the following questions:

Instructor: What did the Elephant's Child do to all his relatives?
Student: *He asked them questions.*

Instructor: What was the last question he asked?
Student: *He asked what the Crocodile ate for dinner.*

Instructor: Did the animals answer his question?
Student: *No, they just spanked him.*

Instructor: What did the Kolokolo Bird tell him to do?
Student: *The bird told him to go to the Limpopo River to find out.*

Then ask the student to narrate again.

Write down the student's narration on Student Page 168 as he watches. You may need to explain that Kipling capitalizes the names of the animals because he is using the names as proper nouns.

DAY TWO: Copywork Exercise   *Student Page 169*

Focus: *Adverbs*

Pull out Student Page 169. Ask the student to write his name and the date. The following model sentences are already printed on it:

> **Then everybody said, "Hush" in a loud and dreadful tone, and they spanked him immediately and directly, without stopping, for a long time.**

Ask the student to point out the direct quote in the sentence ("Hush"). Then ask him to put his finger on the word "immediately." This is an adverb—a word that modifies (tells more about) a verb. The verb is "spanked." How did the animals spank him? They spanked him "immediately." How else did they spank him? They spanked him "directly." Adverbs tell more about verbs. Usually (although not always) they end in –ly.

Watch the student as he copies. If he begins to make a mistake, correct him at once.

DAY THREE: Dictation Exercise

Pull out Student Page 170. Ask the student to write his name and the date.

Dictate the following sentence to the student twice:

> Then everybody said, "Hush" in a loud and dreadful tone, and they spanked him immediately and directly, without stopping, for a long time.

Be sure to use a different voice for the word "Hush." Remind the student that there are four commas in the sentence. Pause for a count of three at each comma.

Watch the student as he writes, and correct him at once if he begins to make an error.

DAY FOUR: Narration Exercise and Dictation

Focus: *Identifying the central narrative thread in a passage*

Pull out Student Pages 171–172. Ask the student to write his name and the date on Student Page 172.

Today's exercise will combine narration and dictation. Read the following passage out loud to the student. Tell the student that this is also from Rudyard Kipling's story "The Elephant's Child." The Elephant's Child has found the Limpopo River—and he has also found the Crocodile. Kipling makes up a word in this part of the story too—he says "hijjus" instead of "hideous."

> "Come hither, Little One," said the Crocodile, "for I am the Crocodile," and he wept crocodile-tears to show it was quite true.
>
> Then the Elephant's Child grew all breathless, and panted, and kneeled down on the bank and said, "You are the very person I have been looking for all these long days. Will you please tell me what you have for dinner?"
>
> "Come hither, Little One," said the Crocodile, "and I'll whisper."
>
> Then the Elephant's Child put his head down close to the Crocodile's musky, tusky mouth, and the Crocodile caught him by his little nose, which up to that very week, day, hour, and minute, had been no bigger than a boot, though much more useful.
>
> "I think," said the Crocodile—and he said it between his teeth, like this—"I think to-day I will begin with Elephant's Child!" . . . .
>
> Then the Elephant's Child sat back on his little haunches, and pulled, and pulled, and pulled, and his nose began to stretch. And the Crocodile floundered into the water, making it all creamy with great sweeps of his tail, and *he* pulled, and pulled, and pulled.
>
> And the Elephant's Child's nose kept on stretching; and the Elephant's Child spread all his little four legs and pulled, and pulled, and pulled, and his

nose kept on stretching; and the Crocodile threshed his tail like an oar, and *he* pulled and pulled, and pulled, and at each pull the Elephant's Child's nose grew longer and longer—and it hurt him hijjus!

Then the Elephant's Child felt his legs slipping, and he said through his nose, which was now nearly five feet long, "This is too butch for me!" . . . and at last the Crocodile let go of the Elephant's Child's nose with a plop that you could hear all up and down the Limpopo.

Then the Elephant's Child sat down most hard and sudden . . . and next he was kind to his poor pulled nose, and wrapped it all up in cool banana leaves, and hung it in the great grey-green, greasy Limpopo to cool.

—From "The Elephant's Child"
by Rudyard Kipling

Ask the following questions to test the student's listening ability. Remind the student to answer in complete sentences.

Instructor: What kind of tears did the Crocodile weep?
Student: *He wept crocodile tears.*

Instructor: What did the Elephant's Child ask the Crocodile?
Student: *He asked, "What do you have for dinner?"*

Instructor: What did the Crocodile do when the Elephant's Child asked his question?
Student: *He grabbed the Elephant's Child by the nose.*

Instructor: What did the Elephant's Child do when the Crocodile grabbed him?
Student: *He pulled back.*

Instructor: What happened to his nose?
Student: *It stretched out longer and longer.*

Instructor: How did the Elephant's Child cool his poor nose?
Student: *He wrapped it in banana leaves and hung it in the river.*

Instructor: What had his nose turned into?
Student: *It had turned into a trunk.*

You will now ask the student to summarize the basic narrative thread in the passage.

You will continue to train the student to summarize without depending on your leading questions. In order to do this, ask the student, "Can you tell me in three sentences what happened in this story?" The student's answer should resemble one of the following:

"The Elephant's Child asked the Crocodile what he ate for dinner. The Crocodile grabbed his nose and pulled. Finally he let go, but the Elephant's Child's nose had been stretched out into a trunk."

"The Elephant's Child found the Crocodile in the river. He put his head down next to the Crocodile, and the Crocodile grabbed his nose. The Elephant's Child pulled back, and his nose stretched and stretched."

"The Elephant's Child found the Crocodile and asked him what he had for dinner. The Crocodile said that he would eat Elephant's Child! He grabbed the Elephant's Child's nose and stretched it out into a trunk."

If the student is unable to produce a narrative summary, *then* ask the following questions:

Instructor: What did the Elephant's Child find in the river?
Student: *He found the Crocodile.*

Instructor: What did he ask the Crocodile?
Student: *He asked what the Crocodile had for dinner.*

Instructor: What did the Crocodile do?
Student: *He grabbed the Elephant's Child's nose.*

Instructor: What happened to the Elephant's Child's nose when the Crocodile pulled on it?
Student: *It stretched out into a trunk.*

Then ask the student to narrate again.

Write down the student's narration on Student Page 171, but do not allow him to see the sentences. Choose one or two of the sentences from the narration to use as a dictation exercise (Student Page 172). Be sure to indicate any unusual punctuation with your voice; give any necessary spelling help.

DAY FIVE (optional): Creative Writing   *Student Pages 173–174*

Pull out Student Pages 173–174. Write the student's name and the date for him as he watches, or ask him to write the name and date independently.

Instructor: In the story "The Elephant's Child," a young elephant gets his nose stretched out by a hungry crocodile. If you had to choose one part of your face to be changed, which part would you choose? Does it get longer or shorter? bigger or smaller? Does that change how the part of your face works? What can your face-part do now that it couldn't do before?

Remind the student to answer you in a complete sentence or sentences. If he answers in fragments, turn the fragments into complete sentences, say them to him, and then ask him to repeat the sentences back to you. Write the student's answer down on the "Instructor" lines of Student Page 173 as he watches. Then have him copy the sentences onto the "Student" lines.

WEEK 26

Day One: Narration Exercise   *Student Page 175*

Focus: *Identifying the central details in a description*

Pull out Student Page 175. Ask the student to write her name and the date.

Read the following passage out loud to the student. Tell the student that this is from a book called *Moominland Midwinter* by Tove Jansson. It is one of a series of books about the Moomins, tiny creatures who live together in little villages deep in the countryside.

You may need to explain that "peat" is a kind of dense, partly decomposed moss that can be burned for fuel.

> Inside, the house was warm and cosy. Heaps of peat were quietly smouldering in the central-heating stove down in the cellar. The moon looked in sometimes at the drawing-room window, lighting on the white winter covers of the chairs and on the cut-glass chandelier in its white gauze bag. And in the drawing-room also, grouped around the biggest porcelain stove of the house, the Moomin family lay sleeping their long winter sleep.
>
> They always slept from November to April, because such was the custom of their forefathers, and Moomins stick to tradition. They all had a good meal of pine needles in their stomachs, just as their ancestors used to have, and beside their beds each had hopefully laid out everything likely to be needed in early spring: spades, burning-glasses and films, wind-gauges, and the like.
>
> The silence was deep and expectant.
>
> Every now and then somebody sighed and curled deeper down under the quilt.
>
> The streak of moonlight wandered from rocking-chair to drawing-room table, crawled over the brass knobs of the bed end, and shone straight in Moomintroll's face.
>
> And now something happened that had never happened before, not since the first Moomin took to his hibernating den. Moomintroll awoke and found that he couldn't go back to sleep again.
>
> He looked at the moonlight and the ice-ferns on the window. He listened to the humming of the stove in the cellar and felt more and more awake and astonished. Finally he rose and padded over to Moominmamma's bed.
>
> He pulled at her ear very cautiously, but she didn't awake. She just curled into an uninterested ball.
>
> "If not even Mother wakes up it's no use trying the others," Moomintroll thought and went along by himself on a round through the unfamiliar and mysterious house. All the clocks had stopped ages ago, and a fine coat of dust covered everything. On the drawing-room table still stood the soup-tureen

with pine-needles left over from November. And inside its gauze dress the cut-glass chandelier was softly jingling to itself.

—From *Moominland Midwinter*
by Tove Jansson

Ask the following questions to test the student's listening ability. Remind the student to answer in complete sentences. If the student does not remember a detail, reread the sentence that contains the answer.

Instructor: Do you remember where the central-heating stove was?
Student: *It was down in the cellar.*

Instructor: In the drawing room, the chairs were covered up for the winter. What was the chandelier covered in?
Student: *It was covered with a white (gauze) bag.*

Instructor: What room were the Moomins sleeping in?
Student: *They were sleeping in the drawing room.*

Instructor: Between what two months did the Moomins sleep?
Student: *They slept from November to April.*

Instructor: What did they eat before they went to sleep?
Student: *They ate pine needles.*

Instructor: What strange thing did Moomintroll do?
Student: *He woke up.*

Instructor: Moomintroll went through the house, looking at everything in it. What did he notice about the clocks?
Student: *The clocks had stopped.*

Instructor: What had covered everything in the house?
Student: *There was dust all over everything.*

Instructor: What was still inside the soup tureen (the soup kettle) on the table?
Student: *There were still pine needles in it.*

Now say to the student, "In two or three sentences, tell me what Moomintroll's house was like in the middle of the winter." The student's answer should resemble one of the following:

"The chairs and chandelier were covered. The clocks had stopped and dust covered everything. There were still pine needles in the soup bowl on the table."

"Dust covered everything and the clocks had stopped. The stoves were keeping the house warm, and the Moomins were sleeping in the drawing room."

"The moonlight came in through the windows. The chairs and the chandelier were covered up. The clocks had stopped."

Write down the student's narration on Student Page 175.

DAY TWO: Copywork Exercise   *Student Page 176*

Focus: *Adverbs, direct quotations*

Pull out Student Page 176. Ask the student to write her name and the date. The following model sentences are already printed on it:

> "Mother, I love you terribly," said Moomintroll. They went strolling slowly down to the bridge.

This sentence comes later in the book—after Moomintroll's mother finally wakes up! Ask the student to point out the direct quote in this sentence. Then ask her to put her finger on the comma that comes after "terribly." Remind her that a comma separates a direct quote from the rest of the sentence.

Now ask the student to put her finger on the word "slowly." The student has already learned that adjectives modify (give more details about) nouns. "Slowly" is a word that modifies (gives more details about) the action verb "strolling." How did Moomintroll and his mother stroll? They strolled *slowly*. "Slowly" is an adverb because it modifies a verb.

Watch the student as she copies. If she begins to make a mistake, correct her at once.

DAY THREE: Dictation Exercise   *Student Page 177*

Pull out Student Page 177. Ask the student to write her name and the date.

Dictate the following sentences to the student twice:

> "Mother, I love you terribly," said Moomintroll. They went strolling slowly down to the bridge.

Be sure to use a different voice for Moomintroll's exact words. Remind the student that there are two commas in the first sentence, and a period between the first and second sentence. Pause for a count of three at each comma, and for a count of five at the period.

Watch the student as she writes, and correct her at once if she begins to make a mistake.

DAY FOUR: Narration Exercise and Dictation   *Student Pages 178–179*

Focus: *Identifying the central narrative thread in a passage*

Pull out Student Pages 178–179. Ask the student to write her name and the date on Student Page 179.

Today's exercise will combine narration and dictation. Read the following passage out loud to the student. Tell the student that Moomintroll has decided to leave the house and explore the countryside in winter. He has never seen winter before. All the doors and windows are frozen shut, so he goes up to the roof and finds the hatch, or trapdoor, that the chimney sweep uses to clean the chimney.

> . . . Moomintroll rushed up to the attic, managed to lift the chimney-sweep's hatch, and clambered out on to the roof.
>
> A wave of cold air received him.
>
> He lost his breath, slipped, and rolled over the edge.
>
> And so Moomintroll was helplessly thrown out into a strange and dangerous world and dropped up to his ears in the first snowdrift of his experience. It felt unpleasantly prickly to his velvet skin, but at the same time his nose caught a new smell. It was a more serious smell than any he had met before, and slightly frightening. But it made him wide awake and greatly interested.
>
> The valley was enveloped in a kind of grey twilight. It also wasn't green any longer, it was white. Everything that had once moved had become immobile. There were no living sounds. Everything angular was now rounded.
>
> "This is snow," Moomintroll whispered to himself. "I've heard about it from Mother, and it's called snow."
>
> Without Moomintroll knowing a thing about it, at that moment his velvet skin decided to start growing woollier. It decided to become, by and by, a coat of fur for winter use. That would take some time, but at least the decision was made. And that's always a good thing.
>
> Meanwhile Moomintroll was laboriously plodding along through the snow. He went down to the river. It was the same river that used to scuttle, transparent and jolly, through Moomintroll's summer garden. Now it looked quite unlike itself. It was black and listless. It also belonged to this new world in which he didn't feel at home.

—From *Moominland Midwinter*
by Tove Jansson

Ask the following questions to test the student's listening ability. Remind the student to answer in complete sentences.

Instructor: How did Moomintroll get out of the house?
Student: He climbed out onto the roof through the hatch (trapdoor).

Instructor: What did Moomintroll fall into?
Student: He fell into a snowdrift.

Instructor: What color was the valley?
Student: The valley had turned white.

Instructor: What did Moomintroll see for the first time?
Student: He saw snow.

Instructor: What did Moomintroll's velvet skin start to become?
Student: *It started to become a coat of fur.*

Instructor: Where did Moomintroll go next?
Student: *He went down to the river.*

Instructor: What color was the river?
Student: *The river was black.*

You will now ask the student to summarize the basic narrative thread in the passage.

You will continue to train the student to summarize without depending on your leading questions. In order to do this, ask the student, "Can you tell me in three sentences what happened in this story?" The student's answer should resemble one of the following:

"Moomintroll climbed out on the roof and fell down into a snowdrift. He had never seen snow before. He plodded down to the river and saw that it was black."

"Moomintroll got out of the house through the attic. The valley had turned white. When he went down to the river, he saw that the river had turned black."

"Moomintroll had never seen snow before. He climbed onto the roof and fell into a snowdrift, and his coat began to grow thicker—like fur. Then he walked down to the river."

If the student is unable to produce a narrative summary, *then* ask the following questions:

Instructor: How did Moomintroll get out of the house?
Student: *He got out onto the roof.*

Instructor: What was different about the outside world? List two things.
Student: *The valley was white; it smelled different; it was quiet; there was snow everywhere; the river was black.*

Instructor: Where did Moomintroll go after he got off the roof?
Student: *He went down to the river.*

Then ask the student to narrate again.

Write down the student's narration on Student Page 178, but do not allow her to see the sentences. Choose one or two of the sentences from the narration to use as a dictation exercise (Student Page 179). Be sure to indicate any unusual punctuation with your voice; give any necessary spelling help.

DAY FIVE (optional): Creative Writing   *Student Pages 180–181*

Pull out Student Pages 180–181. Write the student's name and the date for her as she watches, or ask her to write the name and date independently.

Instructor: Do you live in the countryside, the city, or a neighborhood? What is one thing you like about where you live? If you could add anything to the place where you live, what would you add? (For example–a pizza shop in the middle of your horse pasture, or a green field instead of the parking lot behind your apartment!)

Remind the student to answer you in a complete sentence or sentences. If she answers in fragments, turn the fragments into complete sentences, say them to her, and then ask her to repeat the sentences back to you. Write the student's answer down on the "Instructor" lines of Student Page 180 as she watches. Then have her copy the sentences onto the "Student" lines.

WEEK 27

DAY ONE: Narration Exercise   *Student Page 182*

Focus: *Identifying the central narrative thread in a passage*

Pull out Student Page 182. Ask the student to write his name and the date.

Read the following passage out loud to the student. Tell the student that this is one of the fairy tales written by Hans Christian Andersen. Hans Christian Andersen was born in Denmark more than two hundred years ago. You probably already know some of Hans Christian Andersen's stories, because they have become famous all around the world.

There was once a Prince who wished to marry a Princess; but then she must be a real Princess. He travelled all over the world in hopes of finding such a lady; but there was always something wrong. Princesses he found in plenty; but whether they were real Princesses it was impossible for him to decide, for now one thing, now another, seemed to him not quite right about the ladies. At last he returned to his palace quite cast down, because he wished so much to have a real Princess for his wife.

One evening a fearful tempest arose. It thundered and lightened, and the rain poured down from the sky in torrents: besides, it was as dark as pitch. All at once there was heard a violent knocking at the door, and the old King, the Prince's father, went out himself to open it.

It was a Princess who was standing outside the door. What with the rain and the wind, she was in a sad condition; the water trickled down from her hair, and her clothes clung to her body. She said she was a real Princess.

"Ah! We shall soon see about that!" thought the old Queen-mother; however, she said not a word of what she was going to do; but went quietly into the bedroom, took all the bed-clothes off the bed, and put three little peas on the bedstead. She then laid twenty mattresses one upon another over the three peas, and put twenty feather beds over the mattresses.

Upon this bed the Princess was to pass the night.

The next morning she was asked how she had slept. "Oh, very badly indeed!" she replied. "I have scarcely closed my eyes the whole night through. I do not know what was in my bed, but I had something hard under me, and am all over black and blue. It has hurt me so much!"

Now it was plain that the lady must be a real Princess, since she had been able to feel the three little peas through the twenty mattresses and twenty feather beds. None but a real Princess could have had such a delicate sense of feeling.

The Prince accordingly made her his wife; being now convinced that he had found a real Princess. The three peas were however put into the cabinet of curiosities, where they are still to be seen, provided they are not lost.

Wasn't this a lady of real delicacy?

—From "The Real Princess"
by Hans Christian Andersen

Ask the following questions to test the student's listening ability. Remind the student to answer in complete sentences.

Instructor: What kind of princess did the prince want to marry?
Student: He wanted to marry a real princess.

Instructor: What was the weather like when the princess knocked on the castle door?
Student: There was a terrible storm.

Instructor: How many mattresses did the Queen put on the bed?
Student: She put twenty mattresses on the bed.

Instructor: What did she put on top of the mattresses?
Student: She put twenty feather beds on top.

Instructor: What was underneath all of those mattresses and feather beds?
Student: Three little peas were underneath them.

Instructor: How did the Queen know that the princess was a real princess?
Student: The princess could feel the peas through all the mattresses and feather beds.

Instructor: What happened to the peas?
Student: They were put in a cabinet.

You will now ask the student to summarize the basic narrative thread in the passage.

You will continue to train the student to summarize without depending on your leading questions; however, since this is a complete story, you will give the student some additional help by saying, "Tell me how the Queen found out that the princess was a real princess." If necessary, you can use one of the above questions to prompt the student.

The student's answer should resemble one of the following (note that it isn't necessary for the student to know the difference between a mattress and a feather bed!):

"The Queen put a pea under twenty mattresses and twenty feather beds. The princess could feel the pea through all the mattresses anyway. That's how the Queen knew that she was a real princess."

"The princess was caught in a storm and asked for a place to sleep. The Queen put forty mattresses on top of three peas and told her to sleep there. The next morning, the princess was black and blue from the peas."

"The prince wanted to marry a real princess, so the Queen put three peas under the princess's mattresses. The next morning, the princess said that she could feel the peas all night long. The prince and the Queen knew that she was a real princess because she was so delicate."

Write down the student's narration on Student Page 182 as he watches.

DAY TWO: Copywork Exercise   *Student Page 183*

Focus: *Review interjections, exclamation points, direct quotes*

Pull out Student Page 183. Ask the student to write his name and the date. The following model sentences are already printed on it:

> She said she was a real princess. "Ah! We shall soon see about that!" thought the old queen.

Ask the student to point to the interjection in the sentence ("Ah!"). Remind the student that an interjection expresses sudden or strong feeling. Ask the student to point to the quotation marks on either side of the queen's words. Remind the student that exact words are set off by quotation marks.

Watch the student as he copies. If he begins to make a mistake, correct him at once.

DAY THREE: Dictation Exercise   *Student Page 184*

Pull out Student Page 184. Ask the student to write his name and the date.

Dictate the following sentences to the student twice:

> She said she was a real princess. "Ah! We shall soon see about that!" thought the old queen.

Be sure to use a different voice for the queen's exact words. Pause for a count of five at the first period. Say "Ah!" with great energy and then pause for a count of five before beginning the queen's next sentence. If necessary, remind the student to add the quotation marks and the exclamation at the end of the queen's second sentence.

Watch the student as he writes, and correct him at once if he begins to make a mistake.

DAY FOUR: Narration Exercise and Dictation   *Student Pages 185–186*

Focus: *Identifying the central details in a description*

Pull out Student Pages 185–186. Ask the student to write his name and the date on Student Page 186.

Today's exercise will combine narration and dictation. Read the following passage out loud to the student. Tell the student that this is from the beginning of another, much longer fairy tale by Hans Christian Anderson, "The Brave Tin Soldier." Sometimes this story is called "The Steadfast Tin Soldier" ("steadfast" means "faithful" or "courageous").

There were once five-and-twenty tin soldiers, who were all brothers, for they had been made out of the same old tin spoon. They shouldered arms and looked straight before them, and wore a splendid uniform, red and blue. The first thing in the world they ever heard were the words, "Tin soldiers!" uttered by a little boy, who clapped his hands with delight when the lid of the box, in which they lay, was taken off. They were given him for a birthday present, and he stood at the table to set them up. The soldiers were all exactly alike, excepting one, who had only one leg; he had been left to the last, and then there was not enough of the melted tin to finish him, so they made him to stand firmly on one leg, and this caused him to be very remarkable.

The table on which the tin soldiers stood, was covered with other playthings, but the most attractive to the eye was a pretty little paper castle. Through the small windows the rooms could be seen. In front of the castle a number of little trees surrounded a piece of looking-glass, which was intended to represent a transparent lake. Swans, made of wax, swam on the lake, and were reflected in it. All this was very pretty, but the prettiest of all was a tiny little lady, who stood at the open door of the castle; she, also, was made of paper, and she wore a dress of clear muslin, with a narrow blue ribbon over her shoulders just like a scarf. In front of these was fixed a glittering tinsel rose, as large as her whole face. The little lady was a dancer, and she stretched out both her arms, and raised one of her legs so high, that the tin soldier could not see it at all, and he thought that she, like himself, had only one leg. "That is the wife for me," he thought; "but she is too grand, and lives in a castle, while I have only a box to live in, five-and-twenty of us altogether, that is no place for her. Still I must try and make her acquaintance." Then he laid himself at full length on the table behind a snuff-box that stood upon it, so that he could peep at the little delicate lady, who continued to stand on one leg without losing her balance. When evening came, the other tin soldiers were all placed in the box, and the people of the house went to bed. Then the playthings began to have their own games together, to pay visits, to have sham fights, and to give balls. The tin soldiers rattled in their box; they wanted to get out and join the amusements, but they could not open the lid. The nut-crackers played at leap-frog, and the pencil jumped about the table. There was such a noise that the canary woke up and began to talk, and in poetry too. Only the tin soldier and the dancer remained in their places. She stood on tiptoe, with her legs stretched out, as firmly as he did on his one leg. He never took his eyes from her for even a moment.

—From "The Brave Tin Soldier"
by Hans Christian Andersen

Ask the following questions to test the student's listening ability. Remind the student to answer in complete sentences. If the student does not remember a detail, reread the sentence that contains the answer.

Instructor: How many tin soldiers were there?
Student: *There were twenty-five.*

Instructor: What were they made out of?
Student: *They were made from a tin spoon.* (**Note:** *Just "tin" is not enough detail!*)

Instructor: What kind of present were they?
Student: *They were a birthday present.*

Instructor: What was different about one of the soldiers?
Student: *He only had one leg.*

Instructor: What was the most attractive thing on the table?
Student: *The most attractive thing was a paper castle.*

Instructor: What was the lake in front of the castle made out of?
Student: *It was made out of a looking-glass (mirror).*

Instructor: What swam on the lake?
Student: *Wax swans swam on the lake.*

Instructor: Who stood at the castle door?
Student: *A tiny little lady OR A tiny little dancer stood at the castle door.*

Instructor: Why did the tin soldier think that she only had one leg?
Student: *Her other leg was raised up high.*

Instructor: What did the playthings do when the people went to bed?
Student: *They began to have their own games.*

Now say to the student, "Describe the castle in three sentences. Make sure to tell me about the dancer too!" The student's answer should resemble one of the following:

"The castle was made of paper, and you could see through the windows. There was a lake in front of it made out of a mirror, with wax swans on it. A dancer wearing a blue scarf stood in the doorway."

"The paper castle had a lake in front of it with trees around it and swans swimming on it. The swans were made out of wax. A little lady was standing at the door, wearing a muslin dress with a rose on it."

"The paper castle had windows, and you could see rooms through them. There were trees and a lake made out of a looking glass in front of it. The little dancer at the front door was standing on one leg, and the soldier thought she was very beautiful."

Write down the student's narration on Student Page 185, but do not allow him to see the sentences. Choose one or two of the sentences from the narration to use as a dictation exercise (Student Page 186). Be sure to indicate any unusual punctuation with your voice; give any necessary spelling help.

DAY FIVE (optional): Creative Writing   *Student Pages 187–188*

Pull out Student Pages 187–188. Write the student's name and the date for him as he watches, or ask him to write the name and date independently.

> **Instructor:** Imagine that you get caught in a huge storm. What kind of storm is it? (Rain, wind, snow, ice?) What does the storm do to you? How do you feel when you finally reach shelter?

Remind the student to answer you in a complete sentence or sentences. If he answers in fragments, turn the fragments into complete sentences, say them to him, and then ask him to repeat the sentences back to you. Write the student's answer down on the "Instructor" lines of Student Page 187 as he watches. Then have him copy the sentences onto the "Student" lines.

WEEK 28

DAY ONE: Narration Exercise   *Student Page 189*

Focus: *Identifying the central narrative thread in a passage*

Pull out Student Page 189. Ask the student to write her name and the date.

Read the following passage out loud to the student. Tell the student that this passage is from a book called *The Magic of Oz* by the writer L. Frank Baum, who wrote *The Wonderful Wizard of Oz* and then wrote many other books about Dorothy and her friends in Oz and the magical countries that surround it.

In this story, two friends—a little girl named Trot and a sailor named Cap'n Bill—have sailed off on an expedition, accompanied by an enchanted cat made out of glass. They are trying to find a birthday present for the ruler of Oz, a beautiful princess named Ozma who already has everything she could possibly want. But Trot and Cap'n Bill have heard about a Magic Flower that blooms constantly, with all kinds of different blossoms. It grows on a deserted island in a golden pot, and Trot and Cap'n Bill have just arrived at the deserted island and seen the flower.

So intently did Trot and Cap'n Bill gaze upon the Golden Flowerpot that held the Magic Flower that they scarcely noticed the island itself until the raft beached upon its sands. But then the girl exclaimed: "How funny it is, Cap'n Bill, that nothing else grows here except the Magic Flower."

Then the sailor glanced at the island and saw that it was all bare ground, without a weed, a stone, or a blade of grass. Trot, eager to examine the Flower closer, sprang from the raft and ran up the bank until she reached the Golden Flowerpot. Then she stood beside it motionless and filled with wonder. Cap'n Bill joined her, coming more leisurely, and he, too, stood in silent admiration for a time.

"Ozma will like this," remarked the Glass Cat, sitting down to watch the shifting hues of the flowers. "I'm sure she won't have as fine a birthday present from anyone else."

"Do you 'spose it's very heavy, Cap'n? And can we get it home without breaking it?" asked Trot anxiously.

"Well, I've lifted many bigger things than that," he replied; "but let's see what it weighs."

He tried to take a step forward, but could not lift his meat foot from the ground. His wooden leg seemed free enough, but the other would not budge.

"I seem stuck, Trot," he said, with a perplexed look at his foot. "It ain't mud, an' it ain't glue, but somethin's holdin' me down."

The girl attempted to lift her own feet, to go nearer to her friend, but the ground held them as fast as it held Cap'n Bill's foot. She tried to slide them, or to twist them around, but it was no use; she could not move either foot a hair's breadth.

"This is funny!" she exclaimed. "What do you 'spose has happened to us, Cap'n Bill?"

"I'm tryin' to make out," he answered. "Take off your shoes, Trot. P'raps it's the leather soles that's stuck to the ground." She leaned down and unlaced her shoes, but found she could not pull her feet out of them. The Glass Cat, which was walking around as naturally as ever, now said:

"Your foot has got roots to it, Cap'n, and I can see the roots going into the ground, where they spread out in all directions. It's the same way with Trot. That's why you can't move. The roots hold you fast."

—From *The Magic of Oz*
by L. Frank Baum

Ask the student the following comprehension questions. These are designed to guide the student towards recognizing the need to give you a plot summary (rather than a description).

Instructor: What odd thing did Trot notice about the island?
Student: *Nothing else grew there.*

Instructor: What happened when Cap'n Bill tried to step forward and lift the pot?
Student: *His foot stuck to the ground.*

Instructor: Did both feet stick to the ground?
Student: *No, his wooden foot was free.*

Instructor: What happened when Trot tried to help him?
Student: *She found out that her feet were stuck too.*

Instructor: Did taking off her shoes help?
Student: *No, her feet were still stuck.*

Instructor: The Glass Cat could see the problem. What was it?
Student: *Their feet had grown roots.*

Instructor: Why do you think the Glass Cat's feet and the wooden leg didn't grow roots?
Student: *Only living things grew roots.* (Prompt the student for this answer if necessary.)

Now ask the student the general question, "Can you give me a brief summary of this passage?" The student should respond by telling you what *happens* in the story, rather than with a listing of details. Her answer should resemble one of the following:

"Trot and Cap'n Bill came to the island to get the Magic Flower for Ozma. But their feet grew roots so that they couldn't move."

"The Magic Flower grew on a deserted island. Trot and Cap'n Bill came to the island to get the flower. When they stepped on the island, their feet grew roots."

"Trot and Cap'n Bill came to get the Magic Flower. When they stepped on the island where it grew, their feet grew roots. The Glass Cat's feet didn't grow roots, so it could still walk around."

If the student has difficulty forming a brief summary, ask these three questions:

Why did Trot and Cap'n Bill come to the island?

What happened when they stepped onto the island?

Did the same thing happen to the Glass Cat?

Then have the student repeat her answers in order; this will form her brief summary. Write the student's narration down on Student Page 189 as she watches.

DAY TWO: Dictation Exercise

Student Page 190

Focus: *Review commas*

Pull out Student Page 190. Ask the student to write her name and the date.

Dictate the following sentence to the student three times. Tell the student to listen for the comma, and then pause for a silent count of three at the comma.

> **It was a wild country and little travelled, but the Glass Cat knew every path.**

Tell the student that since the Glass Cat was not caught by the magic island, it set off to find help for Trot and Cap'n Bill. Point out that the writer uses "Glass Cat" as a proper name, so both words should be capitalized.

"Travelled" can also be spelled "traveled."

Watch the student as she writes, and correct her at once if she begins to make a mistake.

DAY THREE: Dictation Exercise

Student Page 191

Pull out Student Page 191. Ask the student to write her name and the date.

Dictate the following sentences to the student three times. Tell the student to listen for the period, and then pause for a count of five at the period.

> **It had a heart made of a blood-red ruby. The eyes were two large emeralds.**

Tell the student that the dictation sentences today are about the Glass Cat. Here is the beginning of the description of the Glass Cat: "This astonishing cat was made all of glass and was so clear and transparent that you could see through it as easily as through a window. In the top of its head, however, was a mass of delicate pink balls which looked like jewels but were intended for brains."

Point out to the student that "blood-red" is a compound adjective (two adjectives together) connected by a hyphen.

Watch the student as she writes, and correct her at once if she begins to make a mistake.

DAY FOUR: Narration Exercise and Dictation   *Student Pages 192–193*

Focus: Identifying the central details in a description

Pull out Student Pages 192–193. Ask the student to write her name and the date on Student Page 193.

Today's exercise will combine narration and dictation. Read the following passage out loud to the student. Tell the student that this scene comes a little later in *The Magic of Oz.* Trot and Cap'n Bill have been standing on the island a very long time, waiting for rescue. They are both getting tired and hungry.

Trot sighed again and watched the wonderful Magic Flower, because there was nothing else to do. Just now a lovely group of pink peonies budded and bloomed, but soon they faded away, and a mass of deep blue lilies took their place. Then some yellow chrysanthemums blossomed on the plant, and when they had opened all their petals and reached perfection, they gave way to a lot of white floral balls spotted with crimson—a flower Trot had never seen before.

"But I get awful tired watchin' flowers an' flowers an' flowers," she said impatiently.

"They're mighty pretty," observed Cap'n Bill.

"I know; and if a person could come and look at the Magic Flower just when she felt like it, it would be a fine thing, but to HAVE TO stand and watch it, whether you want to or not, isn't so much fun. I wish, Cap'n Bill, the thing would grow fruit for a while instead of flowers."

Scarcely had she spoken when the white balls with crimson spots faded away and a lot of beautiful ripe peaches took their place. With a cry of mingled surprise and delight Trot reached out and plucked a peach from the bush and began to eat it, finding it delicious. Cap'n Bill was somewhat dazed at the girl's wish being granted so quickly, so before he could pick a peach they had faded away and bananas took their place. "Grab one, Cap'n!" exclaimed Trot, and even while eating the peach she seized a banana with her other hand and tore it from the bush.

The old sailor was still bewildered. He put out a hand indeed, but he was too late, for now the bananas disappeared and lemons took their place.

"Pshaw!" cried Trot. "You can't eat those things; but watch out, Cap'n, for something else."

Cocoanuts next appeared, but Cap'n Bill shook his head.

"Can't crack 'em," he remarked, "'cause we haven't anything handy to smash 'em with."

"Well, take one, anyhow," advised Trot; but the cocoanuts were gone now, and a deep, purple, pear-shaped fruit which was unknown to them took their place. Again Cap'n Bill hesitated, and Trot said to him:

"You ought to have captured a peach and a banana, as I did. If you're not careful, Cap'n, you'll miss all your chances. Here, I'll divide my banana with you."

Even as she spoke, the Magic Plant was covered with big red apples, growing on every branch, and Cap'n Bill hesitated no longer. He grabbed with both hands and picked two apples, while Trot had only time to secure one before they were gone.

—From *The Magic of Oz*
by L. Frank Baum

Ask the student the following comprehension questions. These are designed to guide the student towards recognizing the need to give you important details about the Magic Flower, rather than telling you what *happens* in the story.

Instructor: Can you list two of the four kinds of flowers that blossom on the Magic Flower while Trot watches?
Student: *There were pink peonies, blue lilies, yellow chrysanthemums, and white balls with crimson (a kind of flower Trot didn't know the name of).*

Instructor: After Trot wished that the Magic Flower would bear fruit, it instantly produced two kinds of fruit. Can you remember one of them?
Student: *It had peaches and bananas.*

Instructor: What two kinds of fruit did Trot and Cap'n Bill decide *not* to pick?
Student: *They didn't pick lemons or coconuts.* (Note that the passage uses an archaic alternate spelling.)

Instructor: After the strange purple fruit, what did the Magic Flower bear?
Student: *It grew big red apples.*

Now ask the student the general question "Can you give me a brief summary of this passage?" The answer should focus on the details in the passage; if the student can't remember the details, read part of the paragraph to her again. Her answer should contain at least three different specific details of fruit and flowers, plus the information that the flower could have both. The student's answer should resemble one of the following:

"The Magic Flower had all kinds of blossoms, like pink peonies and blue lilies. When Trot wished that it would have fruit instead, peaches, bananas, coconuts, and apples grew on it."

"Trot was tired of flowers and wished for fruit. The Magic Flower had peaches, bananas, and apples. It also had lemons and coconuts, but Trot and Cap'n Bill didn't eat those."

"The Magic Flower could have fruit as well as flowers. Trot picked peaches and bananas from it, and Cap'n Bill picked apples."

Write down the student's narration on Student Page 192, but do not allow her to watch. Then dictate one or two of the sentences back to her (Student Page 193). Be sure to indicate any unusual punctuation with your voice; give any necessary spelling help. If appropriate, remind her that Magic Flower is capitalized because the writer treats it like a proper name. Cap'n is also capitalized because it is part of Cap'n Bill's proper name.

Day Five (optional): Creative Writing   *Student Pages 194–195*

From this point onward, dictation will replace copywork. That is why there is no longer a space for instructor lines on the student page.

Pull out Student Pages 194–195. Write the student's name and the date for her as she watches, or ask her to write the name and date independently.

Instructor: In *The Magic of Oz,* Cap'n Bill and Trot get stuck on an island that has a Magic Plant. This Magic Plant grows all sorts of flowers. Imagine that you find a Magic Plant that grows flowers and fruit. What would you like your Magic Plant to grow? List at least three or four things that would appear on the Magic Plant so that you could grab them before they disappear! If you like, draw a picture on student page 195 to accompany your description.

Write the student's answer down on a separate piece of paper. First, read the sentence back to him and then have him repeat it back to you. Finally, have him write the sentence down on his own, without access to the written model. Repeat steps 1–2 if necessary until the student has written the full sentence.

WEEK 29

DAY ONE: Narration Exercise   *Student Page 196*

Focus: *Identifying similarities and contrasts in a passage*

Pull out Student Page 196. Ask the student to write his name and the date.

Read the following passage out loud to the student. Before you begin, tell the student that the passage will explain about three different kinds of people who lived in Greek cities. Ask the student to be alert, and to listen for these three different kinds. When you read the passage, emphasize the words in **bold print.**

You may want to explain that "hereditary" means "by birth." If you have something that is "hereditary," you have had it since you were born; you didn't do anything to deserve it. *Uncle Tom's Cabin* is a novel about African-American slaves in the American South. It was written before the American Civil War by Harriet Beecher Stowe, a woman who felt strongly that slavery was wrong and should be "abolished," or done away with. The novel describes the horror and pain of life as an American slave.

> Every Greek city was composed of a small number of free born **citizens,** a large number of **slaves** and a sprinkling of **foreigners.**
>
> At rare intervals (usually during a war, when men were needed for the army) the Greeks showed themselves willing to confer the rights of citizenship upon the "barbarians," as they called the **foreigners.** But this was an exception. Citizenship was a matter of birth. You were an Athenian because your father and your grandfather had been Athenians before you. But however great your merits as a trader or a soldier, if you were born of non-Athenian parents, you remained a **"foreigner"** until the end of time.
>
> The Greek city, therefore, whenever it was not ruled by a king or a tyrant, was run by and for the free men, and this would not have been possible without a large army of **slaves** who outnumbered the free **citizens** at the rate of six or five to one and who performed those tasks to which we modern people must devote most of our time and energy if we wish to provide for our families and pay the rent of our apartments. The **slaves** did all the cooking and baking and candlestick making of the entire city. They were the tailors and the carpenters and the jewelers and the school-teachers and the bookkeepers and they tended the store and looked after the factory while the master went to the public meeting to discuss questions of war and peace or visited the theatre to see the latest play. . . . Indeed, ancient Athens resembled a modern club. All the freeborn **citizens** were hereditary members and all the **slaves** were hereditary servants, and waited upon the needs of their masters, and it was very pleasant to be a member of the organisation.

But when we talk about slaves, we do not mean the sort of people about whom you have read in the pages of *Uncle Tom's Cabin*. It is true that the position of those **slaves** who tilled the fields was a very unpleasant one, but the average freeman who had come down in the world and who had been obliged to hire himself out as a farm hand led just as miserable a life. In the cities, furthermore, many of the **slaves** were more prosperous than the poorer classes of the free men. For the Greeks, who loved moderation in all things, did not like to treat their **slaves** after the fashion which afterward was so common in Rome, where a slave had as few rights as an engine in a modern factory and could be thrown to the wild animals upon the smallest pretext.

The Greeks accepted slavery as a necessary institution, without which no city could possibly become the home of a truly civilised people. The **slaves** also took care of those tasks which nowadays are performed by the business men and the professional men.

—From *The Story of Mankind*
by Hendrik Van Loon

Ask the student the following comprehension questions. These are designed to highlight the similiarities and differences in the above passage. If the student cannot remember an answer, reread the sentence from the passage in which the answer appears.

Instructor: What were the three kinds of people who lived in every Greek city?
Student: *Every Greek city had citizens, slaves, and foreigners.*

Instructor: How did you become a Greek citizen?
Student: *You were born in a Greek city.*

Instructor: Where were foreigners born?
Student: *They were born somewhere else (not in a Greek city).*

Instructor: Were there more citizens or more slaves in a Greek city?
Student: *There were more slaves.*

Instructor: Can you remember three things that slaves did?
Student: *Slaves did cooking, baking, candlestick making, tended stores, made jewelry, taught school, kept books, and sewed clothes.*

Instructor: Can you remember one thing the masters (the citizens) did while the slaves worked?
Student: *They went to public meetings, discussed questions of war and peace, or went to the theatre.*

Now say to the student, "Tell me about the people who lived in Greek cities, and what made them different." The student's answer should list slaves, citizens, and foreigners. It should contrast slaves with foreigners, and citizens with slaves. If necessary, use the questions above as prompts. The answer should resemble one of the following:

"Slaves, citizens, and foreigners lived in Greek cities. Citizens were born in Greek cities, and foreigners weren't. Slaves did all of the work, while citizens talked about ideas or went to the theatre."

"Greek cities had slaves, who did the work, and citizens, who went to meetings or amused themselves. They also had foreigners. Citizens were born in Greece, but foreigners were born somewhere else."

"Greek cities had slaves, citizens, and foreigners. Slaves did work, like cooking and baking. Citizens were born in Greek cities. Foreigners were born in other places."

Write the student's narration down on Student Page 196 while he watches. Note that the passage uses the British spelling "theatre"; if the student uses this word in the narration, you may choose to use the American spelling "theater" instead.

DAY TWO: Dictation Exercise   *Student Page 197*

Focus: *Articles*

Pull out Student Page 197. Ask the student to write his name and the date.

Dictate the following sentence to the student three times. Tell the student to listen for the comma, and then pause for a silent count of three at each comma.

> **Every Greek city was composed of a small number of free born citizens, a large number of slaves and a sprinkling of foreigners.**

Now read the sentence one more time, emphasizing the bolded words.

> **Every Greek city was composed of a small number of free born citizens, a large number of slaves and a sprinkling of foreigners.**

Tell the student that "a" is an *article*. An article is a small word that modifies (describes) a noun. Articles tell you whether you are talking about one *particular* thing or not. "**A** citizen" could be any citizen in any Greek city. If you wanted to talk about one *particular* citizen, you would say "**the** citizen." This sentence could be talking about any citizens, any slaves, or any foreigners.

Remind the student that "Greek" is capitalized because it refers to the people of Greece.

Watch the student as he writes, and correct him at once if he begins to make a mistake. Give all necessary spelling help.

DAY THREE: Dictation Exercise   *Student Page 198*

Focus: Articles

Pull out Student Page 198. Ask the student to write his name and the date.

Dictate the following sentence to the student three times. Tell the student to listen for the commas, and then pause for a silent count of three at each comma.

> In one corner of the yard the cook, who was a slave, prepared the meal and in another corner the teacher, who was also a slave, taught the children.

Tell the student that this sentence describes part of a day in a Greek household. Now read the sentence again, emphasizing the bolded words.

> In one corner of **the** yard **the** cook, who was a slave, prepared **the** meal and in another corner **the** teacher, who was also a slave, taught **the** children.

This sentence is describing a particular Greek household, with one particular cook, one particular meal, one particular teacher, and one particular set of children. The article "the" modifies that particular household, cook, meal, teacher, and children.

Watch the student as he writes, and correct him at once if he begins to make a mistake.

DAY FOUR: Narration Exercise and Dictation   *Student Pages 199–200*

Focus: Identifying the central details in a description

Pull out Student Pages 199–200. Ask the student to write his name and the date on Student Page 200.

Today's exercise will combine narration and dictation. Read the following passage out loud to the student. Tell the student that this passage is also about the lives of the ancient Greeks.

> As for those household duties which take up so much of the time of your mother and which worry your father when he comes home from his office, the Greeks, who understood the value of leisure, had reduced such duties to the smallest possible minimum by living amidst surroundings of extreme simplicity.

To begin with, their homes were very plain. Even the rich nobles spent their lives in a sort of adobe barn, which lacked all the comforts which a modern workman expects as his natural right. A Greek home consisted of four walls and a roof. There was a door which led into the street but there were no windows. The kitchen, the living rooms and the sleeping quarters were built around an open courtyard in which there was a small fountain, or a statue and a few plants to make it look bright. Within this courtyard the family lived when it did not rain or when it was not too cold. In one corner of the yard the cook (who was a slave) prepared the meal and in another corner, the teacher (who was also a slave) taught the children the alpha beta gamma and the tables of multiplication and in still another corner the lady of the house, who rarely left her domain (since it was not considered good form for a married woman to be seen on the street too often) was repairing her husband's coat with her seamstresses (who were slaves,) and in the little office, right off the door, the master was inspecting the accounts which the overseer of his farm (who was a slave) had just brought to him.

When dinner was ready the family came together but the meal was a very simple one and did not take much time. The Greeks seem to have regarded eating as an unavoidable evil and not a pastime, which kills many dreary hours and eventually kills many dreary people. They lived on bread and on wine, with a little meat and some green vegetables. They drank water only when nothing else was available because they did not think it very healthy. They loved to call on each other for dinner, but our idea of a festive meal, where everybody is supposed to eat much more than is good for him, would have disgusted them. They came together at the table for the purpose of a good talk and a good glass of wine and water, but as they were moderate people they despised those who drank too much.

—From *The Story of Mankind*
by Hendrik Van Loon

Ask the student the following comprehension questions. These are designed to guide the student towards recognizing the need to give you important details about Greek life, rather than tell you what *happens* in the passage.

Instructor: Were there windows in a Greek home?
Student: No, there were no windows.

Instructor: What were the kitchen, living rooms, and bedrooms built around?
Student: They were built around a courtyard.

Instructor: Name two things that might be in the courtyard.
Student: There might be a small fountain, a statue, or a few plants.

Instructor: What did the cook do in one corner of the courtyard?
Student: *The cook prepared the meal.*

Instructor: What did the teacher do?
Student: *He taught the children their letters and numbers.*

Instructor: In the passage, what did the lady of the house do?
Student: *She sewed her husband's coat.*

Instructor: What did the master of the house do?
Student: *He looked at the accounts.*

Instructor: What did the Greeks eat and drink for their meals?
Student: *They ate bread, meat, and green vegetables, and they drank wine.*

Instructor: Why didn't they drink water?
Student: *They didn't think it was healthy.*

Instructor: Did they spend a long time eating?
Student: *No, they spent a short time eating.*

Now ask the student the general question "Can you give me a brief summary of this passage?" The answer should focus on the details in the passage; if the student can't remember the details, read part of the paragraph to him again. His answer should contain something about the way the house looked, something about what the people in the house did during the day, and something about Greek meals. It should not be longer than four sentences and should resemble one of the following:

> "Greek houses had doors that led right into the street and no windows. They had courtyards in the middle. In the courtyards, the cooks and teachers worked. For meals, the Greeks ate bread and vegetables and meat."

> "Greek houses were very plain and had courtyards in the middle. Slaves worked in the courtyards cooking and teaching. The mother would sew in the courtyard. Meals were plain too."

> "The Greeks lived in houses that were built around courtyards. The children went to school in the courtyards, and the slaves worked there. The Greeks didn't think that water was healthy, so they drank wine for their meals instead."

Write down the student's narration on Student Page 199, but do not allow him to watch. Then dictate one or two of the sentences back to him (Student Page 200). Be sure to indicate any unusual punctuation with your voice; give any necessary spelling help. Allow the student to compare his dictation with your written original.

DAY FIVE (optional): Creative Writing   *Student Pages 201–202*

Pull out Student Pages 201–222. Write the student's name and the date for him as he watches, or ask him to write the name and date independently.

> **Instructor:** Imagine you had a time machine and could visit any place in the past. Where would you go? Would you like to see the dinosaurs, visit Ancient Greece, see yourself as a baby, or go somewhere else in history?

Remind the student to answer you in a complete sentence or sentences. If he answers in fragments, turn the fragments into complete sentences, say them to him, and then ask him to repeat the sentences back to you.

Write the student's answer down on a separate piece of paper. First, read the sentence back to him and then have him repeat it back to you. Finally, have him write the sentence down on his own, without access to the written model. Repeat steps 1–2 if necessary until the student has written the full sentence.

WEEK 30

DAY ONE: Narration Exercise

Focus: *Identifying the central details in a description*

Pull out Student Page 203. Ask the student to write her name and the date.

Read the following passage out loud to the student. Tell her that this is from another history of the Greeks, written a few years before *The Story of Mankind* (which you read from in the last lesson). This history was written by Helene Guerber, a historian from America. She is describing life in one particular Greek city—the city of Sparta.

You may need to explain that a "lyre" is a stringed instrument like a small harp. Rushes are thick, long, grass-like plants.

> The Spartan children stayed under their father's roof and in their mother's care until they were seven years old. While in the nursery, they were taught all the beautiful old Greek legends, and listened with delight to the stories of the ancient heroes, and especially to the poems of Homer telling about the war of Troy and the adventures of Ulysses.
>
> As soon as the children had reached seven years of age, they were given over to the care of the state, and allowed to visit their parents but seldom. The boys were put in charge of chosen men, who trained them to become strong and brave; while the girls were placed under some good and wise woman, who not only taught them all they needed to know to keep house well, but also trained them to be as strong and fearless as their brothers. All Spartan boys were allowed but one rough woolen garment, which served as their sole covering by night and by day, and was of the same material in summer as in winter.
>
> They were taught very little reading, writing, and arithmetic, but were carefully trained to recite the poems of Homer, the patriotic songs, and to accompany themselves skillfully on the lyre. They were also obliged to sing in the public chorus, and to dance gracefully at all the religious feasts.
>
> As the Spartans were very anxious that their boys should be strong and fearless, they were taught to stand pain and fatigue without a murmur; and, to make sure that they could do so, their teachers made them go through a very severe training.
>
> Led by one of the older boys, the little lads were often sent out for long tramps over rough and stony roads, under the hot sun; and the best boy was the one who kept up longest, in spite of bleeding feet, burning thirst, and great fatigue.

> Spartan boys were allowed no beds to sleep in, lest they should become lazy and hard to please. Their only couch was a heap of rushes, which they picked on the banks of the Eurotas, a river near Sparta; and in winter they were allowed to cover these with a layer of cat-tail down to make them softer and warmer.

—From *The Story of the Greeks*
by H. A. Guerber

Ask the student the following comprehension questions. These are designed to guide the student towards recognizing the need to give you important details about Greek life, rather than tell you what *happens* in the passage.

Instructor: How old were the children when they were taken away from their parents?
Student: *They were seven years old.*

Instructor: What were the boys given to wear?
Student: *They were given one garment made out of wool.*

Instructor: Did they learn reading, writing, and math?
Student: *No, they did not learn very much reading, writing, or math.*

Instructor: Can you remember three things that they *were* taught to do?
Student: *They were taught to recite Homer's poems, to recite patriotic poems, to play the lyre, to sing, and to dance.*

Instructor: The boys were supposed to be strong and fearless, without complaining. Can you tell me two ways that they were trained to be strong and uncomplaining?
Student: *They were sent out for long marches on rough, stony roads; they weren't allowed to sleep in beds, only on heaps of rushes.*

Instructor: Would you have enjoyed being a Spartan child?
Student: *Let the student express an opinion!*

Now ask the student the general question "Can you give me a brief summary of this passage?" The answer should focus on the details in the passage; if she can't remember the details, read part of the paragraph to her again. Her answer should contain at least one detail about the Spartan boys' schooling, and at least one detail about the boys' training to be strong and uncomplaining. It should not be more than three sentences long and should resemble one of the following:

"Spartan children left home when they were seven. The boys were taught to sing, dance, and recite poems. They went on long, hard marches so they could learn to be strong and not complain."

"Boys from Sparta went away to school when they were seven. They learned Homer's poems. They were also taught how to be fearless and uncomplaining."

"Spartan boys learned to recite Homer's poems and patriotric songs. They were supposed to be brave and fearless. They were sent on long marches and were forced to sleep on piles of grass instead of beds."

Write the student's narration down on Student Page 203 while she watches.

DAY TWO: Dictation Exercise   *Student Page 204*

Focus: *Prepositions*

Pull out Student Page 204. Ask the student to write her name and the date.

Dictate the following sentences to the student three times. Tell the student to listen for the period, and then pause for a silent count of five when you reach the period.

> Spartan boys were not allowed to sleep in beds. Their teachers did not want them to become lazy and hard to please.

Now read the following sentence one more time, emphasizing the bolded word.

> Spartan boys were not allowed to sleep **in** beds.

Tell the student that the word "in" is a *preposition*. A preposition is a word that shows the relationship between two other words. Where did the boys *not* sleep? They did not sleep *in beds.*

Watch the student as she writes, and correct her at once if she begins to make a mistake. Give all necessary spelling help.

DAY THREE: Dictation Exercise   *Student Page 205*

Pull out Student Page 205. Ask the student to write her name and the date.

Dictate the following sentence to the student three times. Tell the student that there are *seven* commas in this sentence! Pause for a silent count of three at each comma.

> The Spartan girls, who were brought up by the women, were, like the boys, taught to wrestle, run, and swim, and to take part in gymnastics of all kinds.

You may need to dictate this sentence a few additional times, so that the student can remember the placement of all of the commas. Ask the student to repeat the sentence back to you. When she can repeat it, ask her to write.

Watch the student as she writes, and correct her at once if she begins to make a mistake. Give all necessary spelling help. You may need to remind the student to capitalize "Spartan" ("Sparta" is the proper name of a town, so words referring to that town such as "Spartan" are also capitalized).

DAY FOUR: Narration Exercise and Dictation   *Student Pages 206–207*

Focus: *Identifying the central details in a description*

Pull out Student Pages 206–207. Ask the student to write her name and the date on Student Page 207.

Today's exercise will combine narration and dictation. Read the following passage out loud to the student. Tell the student that this is another passage from Helene Guerber's history of the Greeks.

> The Spartan girls, who were brought up by the women, were, like the boys, taught to wrestle, run, and swim, and to take part in gymnastics of all kinds, until they too became very strong and supple, and could stand almost any fatigue.
>
> They were also taught to read, write, count, sing, play, and dance; to spin, weave, and dye; and to do all kinds of woman's work. In short, they were expected to be strong, intelligent, and capable, so that when they married they might help their husbands, and bring up their children sensibly. At some public festivals the girls strove with one another in various games, which were witnessed only by their fathers and mothers and the other married people of the city. The winners in these contests were given beautiful prizes, which were much coveted.
>
> Although the women and girls were not often allowed to appear in public, or to witness certain of the Olympic games, there were special days held sacred to them, when the girls also strove for prizes. They too ran races. . . . One of these races was called the torch race, for each runner carried a lighted torch in her hand. All were allowed to try to put out each other's light; and the prize was given to the maiden who first reached the goal with her torch aflame, or to the one who kept hers burning longest.
>
> The prize for the girls was the same as that given to the boys; but the boys took part in more games, and were present in greater numbers, than the girls, and their victories were praised much more than those of their sisters.
>
> —From *The Story of the Greeks*
> by H. A. Guerber

Ask the student the following comprehension questions. These are designed to guide the student towards recognizing the need to give you important details about life in Sparta, rather than tell you what *happens* in the passage.

> **Instructor:** What kinds of physical activities were girls taught to do? The passage lists four; can you tell me two or three?
> **Student:** *The girls were taught to wrestle, run, swim, and do gymnastics.*

> **Instructor:** The passage lists nine other specific things that girls were taught to do. Can you list five? (Note: Be sure to give the student help if necessary!)
> **Student:** *They were also taught to read, write, count, sing, play, dance, spin, weave, and dye.*

> **Instructor:** What were Spartan girls expected to do when they grew up? The passage lists two specific duties.
> **Student:** *They were supposed to help their husbands and bring up their children.*

> **Instructor:** Who was allowed to watch when the girls wrestled or ran races?
> **Student:** *The fathers, mothers, and other married people watched.*

> **Instructor:** In the torch race, what did the girls try to do to each other?
> **Student:** *They tried to put out the torches.*

> **Instructor:** Whose games were considered more important—the boys' or the girls'?
> **Student:** *The boys' games were considered more important.*

Now ask the student the general question "Can you give me a brief summary of this passage?" The answer should focus on the details in the passage; if the student can't remember the details, read part of the paragraph to her again. Her answer should contain at least one detail about the physical skills the girls were taught to do and at least two details about the other specific skills they were taught. It should also mention the games that the girls competed in. Her answer should be no longer than three sentences and should resemble one of the following:

> "Girls in Sparta were taught to wrestle, run, and do gymnastics. They were also taught to read, write, spin, and weave. They had their own games, like the Olympics, where they raced with torches and wrestled."

> "Spartan girls learned how to do gymnastics. They also learned how to do household jobs, like dyeing and spinning. They played games like the boys, but their games were not as important to the Spartans."

> "In Sparta, girls were taught how to run, swim, do gymnastics, read, write, and count. They were taught how to help their husbands and raise children. They played in games like their brothers, but only married people were allowed to watch."

Write down the student's narration on Student Page 206, but do not allow her to watch. Then dictate one or two of the sentences back to her (Student Page 207). Be sure to indicate any unusual punctuation with your voice; give any necessary spelling help. Allow the student to compare her dictation with your written original.

DAY FIVE (optional): Creative Writing   *Student Pages 208–209*

Pull out Student Pages 208–209. Write the student's name and the date for her as she watches, or ask her to write the name and date independently.

> **Instructor:** After reading a little bit about the ancient Spartans, imagine you are a Spartan boy or girl. What would be your favorite part of the day? What would be your least favorite part?

Write the student's answer down on a separate piece of paper. First, read the sentence back to her and then have her repeat it back to you. Finally, have her write the sentence down on her own, without access to the written model. Repeat steps 1–2 if necessary until the student has written the full sentence.

WEEK 31

DAY ONE: Narration Exercise   *Student Page 210*

Focus: *Identifying the central narrative thread in a poem*

Pull out Student Page 210. Ask the student to write his name and the date.

Read the following poem out loud to the student. You may want to explain that a "spat" is a fight.

> The gingham dog and the calico cat
> Side by side on the table sat;
> 'Twas half-past twelve, and (what do you think!)
> Nor one nor t'other had slept a wink!
> The old Dutch clock and the Chinese plate
> Appeared to know as sure as fate
> There was going to be a terrible spat.
> (I wasn't there; I simply state
> What was told to me by the Chinese plate!)
>
> The gingham dog went "bow-wow-wow!"
> And the calico cat replied "mee-ow!"
> The air was littered, an hour or so,
> With bits of gingham and calico,
> While the old Dutch clock in the chimney-place
> Up with its hands before its face,
> For it always dreaded a family row!
> (Now mind: I'm only telling you
> What the old Dutch clock declares is true!)
>
> The Chinese plate looked very blue,
> And wailed, "Oh, dear! what shall we do!"
> But the gingham dog and the calico cat
> Wallowed this way and tumbled that,
> Employing every tooth and claw
> In the awfullest way you ever saw—
> And, oh! how the gingham and calico flew!
> (Don't fancy I exaggerate!
> I got my views from the Chinese plate!)
>
> Next morning where the two had sat
> They found no trace of dog or cat;
> And some folks think unto this day

> That burglars stole the pair away!
> But the truth about the cat and pup
> Is this: They ate each other up!
> Now what do you really think of that!
> (The old Dutch clock it told me so,
> And that is how I came to know.)

—"The Duel"
by Eugene Field

Ask the student the following comprehension questions. These are designed to guide the student towards summarizing the story in the poem.

Instructor: The Dutch clock and the Chinese plate knew that something was going to happen. What did they know?
Student: *They knew that there was going to be a spat (a fight).*

Instructor: Who was going to fight?
Student: *The gingham dog and the calico cat were going to fight.*

Instructor: The poem says that the clock put its "hands before its face." This is a "pun"—a phrase with two meanings. One of the meanings is that the hands of a clock go around its face. What is the other meaning? Can you show me?
Student: *(The student should put his hands up in front of his face.)*

Instructor: After the dog and the cat fought, what happened to them?
Student: *They disappeared OR They ate each other up.*

Instructor: What did people *say* had happened to them?
Student: *People said that burglars stole them.*

Instructor: Who told the narrator of the poem about the cat and the dog?
Student: *The Dutch clock and the Chinese plate told the narrator.*

Now say to the student, "Tell me in one or two sentences what happened in this poem." The student's answer should resemble one of the following:

"The gingham dog and the calico cat had a fight and ate each other up."

"The gingham dog and the calico cat had a fight. People thought that they had been stolen by burglars, but they actually ate each other up."

"The Dutch clock and the Chinese plate saw the dog and the cat fight. The dog and cat disappeared because they ate each other!"

Write the student's narration down on Student Page 210 while he watches.

DAY TWO: Dictation Exercise   *Student Page 211*

Focus: *Lines of poetry*

Pull out Student Page 211. Ask the student to write his name and the date.
    Dictate the following two lines of poetry to the student three times:

> Next morning where the two had sat
>
> They found no trace of dog or cat.

Be sure to pause for a silent count of five at the end of the first line of poetry. Remind the student that each line of traditional poetry is indented from the margin (approximately five spaces; you can suggest that the student put his finger down at the margin and then begin writing on the other side of his finger). Also remind the student that each line of traditional poetry begins with a capital letter. Tell the student that there is no punctuation mark at the end of the first line (it will be impossible for him to tell, since you need to pause at the end of the line).
    Watch the student as he writes, and correct him at once if he begins to make a mistake.

DAY THREE: Dictation Exercise   *Student Page 212*

Focus: *Lines of poetry and prepositions*

Pull out Student Page 212. Ask the student to write his name and the date.
    Dictate the following two lines of poetry to the student three times:

> The gingham dog and the calico cat
>
> Side by side on the table sat.

Be sure to pause for a silent count of five at the end of the first line of poetry. Remind the student that each line of traditional poetry is indented from the margin (approximately five spaces; you can suggest that the student put his finger down at the margin and then begin writing on the other side of his finger). Also remind the student that each line of traditional poetry begins with a capital letter. Tell the student that there is no punctuation mark at the end of the first line (it will be impossible for him to tell, since you need to pause at the end of the line).
    Now read the following lines again, emphasizing the bolded word.

> The gingham dog and the calico cat
>
> Side by side **on** the table sat.

Tell the student that the word "on" is a *preposition*. A preposition is a word that shows the relationship between two other words. Where did the dog and cat sit? They sat *on* the table.

Watch the student as he writes, and correct him at once if he begins to make a mistake. Give all necessary spelling help.

DAY FOUR: Narration Exercise and Dictation   *Student Pages 213–214*

Focus: *Identifying the central narrative thread in a poem*

Pull out Student Pages 213–214. Ask the student to write his name and the date on Student Page 214.

Read the following poem out loud to the student. You may want to explain that "Palace Green" and "Bayswater" are places in England. "Abhors" means "hates." A bust is a statue of someone's head and shoulders.

> A trick that everyone abhors
> In Little Girls is slamming Doors.
> A Wealthy Banker's little Daughter
> Who lived in Palace Green, Bayswater
> (By name Rebecca Offendort),
> Was given to this Furious Sport.
> She would deliberately go
> And Slam the door like Billy-Ho!
> To make her Uncle Jacob start.
> She was not really bad at heart,
> But only rather rude and wild:
> She was an aggravating child.
>
> It happened that a Marble Bust
> Of Abraham was standing just
> Above the Door this little Lamb
> Had carefully prepared to Slam,
> And Down it came! It knocked her flat!
> It laid her out! She looked like that!
>
> Her funeral Sermon (which was long
> And followed by a Sacred Song)
> Mentioned her Virtues, it is true,
> But dwelt upon her Vices too,
> And showed the Dreadful End of One
> Who goes and slams the door for Fun.

> The children who were brought to hear
> The awful Tale from far and near
> Were much impressed, and inly swore
> They never more would slam the Door,
> As often they had done before.

> —"Rebecca, Who Slammed Doors for
> Fun and Perished Miserably"
> by Hilaire Belloc

Ask the student the following comprehension questions. These are designed to guide the student towards summarizing the story in the poem.

Instructor: What obnoxious habit did Rebecca Offendort have?
Student: *She slammed doors.*

Instructor: A marble bust was standing above the door that she slammed. Who was portrayed by the bust?
Student: *It was a bust of Abraham.*

Instructor: What happened when Rebecca slammed the door?
Student: *The bust fell down and knocked her flat.*

Instructor: What was her funeral sermon about?
Student: *It was about children who slam doors, and what happens to them.*

Instructor: What did the children who heard the sermon decide?
Student: *They decided not to slam doors anymore.*

Now say to the student, "Tell me in two or three sentences what happened in this poem." The student's answer should resemble one of the following:

"Rebecca liked to slam doors for fun. One day, she slammed a door and a statue of Abraham fell down and smashed her."

"A statue of Abraham fell down and smashed Rebecca. Her funeral sermon was about slamming doors for fun. The children who heard it decided not to slam doors anymore."

"Rebecca was a little girl who slammed doors. She was smashed flat by a bust of Abraham. The children who came to her funeral swore that they wouldn't slam doors anymore."

Write down the student's narration on Student Page 213, but do not allow him to watch. Then dictate one or two of the sentences back to him (Student Page 214). Be sure to indicate any unusual punctuation with your voice; give any necessary spelling help. Allow the student to compare his dictation with your written original.

DAY FIVE (optional): Creative Writing   *Student Pages 215–216*

Pull out Student Pages 215–216. Write the student's name and the date for him as he watches, or ask him to write the name and date independently.

> **Instructor:** Write a free form poem about one person in your family. I will write down your poem for you to copy into your student book. Make sure to capitalize the first letter of each line. The poem should describe something that you love about the person, or something unique and different that they do.

Write the student's answer down on a separate piece of paper. First, read the poem back to him and then have him repeat it back to you. Finally, have him write the poem down on his own, without access to the written model. Repeat steps 1–2 if necessary until the student has written the full sentence.

Remind your student that for a free form poem, the lines can be any length and they do not have to rhyme. If your student worries that all poems must rhyme, read him some of your favorite non-rhyming poems as examples. Or show the student the following poem by Carl Sandburg:

The fog comes
on little cat feet.
It sits looking
over harbor and city
on silent haunches
and then moves on.

WEEK 32

DAY ONE: Narration Exercise   *Student Page 217*

Focus: *Identifying the central narrative thread in a passage*

Pull out Student Page 217. Ask the student to write her name and the date.

Read the following passage out loud to the student. Tell the student that this passage is about the Gold Rush—the time in the year 1849 when gold was discovered in California, and news about the discovery spread all across the United States.

> Not so many years ago the Mississippi River was the far edge of the United States. Beyond the Mississippi it was wild, wilder, wilderness. Few people had ever been all the way across our country to the Pacific Ocean. There were wild Indians, wild animals, and high, high mountains in the way. Why did people want to go across the country anyway, and what sort of people were they? They were hunters who wanted to hunt wild animals, they were missionaries who wanted to make the Indians Christians, and they were people who were just inquisitive and who wanted to see what the wilderness was like.
>
> Then one day a man told another, that another man had told him, that another man had told him, that still another man had told him that he had found gold in California, a land way off on the edge of the Pacific Ocean—plenty of gold; all you had to do was to dip it up in pans out of the rivers and pick it out of the sand and water.
>
> Gold! Gold! It was almost as if someone had cried, "Fire! Fire!" Thousands of people dropped their tools, stopped their farming, shut up their shops, loaded their beds and cooking things on wagons, put a cover under the wagon so that they could live under it as under a tent, took along a gun, and rushed for the far west to hunt for gold. There were no roads, there were no bridges, there were no sign-boards to tell which was the right way—it was just wild, wilder, wilderness. For months and months they traveled. Many of them died of sickness, many were killed by the Indians, many were drowned in crossing rivers, many lost their way and died of starvation or of thirst—but many also, at last, reached California, found gold just where they heard it was to be found, and made their fortunes. This was in the year 1849, so these people who went west were called "Forty-niners."

—From *A Child's Geography of the World*
by V. M. Hillyer

Ask the student the following comprehension questions. These are designed to guide the student towards recognizing the need to give you a plot summary (rather than a description).

Instructor: What river used to be the far edge of the United States?
Student: The Mississippi used to be the far edge of the United States.

Instructor: The passage gives you three reasons why people might want to go across the country all the way to the Pacific Ocean. Can you remember two of them?
Student: Hunters wanted to hunt wild animals; missionaries wanted to make the Indians Christian; people wanted to see what the wilderness was like.

Instructor: One man told another man about a discovery—and then the news of the discovery spread across the United States. What had been discovered?
Student: Gold had been discovered.

Instructor: What did thousands of people do?
Student: They went west to find gold.

Instructor: What did they travel in?
Student: They travelled in wagons.

Instructor: Was there anything to tell them which way to go?
Student: No, there were no signs or bridges or roads.

Instructor: Can you remember two of the bad things that happened to people as they went west?
Student: They died of sickness, were killed by Indians, drowned in rivers, or died of starvation or thirst.

Instructor: What state did the successful ones reach?
Student: They reached California.

Instructor: What were the people who went west around the year 1849 called?
Student: They were called Forty-Niners.

Now ask the student the general question, "Can you give me a brief summary of this passage?" The student should respond by telling you what *happens* in the story, rather than with a listing of details. Her answer should be no longer than four sentences and should resemble one of the following:

"The west of the United States was wild and far away. Then gold was discovered. Thousands of people went west to find gold. Many died of sickness or starvation or were killed by Indians, but some of them reached California."

"Gold was discovered in the far west. Thousands of people sold their homes and went west in wagons. Some died of sickness or drowned in rivers. But others got to California."

"The Mississippi used to be the edge of the United States. Then gold was discovered. Many people went west to find gold. They were called Forty-Niners because they went west around 1849."

If the student has difficulty forming a brief summary, ask these three questions:

Why did people go west?

What happened to the unfortunate ones?

What did the successful ones manage to do?

Then have the student repeat her answers in order; this will form her brief summary. Write the student's narration down on Student Page 217 while she watches.

DAY TWO: Dictation Exercise   *Student Page 218*

Focus: *Review interjections, direct quotes*

Pull out Student Page 218. Ask the student to write her name and the date.
Dictate the following sentences to the student three times. Tell the student to listen for the interjections and for the direct quotes. Be sure to use an excited voice for "Gold! Gold!" and to use a different voice for "Fire! Fire!"

> Gold! Gold! It was almost as if someone had cried, "Fire! Fire!"
> Thousands of people rushed west to hunt for gold.

Remind the student that the interjections should be followed by exclamation points and that a comma comes before the direct quotes.
Watch the student as she writes, and correct her at once if she begins to make a mistake.

DAY THREE: Dictation Exercise   *Student Page 219*

Focus: *Synonyms*

Pull out Student Page 219. Ask the student to write her name and the date.
Dictate the following sentence to the student three times. Tell the student to listen for the comma; pause for a silent count of three when you reach the comma.

> The explorers who went west faced much danger and peril, but some of
> them found wealth and riches.

Tell the student that this sentence has *synonyms* in it. Synonyms are words which mean the same thing. "Danger" and "peril" are synonyms, because they are two different words for the same thing. Read the sentence again and ask the student if she can find the other two synonyms ("wealth" and "riches").
Watch the student as she writes, and correct her at once if she begins to make a mistake.

DAY FOUR: Narration Exercise and Dictation   *Student Pages 220–221*

Focus: *Identifying the central details in a description*

Pull out Student Pages 220–221. Ask the student to write her name and the date on Student Page 221.

Today's exercise will combine narration and dictation. Read the following passage out loud to the student. Tell the student that this passage is from the same book as the story about the Forty-Niners—*A Child's Geography of the World* by the author V. M. Hillyer. The earlier story was about gold, but this passage is about a different kind of treasure.

> All jewels, such as diamonds, rubies and emeralds, come out of the ground—all except one. But one jewel does not come out of the ground. It comes out of the water, out of an oyster. This jewel is the pearl. The oyster makes a pearl around a grain of sand that has gotten into his shell and annoys him. So at the center of each pearl is a tiny grain of sand. It takes an oyster four or five years to make a pearl the size of a pea.
>
> In the Persian Gulf the finest pearls are found. The oysters are not good to eat, but are gathered for the pearls that are to be found in them. Men dive for the oysters, staying under the water long enough to go down to the bottom, gather a basket of oysters and come up to the top—as long as they can hold their breath. You can probably hold your breath only half a minute, but a pearl-diver can hold his for a minute or longer, and it is said that some have been able to do so for an hour—but that is a fairy-tale. A little boy wrote this composition telling how it is done: "They clamp clothes-pins on their noses and stuff wax in their earses to keep out the waterses. Then they fasten heavy stones to their feetses and jump overboard from small boatses."
>
> Many pearl-divers lose their lives each year. They burst a blood vessel or are drowned or stung to death by a poisonous fish called the ray. But millions of dollars' worth of pearls are gathered each year to ornament the necks and fingers of queens and ladies all over the world.

—From *A Child's Geography of the World*
by V. M. Hillyer

Ask the student the following comprehension questions. These are designed to guide the student towards recognizing the need to give you important details about pearls or pearl divers, rather than telling you what *happens* in the story.

Instructor: Which jewel does not come out of the ground?
Student: *Pearls do not come out of the ground.*

Instructor: What do pearls come out of?
Student: *Pearls come out of oysters.*

Instructor: What is at the center of a pearl?
Student: *An oyster makes a pearl around a grain of sand.*

Instructor: How long does it take an oyster to make a pearl the size of a pea?
Student: *It takes four or five years.*

Instructor: Where are the best pearls found?
Student: *They are found in the Persian Gulf.*

Instructor: How long can a pearl diver hold his breath?
Student: *He can hold his breath for a minute or longer OR He can hold his breath long enough to go down to the bottom, gather a basket of oysters, and come back up.*

Instructor: Pearl diving is dangerous. Can you remember one of the things that might happen to a pearl diver?
Student: *Pearl divers can burst a blood vessel, be drowned, or be stung to death by a stingray.*

Now ask the student, "Can you tell me about pearls in two or three sentences?" The student's answer should resemble one of the following:

> "Pearls are made when an oyster gets a grain of sand in its shell. It takes four or five years for an oyster to make a pearl. Pearl divers collect the oysters from the bottom of the sea."

> "A pearl has a grain of sand at its center. The sand gets into the oyster's shell, and the oyster makes a pearl around it."

> "Pearls are made by oysters. A pearl diver can hold his breath long enough to dive down and collect the oysters. The Persian Gulf is the best place to find pearls."

Write down the student's narration on Student Page 220, but do not allow her to watch. Then dictate one or two of the sentences back to her (Student Page 221). Be sure to indicate any unusual punctuation with your voice; give any necessary spelling help.

DAY FIVE (optional): Creative Writing   *Student Pages 222–223*

Pull out Student Pages 222–223. Write the student's name and the date for her as she watches, or ask her to write the name and date independently.

Instructor: In this week's passage you learned about people who worked very dangerous jobs, like gold mining and pearl diving. If you had to try a dangerous job for a day, which one would you choose: an astronaut, a shark tamer, or a firefighter? Did you choose the job that seemed the least dangerous, or the job that seemed the most interesting? (Or would you like to make up your own dangerous job?)

Write the student's answer down on a separate piece of paper. First, read the sentence back to her and then have her repeat it back to you. Finally, have her write the sentence down on her own, without access to the written model. Repeat steps 1–2 if necessary until the student has written the full sentence.

WEEK 33

DAY ONE: Narration Exercise   *Student Page 224*

Focus: *Identifying the central details in a description*

Pull out Student Page 224. Ask the student to write his name and the date.

Read the following passage out loud to the student. Tell him that this is the beginning of *The Hobbit,* the book that comes before *The Lord of the Rings.*

In a hole in the ground there lived a hobbit. Not a nasty, dirty, wet hole, filled with the ends of worms and an oozy smell, nor yet a dry, bare, sandy hole with nothing in it to sit down on or to eat: it was a hobbit hole, and that means comfort.

It had a perfectly round door like a porthole, painted green, with a shiny yellow brass knob in the exact middle. The door opened on to a tube-shaped hall like a tunnel: a very comfortable tunnel without smoke, with panelled walls, and floors tiled and carpeted, provided with polished chairs, and lots and lots of pegs for hats and coats—the hobbit was fond of visitors. The tunnel wound on and on, going fairly but not quite straight into the side of the hill—The Hill, as all the people for many miles round called it—and many little round doors opened out of it, first on one side and then on another. No going upstairs for the hobbit: bedrooms, bathrooms, cellars, pantries (lots of these), wardrobes (he had whole rooms devoted to clothes), kitchens, dining-rooms, all were on the same floor, and indeed on the same passage. The best rooms were all on the left-hand side (going in), for these were the only ones to have windows, deep-set round windows looking over his garden, and meadows beyond, sloping down to the river.

This hobbit was a very well-to-do hobbit, and his name was Baggins. The Bagginses have lived in the neighbourhood of The Hill for time out of mind, and people considered them very respectable, not only because most of them were rich, but also because they never had any adventures or did anything unexpected: you could tell what a Baggins would say on any question without the bother of asking him. This is a story of how a Baggins had an adventure, and found himself doing and saying things altogether unexpected. He may have lost the neighbours' respect, but he gained—well, you will see whether he gained anything in the end.

The mother of our particular hobbit—what is a hobbit? I suppose hobbits need some description nowadays, since they have become rare and shy of the Big People, as they call us. They are (or were) a little people, about half our height, and smaller than the bearded dwarves. Hobbits have no beards. There is little or no magic about them, except the ordinary everyday sort which helps them to disappear quietly and quickly when large stupid folk like you and me come blundering along, making a noise like elephants which they can hear a mile off. They are inclined to be fat in the stomach; they dress in bright colours (chiefly green and yellow); wear no shoes, because their feet grow natural leathery soles and thick warm brown hair like the stuff on their heads (which is curly); have long clever brown fingers, good-natured faces, and laugh deep fruity laughs (especially after dinner, which they have twice a day when they can get it). Now you know enough to go on with.

—From *The Hobbit*
by J. R. R. Tolkien

Ask the student the following comprehension questions. These are designed to guide the student towards recognizing the need to give you a detail-oriented summary.

Instructor: Where did the hobbit live?
Student: He lived in a hole in the ground.

Instructor: What kind of door did he have?
Student: He had a round green door.

Instructor: What was the hall of his house shaped like?
Student: It was shaped like a tunnel.

Instructor: Why did it have lots of pegs for coats and hats?
Student: The hobbit liked to have company.

Instructor: Why were the best rooms on the left-hand side of the tunnel?
Student: They had windows that looked out over the garden.

Instructor: What was the hobbit's name?
Student: His name was Baggins.

Instructor: People considered them respectable for two reasons. What were the two reasons?
Student: They were rich, and they never had adventures (or did anything unexpected).

Instructor: How tall are hobbits?
Student: They are half as tall as we are (smaller than dwarves).

Instructor: How are they different from dwarves?
Student: They don't have beards.

Instructor: Are they thin or fat?
Student: They are fat in the stomach.

Instructor: What colors do they wear?
Student: They like to wear green and yellow.

Instructor: Why don't they wear shoes?
Student: Their feet have leathery soles and curly hair on them.

Instructor: What do they like to have twice a day, if they can get it?
Student: *They like dinner twice a day.*

Now ask the student, "Can you describe hobbits to me in three sentences?" The student's answer should resemble one of the following:

"Hobbits are smaller than dwarves and don't have beards. They like to wear green and yellow, and they like to eat. They don't need shoes because they have leathery soles and curly warm hair on their feet."

"Hobbits live underground in comfortable holes. They are small and fat in the stomach, and they have curly hair on their heads and on their feet. They can disappear quickly and quietly."

"Hobbits are little people who have hair growing on the tops of their feet. They like to laugh and to eat. They wear bright colors and tend to get fat in the stomach."

Write down the student's narration on Student Page 224 as he watches.

Day Two: Dictation Exercise   *Student Page 225*

Pull out Student Page 225. Ask the student to write his name and the date.
Dictate the following sentence to the student three times. Tell the student to be sure to listen for the commas, and then pause for a silent count of three when you reach each comma.

It had a perfectly round door like a porthole, painted green, with a
shiny yellow brass knob in the exact middle.

Watch the student as he writes, and correct him at once if he begins to make a mistake.

Day Three: Dictation Exercise   *Student Page 226*

Focus: Colons, antonyms

Pull out Student Page 226. Ask the student to write his name and the date.
Today's dictation sentence will be a challenge sentence. It has a new punctuation mark in it: a colon. Allow the student to look at the sentence printed below before you dictate it to him.

Not a nasty, dirty, wet hole, filled with the ends of worms and an oozy
smell, nor yet a dry, bare, sandy hole with nothing in it to sit down on
or to eat: it was a hobbit hole, and that means comfort.

A colon can be used to separate a list from the main part (the "main clause") of the sentence. In this sentence, the main clause is "It was a hobbit hole, and that means comfort." The list comes before the main clause, and tells you all the things that the hole is *not*. It is not nasty, dirty, wet, dry, bare, or sandy.

Today's sentence also has a new kind of word in it: *antonyms*. Synonyms are words that mean the same. Antonyms are opposites. J. R. R. Tolkien says that it is not a "nasty, dirty, wet hole" or a "dry, bare, sandy hole." In those phrases, "wet" and "dry" are *antonyms*. They have opposite meanings.

Now dictate the sentence to the student three times. Tell him to listen for the commas and for the colon, and to remember that the first word after the colon does not begin with a capital letter—even though you will pause at the colon for almost as long as you might pause at a period. Pause for a silent count of three at each comma, and for a silent count of four at the colon.

Repeat the sentence additional times as necessary. Give all spelling and punctuation help. Watch the student as he writes, and correct him at once if he begins to make a mistake.

DAY FOUR: Narration Exercise and Dictation   *Student Pages 227–228*

Focus: *Identifying the central narrative thread in a passage*

Pull out Student Pages 227–228. Ask the student to write his name and the date on Student Page 228.

Today's exercise will combine narration and dictation. Read the following passage out loud to the student. Tell the student that this passage comes a little later in *The Hobbit*. By this point, you have learned that the hobbit who lives under The Hill in Bag End is named Bilbo Baggins.

> By some curious chance one morning long ago in the quiet of the world, when there was less noise and more green, and the hobbits were still numerous and prosperous, and Bilbo Baggins was standing at his door after breakfast smoking an enormous long wooden pipe that reached nearly down to his woolly toes (neatly brushed)—Gandalf came by. Gandalf! If you had heard only a quarter of what I have heard about him, and I have only heard very little of all there is to hear, you would be prepared for any sort of remarkable tale. Tales and adventures sprouted up all over the place wherever he went, in the most extraordinary fashion. He had not been down that way under The Hill for ages and ages, not since his friend the Old Took died, in fact, and the hobbits had almost forgotten what he had looked like. He had been away over The Hill and across The Water on businesses of his own since they were all small hobbit-boys and hobbit-girls.
>
> All that the unsuspecting Bilbo saw that morning was an old man with a staff. He had a tall pointed blue hat, a long grey cloak, a silver scarf over

which his long white beard hung down below his waist, and immense black boots.

"Good Morning!" said Bilbo, and he meant it. The sun was shining, and the grass was very green. But Gandalf looked at him from under long bushy eyebrows that stuck out further than the brim of his shady hat.

"What do you mean?" he said. "Do you wish me a good morning, or mean that it is a good morning whether I want it or not; or that you feel good this morning; or that it is a morning to be good on?"

"All of them at once," said Bilbo. "And a very fine morning for a pipe of tobacco out of doors, into the bargain. If you have a pipe about you, sit down and have a fill of mine! There's no hurry, we have all the day before us!" Then Bilbo sat down on a seat by his door, crossed his legs, and blew out a beautiful grey ring of smoke that sailed up into the air without breaking and floated away over The Hill.

"Very pretty!" said Gandalf. "But I have no time to blow smoke-rings this morning. I am looking for someone to share in an adventure that I am arranging, and it's very difficult to find anyone."

"I should think so—in these parts! We are plain quiet folk and have no use for adventures. Nasty disturbing uncomfortable things! Make you late for dinner! I can't think what anybody sees in them," said our Mr. Baggins, and stuck one thumb behind his braces, and blew out another even bigger smoke-ring. Then he took out his morning letters, and began to read, pretending to take no more notice of the old man. He had decided that he was not quite his sort, and wanted him to go away.

—From *The Hobbit*
by J. R. R Tolkien

Ask the student the following comprehension questions. These are designed to guide the student towards recognizing the need to give you a plot summary (rather than a description).

Instructor: What was Bilbo doing at the beginning of the passage? And where was he doing it?
Student: *He was standing at his door smoking his pipe.*

Instructor: Who came by?
Student: *Gandalf came by.*

Instructor: What did Bilbo say when he saw Gandalf?
Student: *He said, "Good morning!"*

Instructor: Did Gandalf say "Good morning" back?
Student: *No, he didn't!* (If the student wishes, he can explain that Gandalf wanted to know what Bilbo meant by "good morning.")

Instructor: What did Bilbo invite Gandalf to do?
Student: *He invited Gandalf to sit down and smoke a pipe with him.*

Instructor: Did Gandalf sit down with Bilbo?
Student: *No, he didn't!*

Instructor: Gandalf told Bilbo that he was looking for something. What was he looking for?
Student: *He was looking for someone to share an adventure.*

Instructor: Did Bilbo agree to share the adventure?
Student: *No, he said that adventures were uncomfortable and nasty.*

Instructor: What did Bilbo think was wrong with adventures?
Student: *They made you late for dinner.*

Instructor: What did Bilbo do after he told Gandalf that he didn't like adventures?
Student: *He started to read his letters.*

Instructor: What did he want Gandalf to do?
Student: *He wanted Gandalf to go away.*

Now ask the student the general question, "Can you give me a brief summary of this passage?" The student should respond by telling you what *happens* in the story, rather than with a listing of details. His answer should be no longer than four sentences and should resemble one of the following:

> "Bilbo Baggins was smoking his pipe in front of his house when Gandalf came by. Gandalf was looking for someone to go on an adventure. Bilbo said that adventures made you late for dinner, and started to read his letters. He hoped Gandalf would go away."

> "Bilbo Baggins was standing at his door. Gandalf came along, and Bilbo wished him good morning. Gandalf said that he was looking for someone to go on an adventure. Bilbo said that adventures were nasty uncomfortable things."

> "The hobbit Bilbo was smoking his pipe at his front door. Gandalf came along the road, and Bilbo invited him to sit down and smoke a pipe. Gandalf refused because he was looking for someone to have an adventure. But Bilbo didn't want to have an adventure."

If the student has difficulty forming a brief summary, ask these three questions:

> What was Bilbo doing?

> What was Gandalf looking for?

> What did Bilbo think of Gandalf's quest?

Then have the student repeat his answers in order; this will form his brief summary.

Write down the student's narration on Student Page 227, but do not allow him to watch. Then dictate one or two of the sentences back to him (Student Page 228). Be sure to indicate any unusual punctuation with your voice; give any necessary spelling help.

DAY FIVE (optional): Creative Writing   *Student Pages 229–230*

Pull out Student Pages 229–230. Write the student's name and the date for him as he watches, or ask him to write the name and date independently.

Instructor: Bilbo Baggins lived in a comfortable hole in the ground. Imagine that you live somewhere other than a house. Is it on a cliff, in a tree, in the water, or somewhere else? How do you enter your home? What is your favorite place inside it?

Remind the student to answer you in complete sentences. If he answers in fragments, turn the fragments into complete sentences, say them to him, and then ask him to repeat the sentences back to you.

Write the student's answer down on a separate piece of paper. First, read the sentence back to him and then have him repeat it back to you. Finally, have him write the sentence down on his own, without access to the written model. Repeat steps 1–2 if necessary until the student has written the full sentence.

WEEK 34

DAY ONE: Narration Exercise   *Student Page 231*

Focus: *Identifying the central narrative thread in a passage*

Pull out Student Page 231. Ask the student to write her name and the date.

Read the following passage out loud to the student. Tell her that this is from a book by Deborah and James Howe called *Bunnicula: A Rabbit-Tale of Mystery*. It is about a rabbit who has some very strange habits.

Ask the student if she can figure out who the narrator of the passage is.

I shall never forget the time I laid these now tired eyes on our visitor. I had been left home by the family with the admonition to take care of the house until they returned. That's something they always say to me when they go out: "Take care of the house, Harold. You're the watchdog." I think it's their way of making up for not taking me with them. As if I *wanted* to go anyway. You can't lie down at the movies and still see the screen. And people think you're being impolite if you fall asleep and start to snore, or scratch yourself in public. No thank you, I'd rather be stretched out on my favorite rug in front of a nice whistling radiator.

But I digress. I was talking about that first night. Well, it was cold, the rain was pelting the windows, the wind was howling, and it felt pretty good to be indoors. I was lying on the rug with my head on my paws just staring absently at the front door. My friend Chester was curled up on the brown velvet armchair, which years ago he'd staked out as his own. I saw that once again he'd covered the whole seat with his cat hair, and I chuckled to myself, picturing the scene tomorrow. (Next to grasshoppers, there is nothing that frightens Chester more than the vacuum cleaner.)

In the midst of this reverie, I heard a car pull into the driveway. I didn't even bother to get up and see who it was. I knew it had to be my family—the Monroes—since it was just about time for the movie to be over. After a moment, the front door flew open. There they stood in the doorway: Toby and Pete and Mom and Dad Monroe. There was a flash of lightning, and in its glare I noticed that Mr. Monroe was carrying a little bundle—a bundle with tiny glistening eyes.

Pete and Toby bounded into the room, both talking at the top of their lungs. Toby shouted, "Put him over here, Dad."

"Take your boots off. You're soaking wet," replied his mother, somewhat calmly I thought, under the circumstances.

"But Mom, what about the—"

"First, stop dripping on the carpet."

"Would somebody like to take this?" asked Mr. Monroe, indicating the bundle with the eyes. "I'd like to remove my coat."

"I will," Pete yelled.

"No, I will," said Toby. "I found him."

—From *Bunnicula: A Rabbit-Tale of Mystery*
by Deborah and James Howe

Ask the student the following comprehension questions. They are designed to guide the student towards recognizing the need to give you a plot summary (rather than a description).

Instructor: Who is the narrator of the passage?
Student: *The narrator is Harold, the family dog.*

Instructor: Where did the family go while Harold was waiting at home?
Student: *They went to the movies.*

Instructor: What was the weather like?
Student: *It was cold and rainy, and the wind was howling.*

Instructor: What kind of animal is Chester?
Student: *Chester is a cat.*

Instructor: What did Harold hear in the driveway?
Student: *He heard a car OR the family returning home.*

Instructor: What were the names of the two boys in the family?
Student: *Their names were Pete and Toby.*

Instructor: What were they carrying?
Student: *They were carrying a little bundle with glittering eyes.*

Now ask the student the general question, "Can you give me a brief summary of this passage?" The student should respond by telling you what *happens* in the story, rather than with a listing of details. Her answer should be no longer than three sentences and should resemble one of the following:

"Harold, the dog, was waiting for his family to come back from the movies. It was a cold, rainy night, and the wind was blowing. When the family came home, they were carrying a little bundle with glittering eyes."

"Harold's family went to the movies and left him home. When they came back, they were carrying something with them. It was a little bundle with glittering eyes."

"Harold the dog and Chester the cat were inside on a cold, stormy night. Their family had gone to the movies. Finally, the family came back with a mysterious little bundle."

If the student has difficulty forming a brief summary, ask these three questions:

What was Harold waiting for?

What kind of night was it?

When the family came home, what did they have?

Then have the student repeat her answers in order; this will form her brief summary. Write down the student's narration on Student Page 231.

DAY TWO: Dictation Exercise   *Student Page 232*

Focus: *Direct quotations, synonyms*

Pull out Student Page 232. Ask the student to write her name and the date.

Dictate the following sentence to the student three times. Be sure to use a different voice for the mother's exact words. Pause for a silent count of five at the period and for a silent count of three at each comma.

> "Take your boots off. You're soaking wet," replied his mother, somewhat calmly I thought, under the circumstances.

Tell the student that this sentence has a contraction in it. Read it one more time, asking the student to listen for the contraction ("You're"). Ask her what this contraction is short for ("You are"). Remind her that the apostrophe goes where letters have been left out of the word.

Remind the student that quotation marks go on either side of a direct quote. Read the direct quote ("Take your boots off. You're soaking wet") one more time, asking the student to listen for the period that separates the two sentences in the direct quote.

Remind the student that a comma comes between the end of the quote and the words "replied his mother."

Now tell the student that you will read the sentence one more time. She should listen for the synonyms—two words that mean the same (or almost the same) thing. Can she find them? (The synonyms are "soaking" and "wet").

Watch the student as she writes, and correct her at once if she begins to make a mistake.

DAY THREE: Dictation Exercise   *Student Page 233*

Pull out Student Page 233. Ask the student to write her name and the date.

Dictate the following sentence to the student three times. Pause for a silent count of three at each comma, but do not tell the student ahead of time how many commas are in the sentence.

> A rabbit, I concluded, is cute to look at, but is generally useless, especially as a companion to dogs.

Now ask the student to write. If she begins to leave out a comma, stop her and read that part of the sentence again, pausing for a silent count of three at each comma.

If she makes other errors in spelling or puncutation, be sure to stop and correct her.

DAY FOUR: Narration Exercise and Dictation   *Student Pages 234–235*

Focus: Identifying the central element in a plot

Pull out Student Pages 234–235. Ask the student to write her name and the date on Student Page 235.

Today's exercise will combine narration and dictation. Read the following passage out loud to the student. It comes from a little later in the book *Bunnicula*. The little bundle with glittering eyes turned out to be a baby rabbit that the family found. The boys raise the rabbit and name it Bunnicula—but it is a very strange rabbit.

> At first I thought I could strike up a friendship with Bunnicula and maybe teach him a few tricks. But I could never wake him up. He was always waking up just about sunset, when I wanted to take a snooze. A rabbit, I concluded, is cute to look at, but is generally useless, especially as a companion to dogs. So, I would retire each day with my favorite shoe to the rug and chew.
>
> Now, some people (especially Mr. and Mrs. Monroe) can't understand my taste for shoes and yell at me for snacking on them. But I always say there's no accounting for taste. For instance, I remember one evening when Mr. Monroe picked some of his sour balls out of the bowl by his chair and dropped a green one on the floor. He didn't notice as it rolled across the room and landed near my nose. I decided this was a perfect opportunity to try one for myself. I placed it in my mouth . . . and wished immediately that I hadn't. As the tears started running out of my eyes, I thought, What's wrong with my mouth?! It's turning inside out!
>
> Mr. Monroe immediately noticed that something had happened. "What's the matter, Harold? Are you looking for someone to kiss?"
>
> "Help! Help!" I wanted to cry, but all that came out was an "*ooooo*" sound. I "*ooooo*"-ed for days.
>
> So how can anyone who likes green sourballs criticise me for preferring a nice penny loafer or a bedroom slipper?
>
> But back to the matter at hand:
>
> One morning, Chester had news.

"That bunny," he whispered to me across our food bowls, "got out of his cage last night."

"Don't be ridiculous," I said. "How could he break through that wire? Look how little he is."

"That's just it! He didn't break through any wire. He got out of his cage without breaking anything, or opening any doors!"

—From *Bunnicula: A Rabbit-Tale of Mystery*
by Deborah and James Howe

Ask the following questions to test the student's listening ability:

Instructor: Why was Bunnicula useless as a companion?
Student: *He was hard to wake up.*

Instructor: What did Harold do instead?
Student: *He chewed on his favorite shoe.*

Instructor: What kind of candy did Harold try to chew on?
Student: *He tried to eat sour balls.*

Instructor: What did Chester tell Harold about Bunnicula?
Student: *He told Harold that Bunnicula got out of his cage.*

Instructor: What was strange about the way that Bunnicula got out of his cage?
Student: *He got out without breaking the wires or opening the doors.*

Now say to the student, "There were a lot of different details in this passage, but only one thing was really important. Can you guess what it is?" The answer is: Bunnicula got out of his cage without opening the gate or breaking the wires.

If the student says that Bunnicula's sleeping is the important thing, say, "Is it really strange if a rabbit sleeps?"

If the student says, "Howard chewed up a shoe," say, "Is it really strange if a dog chews on a shoe?"

If the student says, "The dog ate a sour ball," say, "Is that actually happening in the book, or is he just remembering it? The important thing is happening in the book itself."

Once the student is able to answer the question correctly, help her to put this information into one sentence. Write the sentence down on Student Page 234, but do not allow her to watch. Then dictate the sentence back to her (Student Page 235), giving all necessary help with spelling and punctuation.

DAY FIVE (optional): Creative Writing   *Student Pages 236–237*

Pull out Student Pages 236–237. Write the student's name and the date for her as she watches, or ask her to write the name and date independently.

> **Instructor:** In the story *Bunnicula*, a rabbit becomes a vampire. Instead of sucking blood, like a regular vampire, Bunnicula sucks up the juice in vegetables (because rabbits love veggies!). If one thing in your house became a vampire, what would it eat? It cannot be human. For example, if your pencil turned into a vampire, would it suck up drawings and writing off of pieces of paper? Or if a coffee cup became a vampire, would it suck up coffee and tea?

Remind the student to answer you in complete sentences. If she answers in fragments, turn the fragments into complete sentences, say them to her, and then ask her to repeat the sentences back to you.

Write the student's answer down on a separate piece of paper. First, read the sentence back to her and then have her repeat it back to you. Finally, have her write the sentence down on her own, without access to the written model. Repeat steps 1–2 if necessary until the student has written the full sentence.

WEEK 35

DAY ONE: Narration Exercise   *Student Page 238*

Focus: *Identifying the central narrative thread in a passage*

Pull out Student Page 238. Ask the student to write his name and the date.

Read the following passage out loud to the student. Tell him that this is from the book *Doctor Dolittle.* We read stories from it earlier in the year. Doctor Dolittle has decided to give up seeing human patients, and to just be an animal doctor instead.

You may need to explain that "spavins" are an injury to the bone in a horse's leg; spavins can make a horse go lame. A mustard-plaster is an old-fashioned remedy for a cough (the vet would mix mustard powder, flour, and egg white together, plaster it onto a cloth, and put it on the horse's chest or neck).

> One day a plow-horse was brought to him; and the poor thing was terribly glad to find a man who could talk in horse-language.
>
> "You know, Doctor," said the horse, "that vet over the hill knows nothing at all. He has been treating me six weeks now—for spavins. What I need is SPECTACLES. I am going blind in one eye. There's no reason why horses shouldn't wear glasses, the same as people. But that stupid man over the hill never even looked at my eyes. He kept on giving me big pills. I tried to tell him; but he couldn't understand a word of horse language. What I need is spectacles."
>
> "Of course—of course," said the Doctor. "I'll get you some at once."
>
> "I would like a pair like yours," said the horse, "only green. They'll keep the sun out of my eyes while I'm plowing the Fifty-Acre Field."
>
> "Certainly," said the Doctor. "Green ones you shall have."
>
> "You know, the trouble is, Sir," said the plow-horse as the Doctor opened the front door to let him out, "the trouble is that ANYBODY thinks he can doctor animals—just because the animals don't complain. As a matter of fact it takes a much cleverer man to be a really good animal-doctor than it does to be a good people's doctor. My farmer's boy thinks he knows all about horses. I wish you could see him—his face is so fat he looks as though he had no eyes—and he has got as much brain as a potato-bug. He tried to put a mustard-plaster on me last week."
>
> "Where did he put it?" asked the Doctor.
>
> "Oh, he didn't put it anywhere—on me," said the horse. "He only tried to. I kicked him into the duck-pond."
>
> "Well, well!" said the Doctor.
>
> "I'm a pretty quiet creature as a rule," said the horse, "very patient with people—don't make much fuss. But it was bad enough to have that vet giving me the wrong medicine. And when that red-faced booby started to monkey with me, I just couldn't bear it any more."

"Did you hurt the boy much?" asked the Doctor.

"Oh, no," said the horse. "I kicked him in the right place. The vet's looking after him now. When will my glasses be ready?"

"I'll have them for you next week," said the Doctor. "Come in again Tuesday. Good morning!"

Then John Dolittle got a fine, big pair of green spectacles; and the plow-horse stopped going blind in one eye and could see as well as ever.

And soon it became a common sight to see farm-animals wearing glasses in the country round Puddleby; and a blind horse was a thing unknown.

And so it was with all the other animals that were brought to him. As soon as they found that he could talk their language, they told him where the pain was and how they felt, and of course it was easy for him to cure them.

—From *Doctor Dolittle*
by Hugh Lofting

Ask the student the following comprehension questions. They are designed to guide the student towards recognizing the need to give you a plot summary (rather than a description).

Instructor: What was wrong with the horse who came to see Doctor Dolittle?
Student: *He needed glasses.*

Instructor: Why didn't the other vet realize that the horse needed glasses?
Student: *He couldn't speak horse language.*

Instructor: What color glasses did the horse ask for?
Student: *He asked for green glasses.*

Instructor: What happened when the farmer's boy tried to put a mustard-plaster on the horse?
Student: *The horse kicked him into the duck-pond.*

Instructor: After the plow-horse started wearing glasses, what happened?
Student: *Other animals started to wear glasses too.*

Now ask the student the general question, "Can you give me a brief summary of this passage?" The student should respond by telling you what *happens* in the story, rather than with a listing of details. His answer should be no longer than three sentences and should resemble one of the following:

"The plow-horse needed glasses, but the vet couldn't understand what was wrong with him. So the horse came to Doctor Dolittle and asked for glasses. Doctor Dolittle got him green glasses so that he could see."

"The horse tried to tell the vet that he needed glasses, but the vet didn't understand him. Doctor Dolittle could understand him, though. Soon all the animals were going to Doctor Dolittle because he could understand their language."

"The vet didn't understand that the horse needed glasses. The farmer's boy tried to put a mustard-plaster on him, and the horse kicked the boy into the pond. Finally the horse told Doctor Dolittle that he needed glasses, and Doctor Dolittle understood him."

If the student has difficulty forming a brief summary, ask these three questions:

What problem did the horse have with the first vet?

Why didn't he have the same problem with Doctor Dolittle?

What did Doctor Dolittle do to help the horse?

Then have the student repeat his answers in order; this will form his brief summary. Write down the student's narration on Student Page 238.

DAY TWO: Dictation Exercise   *Student Page 239*

Focus: *Review commas*

Pull out Student Page 239. Ask the student to write his name and the date.
    Dictate the following sentence to the student three times. Pause for a silent count of three at each comma.

> As soon as they found that he could talk their language, they told him where the pain was and how they felt, and of course it was easy for him to cure them.

Tell the student that you will read the sentence one more time, and that you would like him to count the commas. When he has discovered the correct number of commas, watch him write the sentence. Correct him at once if he begins to make a mistake.

DAY THREE: Dictation Exercise   *Student Page 240*

Pull out Student Page 240. Ask the student to write his name and the date.
    Today's sentence is a challenge. It is only one sentence—but it is very long! Tell the student that you will read it to him until he is able to repeat it back to you. Pause for a silent count of three at each comma.

> And whenever any creatures got sick, not only horses and cows and dogs but all the little things of the fields, like harvest mice and water voles, badgers and bats, they came at once to his house on the edge of the town, so that his big garden was nearly always crowded with animals trying to get in to see him.

Watch the student write, and correct him at once if he begins to make a mistake. Give all necessary help.

DAY FOUR: Narration Exercise and Dictation   *Student Pages 241–242*

Focus: Identifying the central details in a description

Pull out Student Pages 241–242. Ask the student to write his name and the date on Student Page 242.

Today's exercise will combine narration and dictation. Read the following passage out loud to the student. This passage also comes from the book *Doctor Dolittle*.

Now all these animals went back and told their brothers and friends that there was a doctor in the little house with the big garden who really WAS a doctor. And whenever any creatures got sick, not only horses and cows and dogs but all the little things of the fields, like harvest mice and water voles, badgers and bats, they came at once to his house on the edge of the town, so that his big garden was nearly always crowded with animals trying to get in to see him.

There were so many that came that he had to have special doors made for the different kinds. He wrote "HORSES" over the front door, "COWS" over the side door, and "SHEEP" on the kitchen door. Each kind of animal had a separate door—even the mice had a tiny tunnel made for them into the cellar, where they waited patiently in rows for the Doctor to come round to them. . . . and soon now the Doctor began to make money again; and his sister, Sarah, bought a new dress and was happy. Some of the animals who came to see him were so sick that they had to stay at the Doctor's house for a week. And when they were getting better they used to sit in chairs on the lawn.

And often even after they got well, they did not want to go away—they liked the Doctor and his house so much. And he never had the heart to refuse them when they asked if they could stay with him. So in this way he went on getting more and more pets.

Once when he was sitting on his garden wall, smoking a pipe in the evening, an organ-grinder came round with a monkey on a string. The Doctor saw at once that the monkey's collar was too tight and that he was dirty and unhappy. So he took the monkey away from the organ-grinder, gave the man a shilling and told him to go. The organ-grinder got awfully angry and said that he wanted to keep the monkey.

But the Doctor told him that if he didn't go away he would punch him on the nose. John Dolittle was a strong man, though he wasn't very tall. So the organ-grinder went away saying rude things and the monkey stayed with Doctor Dolittle and had a good home. The other animals in the house called him "Chee-Chee"—which is a common word in monkey-language, meaning "ginger."

And another time, when the circus came to Puddleby, the crocodile who had a bad tooth-ache escaped at night and came into the Doctor's garden. The Doctor talked to him in crocodile-language and took him into the house and made his tooth better. But when the crocodile saw what a nice house it was—with all the different places for the different kinds of animals—he too wanted to live with the Doctor. He asked couldn't he sleep in the fish-pond at the bottom of the garden, if he promised not to eat the fish. When the circus-men came to take him back he got so wild and savage that he frightened them away. But to every one in the house he was always as gentle as a kitten.

—From *Doctor Dolittle*
by Hugh Lofting

Ask the student the following comprehension questions. These are designed to guide the student towards recognizing the need to give you a detail-oriented summary.

Instructor: Can you tell me four different kinds of animals that came to see the doctor?
Student: There were horses, cows, dogs, mice, voles, badgers, and bats.

Instructor: What special thing did the doctor make for each kind of animal?
Student: He made special doors for each kind of animal.

Instructor: What kind of door did the mice have?
Student: They had a tunnel in the cellar.

Instructor: What did the animals do while they were getting better?
Student: They sat in chairs on the lawn.

Instructor: Where did Doctor Dolittle get Chee-Chee the monkey?
Student: He took the monkey from an organ-grinder.

Instructor: Where did the crocodile come from?
Student: He came from a circus.

Instructor: Why did he come to see the doctor?
Student: He had a toothache.

Instructor: Where did he sleep, when he decided to stay?
Student: He slept in the fishpond.

Now say to the student, "Tell me what Doctor Dolittle's house was like, in two or three sentences." The student's answer should resemble one of the following:

"Doctor Dolittle had so many patients that he had to make different doors for the different kinds of animals. There were animals everywhere. Animals sat in chairs on the lawn, and a crocodile slept in the fishpond in the garden."

"Doctor Dolittle's house was filled with animals—horses, cows, mice, a monkey, and even a crocodile. There were so many animals that he had to make a special door for each kind of animal."

"Doctor Dolittle had a house full of animals. Each kind of animal had its own kind of door. There were animals everywhere—even in chairs on the lawn."

Write the student's narration down on Student Page 241, but do not allow him to watch. Choose one or two of the sentences from the narration and dictate the sentences back to the student (Student Page 242). Allow the student to compare his sentences with the original narration.

DAY FIVE (optional): Creative Writing   *Student Pages 243–244*

Pull out Student Pages 243–244. Write the student's name and the date for him as he watches, or ask him to write the name and date independently.

> **Instructor:** Imagine that you were one of the animals that lived in Dr. Dolittle's house. What is your favorite thing about Dr. Dolittle? Or what is your favorite thing about Dr. Dolittle's house? Or who is your favorite animal friend who also lives in the house?

Remind the student to answer you in complete sentences. If he answers in fragments, turn the fragments into complete sentences, say them to him, and then ask him to repeat the sentences back to you.

Write the student's answer down on a separate piece of paper. First, read the sentence back to him and then have him repeat it back to you. Finally, have him write the sentence down on his own, without access to the written model. Repeat steps 1–2 if necessary until the student has written the full sentence.

WEEK 36: EVALUATION

Before moving to Level Three, the student should be able to take one long sentence (12–15 words) or two short sentences from dictation, after two repetitions. She should also be able to answer questions about a passage of five to six paragraphs, and then to summarize the passage in a two- to three-sentence narration. Finally, she should be able to take a sentence of her own narration down as a dictation exercise.

Use the following assignments to evaluate the student's mastery of these skills; you may do these over several days or all at once, depending on the student's maturity.

If the student still struggles with narration or dictation, spend a few more weeks on these skills before moving on.

NARRATION EVALUATION *Evaluation Pages 1–2*

Pull out Evaluation Pages 1–2. Ask the student to write her name and the date on Evaluation Page 2.

Read the following passage out loud to the student. This is from the novel *Peter Pan* by J. M. Barrie. Peter Pan has come to visit the three Darling children, Wendy, John, and the youngest child, Michael, while their parents are at a dinner party next door. Peter Pan wants the three children to come back to Neverland with him. He tells them that they can fly to Neverland if they just have wonderful thoughts—but even while they are thinking wonderful thoughts, they can't get off the ground. You should explain to the student that *Cave* is a Latin word that means "Beware!" or "Lookout!" "Nana" is the children's dog.

> Of course Peter had been trifling with them, for no one can fly unless the fairy dust has been blown on him. Fortunately, as we have mentioned, one of his hands was messy with it, and he blew some on each of them, with the most superb results.
>
> "Now just wiggle your shoulders this way," he said, "and let go."
>
> They were all on their beds, and gallant Michael let go first. He did not quite mean to let go, but he did it, and immediately he was borne across the room.
>
> "I flewed!" he screamed while still in mid-air.
>
> John let go and met Wendy near the bathroom.
>
> "Oh, lovely!"
>
> "Oh, ripping!"
>
> "Look at me!"
>
> "Look at me!"
>
> "Look at me!"
>
> They were not nearly so elegant as Peter, they could not help kicking a little, but their heads were bobbing against the ceiling, and there is almost

nothing so delicious as that. Peter gave Wendy a hand at first, but had to desist, Tink was so indignant.

Up and down they went, and round and round. Heavenly was Wendy's word.

"I say," cried John, "why shouldn't we all go out?"

Of course it was to this that Peter had been luring them.

Michael was ready: he wanted to see how long it took him to do a billion miles. But Wendy hesitated.

"Mermaids!" said Peter again.

"Oo!"

"And there are pirates."

"Pirates," cried John, seizing his Sunday hat, "let us go at once."

It was just at this moment that Mr. and Mrs. Darling hurried with Nana out of 27. They ran into the middle of the street to look up at the nursery window; and, yes, it was still shut, but the room was ablaze with light, and most heart-gripping sight of all, they could see in shadow on the curtain three little figures in night attire circling round and round, not on the floor but in the air.

Not three figures, four!

In a tremble they opened the street door. Mr. Darling would have rushed upstairs, but Mrs. Darling signed him to go softly. She even tried to make her heart go softly.

Will they reach the nursery in time? If so, how delightful for them, and we shall all breathe a sigh of relief, but there will be no story. On the other hand, if they are not in time, I solemnly promise that it will all come right in the end.

They would have reached the nursery in time had it not been that the little stars were watching them. Once again the stars blew the window open, and that smallest star of all called out:

"*Cave*, Peter!"

Then Peter knew that there was not a moment to lose. "Come," he cried imperiously, and soared out at once into the night, followed by John and Michael and Wendy.

Mr. and Mrs. Darling and Nana rushed into the nursery too late.

The birds were flown.

—From *Peter Pan*
by J. M. Barrie

Ask the student the following questions. Remember that she should respond in complete sentences; you may remind her of this, but you shouldn't have to form the complete sentences for her.

Instructor: What else, besides wonderful thoughts, did the children need in order to fly?
Student: *They needed fairy dust.*

Instructor: Where did Peter get his fairy dust?
Student: *It was on his hand.*

Instructor: After fairy dust was blown on them, what did the children have to do to fly?
Student: *They had to wiggle their shoulders.*

Instructor: What were the two things that Peter promised them they would see in Neverland?
Student: *There would be mermaids and pirates.*

Instructor: What did Mr. and Mrs. Darling see when they looked up at the nursery window?
Student: *They saw four figures flying in the air.*

Instructor: Who warned Peter that it was time to go?
Student: *A little star called to him.*

Instructor: What did Peter do at once?
Student: *He called the children and flew out into the night.*

Instructor: Did Mr. and Mrs. Darling reach the nursery in time?
Student: *No, the children were already gone.*

Now ask the student, "What happened in this passage?" The narration should resemble one of the following:

"Peter Pan blew fairy dust on the children so that they could fly. They all flew out of the window to Neverland before their parents could come back."

"The children thought wonderful thoughts, had fairy dust blown on them, and wiggled their shoulders. Then they could fly. They flew out of the window with Peter Pan."

"The children were getting ready to fly to Neverland when their parents came home. A star warned Peter, and he led them out of the window before their parents could reach the nursery."

"Peter Pan taught the children to fly and promised them that they would see mermaids and pirates. All four of them flew out of the window before their parents could get to them."

Write the student's narration down on Evaluation Page 1, but do not allow her to watch. Then dictate one of the sentences back to the student (Evaluation Page 2). Help her with any difficult spelling, and indicate unusual punctuation with your voice.

DICTATION EVALUATION   *Evaluation Page 3*

Pull out Evaluation Page 3. Ask the student to write her name and the date.

Tell the student that these two dictation selections come from Chapter 9 of *Peter Pan*, "The Never Bird." Peter Pan is trapped on a rock by the rising tide, but a bird who has her nest on the rock pushes the nest out for him to use as a raft. She is afraid that he will crush her eggs, but instead he puts her eggs into a top hat.

You may do these selections in two different sessions, if necessary. Be sure to use your voice to indicate the period in the first selection.

> Peter put the eggs into this hat and set it on the lagoon. It floated beautifully.

> At the same moment the bird fluttered down upon the hat and once more sat snugly on her eggs.

You may help the student with spelling if necessary, but you should not have to help her with punctuation.

WRITING WITH EASE, REVISED EDITION

Level Two

part of *The Complete Writer*

STUDENT PAGES

By

Susan Wise Bauer
and Susanna Jarrett

18021 The Glebe Lane
Charles City, VA 23030
www.welltrainedmind.com

Names:
Bauer, Susan Wise, author. | Jarrett, Susanna, author.
Title:
Writing with ease. Level two, Student pages / by Susan Wise Bauer and Susanna Jarrett.
Description:
Revised edition. | Charles City, VA : Well-Trained Mind Press, [2024] | Series: The complete writer | Interest age level: 007-008.
Identifiers:
ISBN: 978-1-945841-54-5 (paperback)
Subjects:
LCSH: English language--Rhetoric--Study and teaching (Elementary) | English language-- Composition and exercises--Study and teaching (Elementary) | LCGFT: Problems and exercises. | BISAC: EDUCATION / Teaching / Subjects / Language Arts. | JUVENILE NONFICTION / Language Arts / Composition & Creative Writing.
Classification:
LCC: LB1576 .B382 2024 | DDC: 372.62/3--dc23

1 2 3 4 5 6 7 8 9 10 B&B 32 31 30 29 28 27 26 25 24

© 2024 Well-Trained Mind Press
All rights reserved.
Cover Design by Shane Klink

Narration Exercise

From "The Owl and the Grasshopper" by Aesop

Copywork Exercise

Do not let flattery throw you off your guard against an enemy.

The First Dictation Exercise

Narration Exercise and Dictation

From "The Fox and the Stork" by Aesop

Narration Exercise and Dictation

From "The Fox and the Stork" by Aesop

Instructor

Student

Narration Exercise

From *The Patchwork Girl of Oz* by L. Frank Baum

Copywork Exercise

So I cut up the quilt and made from it a girl, which I
stuffed with cotton.

Name _____

Dictation Exercise

Narration Exercise and Dictation

From *The Patchwork Girl of Oz* by L. Frank Baum

Narration Exercise and Dictation

From *The Patchwork Girl of Oz* by L. Frank Baum

_____

_____

_____

_____

_____

_____

_____

_____

_____

_____

_____

_____

_____

_____

_____

Creative Writing

Instructor

Student

Narration Exercise

From *Mrs. Piggle-Wiggle* by Betty MacDonald

Patsy refused to take a bath. She was so dirty that she could not go outside.

Dictation Exercise

Narration Exercise and Dictation

From *Mrs. Piggle-Wiggle* by Betty MacDonald

Narration Exercise and Dictation

From *Mrs. Piggle-Wiggle* by Betty MacDonald

Creative Writing

Creative Writing

Instructor

Student

Narration Exercise

From *Doctor Dolittle* by Hugh Lofting

Copywork Exercise

How can you expect sick people to come and see you when you keep all these animals in the house? Do not keep the parlor full of hedgehogs and mice!

Name _____

Dictation Exercise

Narration Exercise and Dictation

From *Doctor Dolittle* by Hugh Lofting

Narration Exercise and Dictation

From *Doctor Dolittle* by Hugh Lofting

Creative Writing

Instructor

_____

Student

_____

Name _____

Narration Exercise

From *Misty of Chincoteague* by Marguerite Henry

Copywork Exercise

The ponies arrived on the island in the summer. Soon
winter came, and snow covered the grass.

Dictation Exercise

Narration Exercise and Dictation

From *Misty of Chincoteague* by Marguerite Henry

Name _____

Narration Exercise and Dictation

From *Misty of Chincoteague* by Marguerite Henry

Instructor

Student

Name _____

"My Shadow" by Robert Louis Stevenson

Copywork Exercise

I have a little shadow that goes in and out with me,

And what can be the use of him is more than I can see.

Name _____

Dictation Exercise

Narration Exercise and Dictation

"The Owl and the Pussycat" by Edward Lear

Narration Exercise and Dictation

"The Owl and the Pussycat" by Edward Lear

Name _____

Creative Writing

Instructor

Student

Narration Exercise

From *Ginger Pye* by Eleanor Estes

Copywork Exercise

Jerry would teach his puppy to heel, play dead, sneeze, beg, and walk on his hind legs.

Jerry's puppy will be smart, hungry, wiggly, and noisy.

Jerry's pet could be a cat, dog, mouse, goldfish, or hamster.

Date _____

Name _____

Dictation Exercise

Narration Exercise and Dictation

From *Ginger Pye* by Eleanor Estes

Narration Exercise and Dictation

From *Ginger Pye* by Eleanor Estes

Creative Writing

Instructor

Student

Name _____

Date _____

Narration Exercise

From *The Jungle Book* by Rudyard Kipling

Copywork Exercise

They are evil, dirty, shameless, and they desire to be
noticed by the Jungle People.

Name _____

Dictation Exercise

Narration Exercise and Dictation

From *The Jungle Book* by Rudyard Kipling

Narration Exercise and Dictation

From *The Jungle Book* by Rudyard Kipling

Name _____

Creative Writing

Instructor

Student

Date _____

Name _____

From *Pippi Longstocking* by Astrid Lindgren

Copywork Exercise

The little monkey was dressed in blue pants, yellow jacket, and a white straw hat.

Name _____

Narration Exercise and Dictation

From *Pippi Longstocking* by Astrid Lindgren

Narration Exercise and Dictation

From *Pippi Longstocking* by Astrid Lindgren

Name _____

Creative Writing

Instructor

_____
- -
_____
- -
_____
- -
_____
- -
_____
- -
_____

Student

- -
_____
- -
_____
- -
_____
- -
_____
- -
_____

Name _____

Narration Exercise

From *Nurse Matilda* by Christianna Brand

I shall give you half an hour to be up, dressed, washed, teeth cleaned, pajamas folded, windows opened, and beds turned back.

Dictation Exercise

Narration Exercise and Dictation

From *Nurse Matilda* by Christianna Brand

Narration Exercise and Dictation

From *Nurse Matilda* by Christianna Brand

Creative Writing

Creative Writing

Instructor

Student

Name _____

Date _____

Narration Exercise

From *The Hundred and One Dalmatians* by Dodie Smith

Copywork Exercise

The soup was dark purple. And what did it taste of?
Pepper!

Dictation Exercise

Narration Exercise and Dictation

From *The Hundred and One Dalmatians* by Dodie Smith

Narration Exercise and Dictation

From *The Hundred and One Dalmatians* by Dodie Smith

Creative Writing

Creative Writing

Instructor

Student

Narration Exercise

From *Pilgrim's Progress* by John Bunyan

Copywork Exercise

The man was wearing rags. He was holding a book in his hand, and he was carrying a great burden upon his back.

Dictation Exercise

Narration Exercise and Dictation

From *Pilgrim's Progress* by John Bunyan

Narration Exercise and Dictation

From *Pilgrim's Progress* by John Bunyan

Name _____

Creative Writing

Instructor

Student

Narration Exercise

From *The Borrowers* by Mary Norton

Copywork Exercise

I don't mean the whole potato. Take the scissor, can't you, and cut off a slice.

Dictation Exercise

Narration Exercise and Dictation

From *The Borrowers* by Mary Norton

Narration Exercise and Dictation

From *The Borrowers* by Mary Norton

Creative Writing

Once upon a time I woke up and realized that I had shrunk to be just three inches tall...

Instructor

_____

- -

_____

- -

_____

- -

_____

- -

_____

Student

- -

_____

- -

_____

- -

_____

- -

_____

Narration Exercise

From *The Boxcar Children* by Gertrude Chandler Warner

Copywork Exercise

"Oh, don't you worry," Jess said. "We'll have a surprise for you when you come back. Just you wait and see!"

Dictation Exercise

Narration Exercise and Dictation

From *The Boxcar Children* by Gertrude Chandler Warner

Narration Exercise and Dictation

From *The Boxcar Children* by Gertrude Chandler Warner

Creative Writing

Instructor

Student

Name _____ Date _____

Narration Exercise

From *Mrs. Frisby and the Rats of NIMH* by Robert C. O'Brien

Copywork Exercise

She wished she knew where to find a bit of green lettuce,
or a small egg, or a taste of cheese, or a corn muffin.

Name _____

Narration Exercise and Dictation

From *Mrs. Frisby and the Rats of NIMH* by Robert C. O'Brien

Narration Exercise and Dictation

From *Mrs. Frisby and the Rats of NIMH* by Robert C. O'Brien

Creative Writing

Instructor

Student

Narration Exercise

Adapted from "The Young Man and the Cat" from *The Crimson Fairy Book* by Andrew
Lang

_____

_____

_____

_____

_____

_____

_____

_____

_____

_____

The strange animal was grey. Its eyes were large and bright, and it seemed to be singing in an odd way.

Date _____

Name _____

Dictation Exercise

Narration Exercise and Dictation

Adapted from "The Young Man and the Cat" from *The Crimson Fairy Book* by Andrew Lang

Narration Exercise and Dictation

Adapted from "The Young Man and the Cat" from *The Crimson Fairy Book* by Andrew Lang

Creative Writing

Instructor

Student

Narration Exercise

From "The Pied Piper of Hamelin" by Robert Browning

Copywork Exercise

Rats! They fought the dogs and killed the cats. Oh, how I wish we had a trap!

Name _____

Dictation Exercise

Narration Exercise and Dictation

From "The Pied Piper of Hamelin" by Robert Browning

Narration Exercise and Dictation

From "The Pied Piper of Hamelin" by Robert Browning

Name _____

Creative Writing

Instructor

Student

Narration Exercise

From "The Midnight Ride" from *Fifty Famous People* by James Baldwin

Copywork Exercise

I will stir up all the farmers between here and Concord, and those fellows will have a hot time of it. But you must help me.

Dictation Exercise

Narration Exercise and Dictation

From "The Midnight Ride" from *Fifty Famous People* by James Baldwin

Narration Exercise and Dictation

From "The Midnight Ride" from *Fifty Famous People* by James Baldwin

Name _____

Creative Writing

Instructor

Student

Narration Exercise

From *Five Children and It* by Edith Nesbit

Copywork Exercise

"Good morning," it said. "I did that quite easily! Everyone wants him now."

Name _____

Date _____

Dictation Exercise

Narration Exercise and Dictation

From *Five Children and It* by Edith Nesbit

Narration Exercise and Dictation

From *Five Children and It* by Edith Nesbit

Creative Writing

Instructor

Student

Narration Exercise

From "Alexander the Great and His Horse" from *Tales from Far and Near* by Arthur Guy Terry

Copywork Exercise

"Your words are bold," the king said to Alexander, "but are you bold enough to mount the horse yourself?"

Dictation Exercise

Narration Exercise and Dictation

From *The Story of the World, Volume One* by Susan Wise Bauer

Name _____

Date _____

Narration Exercise and Dictation

From *The Story of the World, Volume One* by Susan Wise Bauer

Creative Writing

_____

Creative Writing

Instructor

_____
_____
_____
_____
_____
_____
_____

Student

_____
_____
_____
_____
_____
_____
_____

Narration Exercise

From *Nurse Matilda* by Christianna Brand

Copywork Exercise

Nurse Matilda only looked politely puzzled and said, "Did you ask for more porridge?"

Dictation Exercise

Narration Exercise and Dictation

From "The Horse That Aroused the Town" from *Junior Classics: Animal and Nature Stories* by Lillian M. Gask, abridged by Susan Wise Bauer

Narration Exercise and Dictation

From "The Horse That Aroused the Town" from *Junior Classics: Animal and Nature Stories* by Lillian M. Gask, abridged by Susan Wise Bauer

Name _____

Instructor

Student

Narration Exercise

From "The Hare That Ran Away" from *Eastern Stories and Legends* by
Marie L. Shedlock

Copywork Exercise

The little hare told the other brother hare that the earth was falling in.

The little hare told the other brother hare, "The earth is falling in!"

Dictation Exercise

Narration Exercise and Dictation

From "The Hare That Ran Away" from *Eastern Stories and Legends* by
Marie L. Shedlock

Name _____ Date _____

Narration Exercise and Dictation

From "The Hare That Ran Away" from *Eastern Stories and Legends* by

Marie L. Shedlock

Creative Writing

"Once upon a time I woke up and my hands had turned into feet!"

Instructor

_____

- -

_____

- -

_____

- -

_____

Student

- -

_____

- -

_____

- -

_____

- -

_____

Creative Writing

Narration Exercise

From *Little Women* by Louisa May Alcott

Copywork Exercise

"I shall take the cream and the muffins," added Amy, heroically giving up the articles she most liked.

Amy said that she would bring the cream and the muffins, heroically giving up the articles she most liked.

Dictation Exercise

Narration Exercise and Dictation

From *Invincible Louisa* by Cornelia Meigs

Date _____

Name _____

Narration Exercise and Dictation

From *Invincible Louisa* by Cornelia Meigs

Creative Writing

Instructor

Student

Narration Exercise

From *The Plant That Ate Dirty Socks* by Nancy McArthur

Copywork Exercise

When Michael had any clear space, he told Norman, "Your neatness is oozing over on my side! Ugh!"

Dictation Exercise

Narration Exercise and Dictation

From *The Plant That Ate Dirty Socks* by Nancy McArthur

Narration Exercise and Dictation

From *The Plant That Ate Dirty Socks* by Nancy McArthur

Creative Writing

Instructor

Student

Narration Exercise

From "The Elephant's Child" by Rudyard Kipling

Copywork Exercise

Then everybody said, "Hush" in a loud and dreadful tone, and they spanked him immediately and directly, without stopping, for a long time.

Dictation Exercise

Narration Exercise and Dictation

From "The Elephant's Child" by Rudyard Kipling

Narration Exercise and Dictation

From "The Elephant's Child" by Rudyard Kipling

Instructor

Student

From *Moominland Midwinter* by Tove Jansson

Copywork Exercise

"Mother, I love you terribly," said Moomintroll. They went strolling slowly down to the bridge.

Dictation Exercise

Name _____

Date _____

Narration Exercise and Dictation

From *Moominland Midwinter* by Tove Jansson

Narration Exercise and Dictation

From *Moominland Midwinter* by Tove Jansson

Creative Writing

Instructor

_____
- -
_____
_____
- -
_____
_____
- -
_____
_____
- -
_____

Student

- -
_____
_____
- -
_____
_____
- -
_____
_____
- -
_____
_____
- -
_____

Narration Exercise

From "The Real Princess" by Hans Christian Andersen

_____

- -

_____

- -

_____

- -

_____

- -

_____

- -

_____

- -

_____

- -

_____

- -

_____

- -

_____

- -

_____

Copywork Exercise

She said she was a real princess. "Ah! We shall soon see about that!" thought the old queen.

Dictation Exercise

Narration Exercise and Dictation

From "The Brave Tin Soldier" by Hans Christian Andersen

Narration Exercise and Dictation

From "The Brave Tin Soldier" by Hans Christian Andersen

Name _____

Creative Writing

Instructor

Student

From *The Magic of Oz* by L. Frank Baum.

Dictation Exercise

Date _____

Name _____

Dictation Exercise

Narration Exercise and Dictation

From *The Magic of Oz* by L. Frank Baum

Narration Exercise and Dictation

From *The Magic of Oz* by L. Frank Baum

Creative Writing

Student

Narration Exercise

From *The Story of Mankind* by Hendrik Van Loon

Name _____

Dictation Exercise

Name _____

Date _____

Dictation Exercise

Narration Exercise and Dictation

From *The Story of Mankind* by Hendrik Van Loon

Narration Exercise and Dictation

From *The Story of Mankind* by Hendrik Van Loon

Name _____

Date _____

Creative Writing

Student

Name _____

Narration Exercise

From *The Story of the Greeks* by H. A. Guerber

Dictation Exercise

Dictation Exercise

Narration Exercise and Dictation

From *The Story of the Greeks* by H. A. Guerber

Narration Exercise and Dictation

From *The Story of the Greeks* by H. A. Guerber

_____

_____

_____

_____

_____

_____

_____

_____

_____

_____

_____

_____

_____

_____

_____

_____

_____

_____

Creative Writing

Student

Narration Exercise

"The Duel" by Eugene Field

Name _____

Dictation Exercise

Date _____

Name _____

Dictation Exercise

Narration Exercise and Dictation

"Rebecca, Who Slammed Doors for Fun and Perished Miserably"

by Hilaire Belloc

Narration Exercise and Dictation

"Rebecca, Who Slammed Doors for Fun and Perished Miserably"

by Hilaire Belloc

_____

_____

_____

_____

_____

_____

_____

_____

_____

_____

_____

_____

Creative Writing

Student

Name _____

Date _____

Narration Exercise

From *A Child's Geography of the World* by V. M. Hillyer

Name _____

Date _____

Dictation Exercise

Dictation Exercise

Narration Exercise and Dictation

From *A Child's Geography of the World* by V. M. Hillyer

Narration Exercise and Dictation

From *A Child's Geography of the World* by V. M. Hillyer

Name _____

Student

Narration Exercise

From *The Hobbit* by J. R. R. Tolkien

Dictation Exercise

Dictation Exercise

Narration Exercise and Dictation

From *The Hobbit* by J. R. R Tolkien

Narration Exercise and Dictation

From *The Hobbit* by J. R. R Tolkien

Creative Writing

Student

_____
- -
_____
- -
_____
- -
_____
- -
_____
- -
_____
- -
_____
- -
_____
- -
_____

Name _____

Date _____

Narration Exercise

From *Bunnicula: A Rabbit-Tale of Mystery* by Deborah and James Howe

Dictation Exercise

Name _____

Dictation Exercise

Narration Exercise and Dictation

From *Bunnicula: A Rabbit-Tale of Mystery* by Deborah and James Howe

Narration Exercise and Dictation

From *Bunnicula: A Rabbit-Tale of Mystery* by Deborah and James Howe

Name _____

Student

Narration Exercise

From *Doctor Dolittle* by Hugh Lofting

Dictation Exercise

Dictation Exercise

Narration Exercise and Dictation

From *Doctor Dolittle* by Hugh Lofting

Narration Exercise and Dictation

From *Doctor Dolittle* by Hugh Lofting

Name _____

Creative Writing

Student

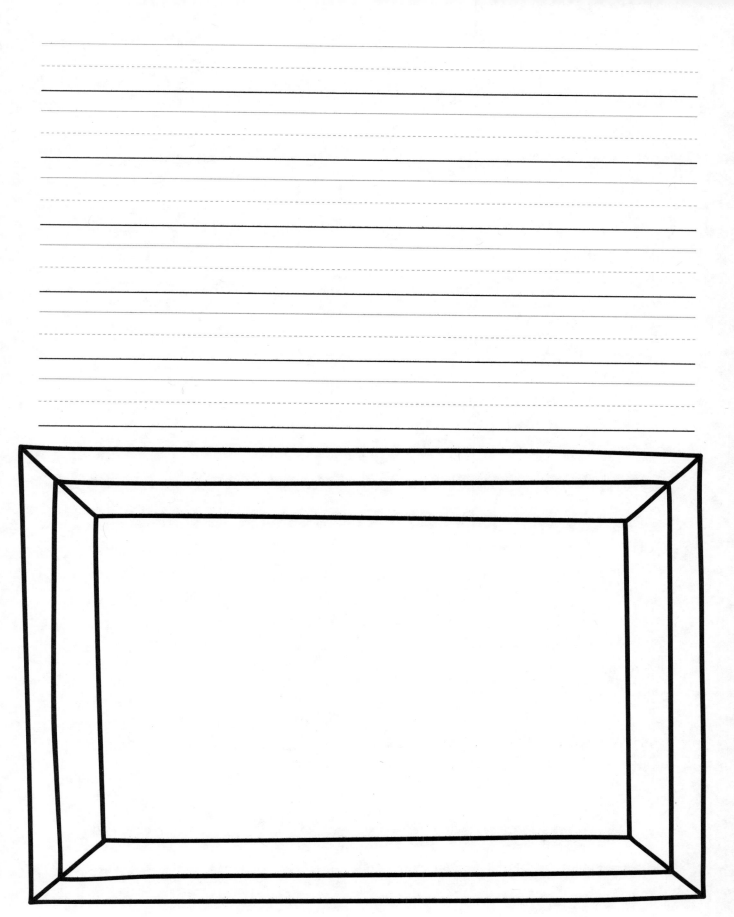

Narration Evaluation

From *Peter Pan* by J. M. Barrie

Narration Evaluation

From *Peter Pan* by J. M. Barrie

_____
- -
_____
- -
_____
- -
_____
- -
_____
- -
_____
- -
_____
- -
_____
- -
_____
- -
_____
- -
_____

Dictation Evaluation